BACK TO TURMOIL, SEQUEL TO STANLEY'S COAT

CHAPTER 1

Twenty-one years old, and most of those years have been squandered. My mind is still in turmoil, still searching for answers. My father has finally admitted that I am his son, but he still won't speak to me like a human being. I honestly cannot understand why he beat me all those years, and why he cannot get over his anger towards me, I did not ask to be born and often wish I hadn't. I am back living at home and back to the tormented state of mind, which eventually seeped into me like cancer.

I don't know why I still have any respect for him after what he has done to my mind and body over the years. Many times, I had wished that I was dead. When my parents denied me a voice, blamed me for all the traumatic events I experienced growing up, while still openly denying that there were ever any wrong doings. I never had a proper relationship with my parents; we only lived under the same roof.

"What's the fucking face for? It's bad enough, you live in my house, without having to look at your fucking miserable cunt face."

Dad was just back from the pub and in a bad mood.

"What's this shite you lot are watching on the

telly? Get it turned over to something decent, or turn it fucking off."

He disappeared into the kitchen for about five minutes and stumbled back into the living room with a bottle of Grouse whisky.

Nobody had answered his question, and he never got an answer. Margaret and James had disappeared to the sanctuary outside while Dad was in the kitchen, so there was only my mum and I left in the house with him.

"I go out for a fucking pint and come home to this shite. Switch the telly off and put the records on, Johnny Cash or Jim Reeves or something decent like that."

He turned to look at me with a scowl on his face filled with hatred. His lips were furling up at the side of his snarling mouth, his eyes half closed as he eyed me up and down with disgust

"How long are you planning to stay in my house this time? Your no fucking man enough to keep a house of your own. You have to come running back home to torment us with your imaginary illnesses. Pansy suits you for a name. I definitely chose the right name for you, gay boy."

That was it for me. I got up, packed a bag and headed out the front door without speaking a word, and headed for the pub. My mind was racing; memories of my past were flooding back in torrents, and tears came trickling down my face. I was angry, but could do nothing about it. He was controlling my mind and controlling my thoughts. Should I go back and stab him when he falls asleep drunk like he always does, what could I do to his car so it would almost certainly burst into flames when he turned the ignition key.

The steep hill I walked down was narrow, and I could hear my footsteps echoing off the walls of the two-storey houses on both sides of the road all the way down, amplified by my agitated state of mind. I reached the Ogilvy Arms Hotel and half opened the door to see who was inside. The place was quiet, so I went to the bar and ordered a pint of lager and sat down. I sat at a table on my own, wondering if mum was getting beaten up, but did not care if she was. She had stood by and let me be a punching bag for most of my life so far. It is something that has always bothered me, why a mother could allow that to happen, and turn a blind eye to save herself from a beating.

I sat watching the antics of the few people at the bar. Old Jimmy was pulling scraps of thinly sliced spam from his jacket pocket. It was the cheapest sliced meat you could get from the butcher, and he never got it put it in a bag, just straight into his pocket. He slid his hand in and broke a fragment of spam off and ate it. Davie the barman topped Jimmies pint up with the dregs of the slop tray under the beer taps, any tap, it did not matter to Jimmy as long as it was alcohol. Jimmy drank a mouthful of his pint, and he shoved another scrap of spam into his mouth with his grubby fingers.

Grace was parading back and forth the floor showing off her new red shiny patent leather court shoes she had just bought in Dundee. The short leather skirt she was wearing was more like a belt than a skirt. I sat in silence, watching how happy they both seemed compared to me. I could not remember the last time I had laughed like Grace was laughing or Jimmy, who was happy for anything he got in life.

"What are you doing out Peedie, you are not usually out on a Sunday."

Something jolted my mind back to reality. Shug had appeared from the toilets after being sick. He must have been in there for ages.

"Do you fancy coming to Forfar? There is a party at Mamie's house. Come on, it will cheer you up, you look like you need it."

"Let's go then Shug, we will get a taxi down and I will pay for it. I was not planning to go back home tonight anyway, and this party will take my mind off my father for a while at least". Shug knew how I had been brought up, and he knew my father.

The taxi driver shouted in through the open pub door.

"Come on Shug, I have other fares lined up, so I can't wait any longer, gulp down your drinks, or you are getting left."

"Come on Shug, I told you that you did not

have time for another one."

Shug gulped down his pint of lager, and he downed it in one go, not stopping for breath.

"Right, let's go then, a party awaits."

Shug was staggering and had to stop momentarily to steady himself on the door frame.

"I must have had more drink than I thought Peedie, and I vomited most of it down the toilet, what a waste, but it has made room for more."

Shug sat in the front seat of the taxi, and I sat behind the driver. The five miles to Forfar seemed to take ages, but we finally arrived. Shug did not look very well, he started to change colour.

"Stop the taxi, I am going to be sick."

Shug had just got the last word out, and a stream of putrid projectile vomit sprayed out of his mouth and all over the dashboard of the taxi and splattered on the windscreen and over the driver's trousers.

The smell was vile, but I laughed and laughed at the look of horror on the driver's face. Shug laughed as well.

"Get out of my taxi you pair of bastards, which one of you are paying to clean this up."

I got out of the taxi and ran, and Shug followed. We headed down Castle Street and went into the walkway under the Royal Hotel, and emerged into the car park, then up the steps past the Post office. We got away without paying the fare, never mind paying to clean up the vomit.

Shug was a mess, covered in vomit, even his shoes and socks were splattered.

"Come on Peedie I will go to my brother's house at Graham Crescent to get a clean pair of jeans, then we will head to the party."

Trousers and socks changed, we headed towards the address where the party was. I could hear the music coming from the house, long before we arrived at the door. Shug knocked on the window and stood there waiting, but nobody answered.

"Why don't you just knock on the door like a normal person Shug?"

"No cunt would answer it, that's why you always knock on the window."

The curtain flicked back, and somebody looked out.

"Oh, it's you Shug, who is that big cunt with the beard with you?"

"It's all right, it's my friend Peedie, he is sound, come on let us in."

The door eventually opened, and we were led into the living room. There were people sitting everywhere, and a strange smell filled the air, one I had never encountered before. The room was filled with a cloud of hazy smoke, engulfing everyone in the room. The living room was small, and some people sat on the floor around the walls. One of them had a Pink Floyd record album cover on his knee, licking cigarette papers and sticking them together. I sat down in the space on the floor beside him. I watched him with interest as he opened a cigarette and emptied the tobacco into the long paper he had created, then he crumbled a green noxious smelling substance all along the tobacco. He twisted the end of his creation, then continued to make another four. He put one in his mouth and lit it, inhaled, but did not exhale for ages, then he passed it to me.

"I don't smoke." I could not believe I just said that, but I did.

"Go on, give it a try mate, it's better than drink any day."

I put it to my mouth and inhaled and nearly choked. Everybody laughed, and that broke the ice. I took another draw and another, my mind seemed to settle, I was not thinking of him anymore, I was in another place now, one I had never been before.

"Come on Peedie, stop hogging the joint, pass it round, you cunt."

I must have been smoking it for ages because the feeling that was engulfing me was fabulous. I felt alive at last. Every single note of Pink Floyd I heard was singled out, amplified, reaching parts of my brain I never knew existed, and swirling uncontrollably round the inside of my skull and down my spine, draining into the floor. I was sitting on the floor, but felt I was levitating. The patterned carpet was moving backwards and forwards like waves, crashing up one wall, then the other. My feet felt like they had pins and needles, and they were hard to keep on the floor as they were floating up by themselves. I was not here anymore, and I did not know where I was, but it was good.

I talked, but my voice was coming out through my ears, my mouth was not working, it felt rubbery, strange, I could not move my lips.

"Anybody want a cake, freshly baked this morning?"

Mamie had baked a big batch of hash cakes, that's what she called them because she had filled them with cannabis. The plate was getting handed round the room and got handed to me. I took one and passed the plate to Shug. I peeled the paper case off and took a bite. It had a strange taste which I had never had before, but I ate it and never gave it another thought. Thirty minutes later that changed. My whole body got numb from the inside outwards. My skin felt like foam to the touch. There was a photograph of a small girl on top of the television. Every time I looked at it, the girl stuck her tongue out at me, jumped out of the frame, and landed on the top of the television, and waved, and as I looked away, she turned back to the way she was before.

"Shug look at that girl in the photo, do you see what she is doing, sticking her tongue out at us. Look at her, she has just stepped out of the frame and on to the television."

"Yes, I have been watching her as well, she

runs right out of the frame and back in again. She isn't there now, she must have slid down the back of the television. Amazing, eh."

We both laughed, and we could not stop. I felt like I was laughing through my nose. Tears were running down my face. Other people joined in, and soon everybody was laughing uncontrollably, but they did not know what they were laughing at.

"What are we laughing at Shug?"

"Fuck knows."

That was it, we were laughing again. Nobody dared look at anyone else or they burst out laughing, squeaky sounding, through the nose laughs

.

CHAPTER 2

I woke up wondering where I was, having no recollection of settling down to sleep, or even what day it was. I was in a bed and an arm was cuddling round me, I carefully moved the arm and sat up, swung my legs round, and sat on the edge of the bed and looked around me. I could make out in the dim light that there was another person on the other side of the bed apart from the one who had their arm round me. There was another double bed at the other side of the room with sleeping occupants draped over each other; one of them was snoring loudly. I think that must have been what woke me up. I sat there still for a few more minutes, trying to piece together the events of last night, and why I did not have a hangover.

"Just come back to bed. It's the middle of the bloody night."

I recognised the voice, it was Mamie, and she had been the one cuddling into me. I lay back down beside her and settled down, but could not get back to sleep. Mamie put her arm around me again, and we lay like that until I must have drifted off.

We all woke up because someone was banging aggressively on the bedroom window.

"Come on, open your door. It is the police."

Several people appeared in the room, one of them was carrying a pillow.

"They're coming in through the window. They're coming in through the window."

Suddenly, a man with long hair and a straggly beard started bashing the policeman over the head with his pillow.

"The aliens are coming in the window, get them out, they are coming for me "

The police man, who at this time had his head and shoulders through the sash window, retreated back to the safety of the garden outside.

"Go away, you're not getting in."

This was the funniest thing I think I had ever seen He looked like Rasputin with his hair and beard. He talked like he was crazy, rambling on about aliens coming to take him away.

"Open up or we will just get a warrant to come in. It will go better for you if you just open the door and let us in."

"Go away you are spoiling my stone, fuck off you had better go and get your warrant, and you are not getting in."

The police gave in trying and left, and strangely never returned with a warrant. They must have been bored or had time to kill before the end of their shift.

"They are here at least once a month annoying me, fucking D.S. Adams and his crew, he must have run out of hash. If he finds any here, he always slips it in his pocket and says fuck all. He must have heard we had Nepalese Temple Balls, the best stone in the world. Well, he won't be getting a free joint from me. I am giving this flat up in two weeks. My sister Carol is fed up with this lifestyle and she wants to leave now and move back home, but we have to give notice."

"Mamie what if I take over the flat, would your landlord let you leave early?"

"I will take you next door later to see the landlord. He owns the shop through the wall from here. The grumpy cunt will be glad to get rid of Carol and me, we are behind with the rent by about three months. Don't mention that you know us, nor that you stayed there last night, or you will have no chance."

We both went to the shop, the landlord was an older man, and he seemed to be respectable. I introduced myself and shook his hand.

"I will give you the flat on one condition, and that is to decorate it yourself, and I will supply the paint for you. When can you take over the lease? If you can do it soon, it will save me advertising it and all the people phoning me."

"I can move in later today. Don't you worry about the decorating sir, I am a time served painter and decorator, but currently working in the timber industry."

"You have not heard what the rent is yet. You might change your mind when you get told. It is £10.00 per week upfront. The flat is furnished with everything you need, except for a television."

I could have burst out laughing, I was earning around £200.00 a week over double what my father earned.

"Here is a month in advance in cash. I will be a good tenant, sir, and will look after the place like it was my own."

"Mamie, when will you be moving out? Just so I can write a date on the lease."

I will leave in the next hour, no later, so you can put today's date on it if you like."

I signed the lease and was given the keys by Mamie. A taxi appeared an hour later, and Mamie and Carol loaded all their belongings into the boot, and left.

I had a place of my own. There would be nobody controlling my life, nor my mind. Nobody staring at the back of my head so intensely that I just had to turn around to look. That man had so much effect on me, I was at breaking point again. Because they had admitted me to Sunnyside Royal psychiatric hospital when I was fifteen, this was his retort every time he wanted to rile me up. It always started with the ridicule of having Electro-convulsive therapy

"The only cunt around who needs a fucking jump start to waken his pansy gay brain. No fucking wonder you don't have a girlfriend. Your girlfriend would need a cock to fancy you because you are a gay pansy bastard."

Everyone had left the flat by now so I tidied the place up a bit. It was a tip; rubbish littered the whole place. I filled a bin bag to the top with beer cans and bottles before I even started on the bedroom. There was a knock at the door, so I went to answer it.

"We have a warrant to search this flat. Could you get Mamie to come to the door? The warrant is in her name."

I showed D.S. Adams my lease, and he almost burst into tears. I gave him the option to come inside to look, but he declined.

"The bitch, she has no idea how hard it was to get this warrant. Do you know where she has moved to?"

I knew she was moving back to Australia to live with her parents. Her father had sent the fares for her and Carol, all they had to do was book the flights. There was no chance I would grass them up and spoil that. They were only half a mile away, but I did not give the address away to him.

He left me standing on the doorstep after grilling me for fifteen minutes, then he and his goons drove away at speed. I went back inside and locked the door. This was my flat now, and it would be me that decided what I would watch on television, me that decided what was cooked and eaten, who could visit, or who could stay. Dad will be furious when he finds out, there would be less drink for him now because he would get no more board money from me, not a penny. I laughed at the thought of him calculating how many pints he had lost in financial terms. He would not be thinking he had just lost a son living at home, he would be happy with that, only the money loss would bother him.

Soon the whole place was clean and tidy, including the bathroom which did not look like it had seen a cloth for weeks. I was proud of my new flat, pleased that I did not have to live where I was not wanted, and where I would not get rudely wakened up from a deep sleep with him pulling me by the ankles, and on to the floor from my bed when he was drunk. Then having to listen to him laughing so uncontrollably just outside my bedroom door at my panicking reaction, that he nearly stopped breathing.

I would not have to listen to the constant criticism I received for anything I did. I have always been blamed by my father for ruining his life just by being born. He has blamed me for the fights between him and mum, my brothers and sisters. Lack of money was always my blame because if I had not been born, he would not have to feed and clothe me. I have been blamed for so much and learned to try so hard that I don't know the truth any more, even after twenty-one years. I think I must have been brainwashed to believe that the root of the problem must have been me. I was finally free of him physically, but not mentally. He was etched into my brain like a tattoo. I imagined this feeling of freedom I was experiencing was like a prisoner getting released after a long prison sentence. I was institutionalised to think I was worthless, and so used to ridicule that I waited on a sarcastic hurtful remark, or expected his hand to grab me at any moment, punch me in the stomach, and then grab my testicles, just to get a reaction.

CHAPTER 3

I woke the next morning with a sense of purpose. I planned to go up to Paddy's Market to buy a new kettle and some cups. Then I would decorate the whole place. I just had to pop next door to the shop when I was ready to start. The landlord had already bought the paint and had it in his store. The living-room was small with a kitchen along the window wall, and there was only a bedroom, bathroom, and a small hallway. It would not take me long to decorate my new home. The whole place was going to be painted magnolia from one end to another.

I finished decorating at sat down to watch the television Mamie had left for me. It was strange to be able to watch a whole program uninterrupted, usually, dad would flick from channel to channel with no good reason, other to show he was in charge. My mind wandered; I could not concentrate. Everything I did in my life involved him; he was everywhere, in all my thoughts, even when I was sleeping. I had nightmares about him, but always woke before he killed me. His car raced towards me at speed. I was not able to move out of the way, then he slammed on his brakes just before he hit me, and sat grinning at me through the windscreen. He reversed back up the road and raced towards me again. This nightmare was a frequent one, and I was powerless to get it out of my mind. That bastard was flowing through my veins and oozing out every pore in my body. He was like a disease without a cure, a pariah, an untouchable leper.

I took a minute to register, but I knew that someone was knocking on my window. The knock was not loud, more like a quiet, soft tap on the glass with a coin or something similar.

"Who is it? Who are you looking for?"

"I was here last night, don't you remember, its Chunks, remember, I hit that copper with the pillow."

"Go to the door. It's not locked. Just come in Chunks, but watch the paint beside the front door. It might still be wet."

"Has the aliens left the building yet?

"They must have because I have never seen any, only on television."

Chunks was definitely crazy like people said he was. Last week the police had arrested him for being naked on a traffic island. He had set light to his clothes so that people would see the smoke and rescue him. Cars were driving past him on the roundabout and circling again to blast their horn at him. The police arrived and covered him up and quelled the flames. They sent for a doctor, but he could do nothing with him. They charged him with a breach of the peace and released him, and here he was sitting on the sofa beside me. I did not see him as crazy; I saw a different side to him, and I had only just met him. He was different alright, his long brown hair touched his shoulders, and his beard was long. He looked like Rasputin, and he talked with a soft, husky voice.

"Skin up Peedie, have you got any skins, I've got Gold Lebanese, fucking brilliant gear.

"No Chunks I have never rolled a joint before in my life."

Chunks licked the papers and stuck them together, showing me how to do it. He broke open a cigarette and spread the tobacco along the entire length. He heated the Leb with his lighter and crumbled plenty into the joint. I don't know how he managed, but he licked the papers and rolled it into an almost perfect wrinkle free joint.

"Come on min, let's light the beauty up, and let's get blasted."

Chunks lit it and took a long draw and then handed it to me.

"Peedie, suck the nectar in, and don't breathe out."

I inhaled and held my breath for what seemed an eternity. An instant feeling of euphoria filled my entire body from the inside outwards, magnifying my thoughts, until another thought took me on a different tangent. I could not concentrate on what was happening to my body and my mind. I took another long draw and held my breath for so long that when I exhaled, no smoke came out of my mouth. Chunks was talking, but my mind was not registering what was getting said. His voice sounded like he was talking through a pipe, it was like he was talking somewhere else, but it was not here. Random words kept entering my mind, flicking about and pinging off my skull at random places, nonsensical words which had no meaning, concocted by my messed-up brain. I felt myself repeating the ludicrous words over and over in my head. This feeling was the best feeling ever. I was safe here in this state. I was in control of my thoughts and what my mind was thinking. I could make things happen only by thinking. This was good, and I wished I could stay here forever in my own Narnia, my own world where I was in charge.

"Come on Peedie give me the joint back, stop hogging it, you are wasting my getting stoned time."

We both looked round at each other when I handed Chunks the joint. For no reason whatsoever we both laughed and could not stop. It felt like I was laughing through my ears and my nose. My chest was aching with laughing, but I could not stop, nor could Chunks.

"Have you got anything to eat Peedie? I am starving, I have the munchies."

"I have not been proper shopping yet, but I have a big tin of Rover biscuits not even opened yet. I found them in the cupboard."

Chunks tore the sellotape seal from the tin and pulled the lid off. We ate them one after another. It was a strange feeling eating being stoned like this, the biscuits felt funny in my mouth, like eating fish or foam, but not biscuits. We pigged out until the tin was almost empty without stopping. If this what he meant by the munchies, I had better start buying plenty of food.

"Do you fancy going round some of the bars to see who is out."

Chunks was needing a nose round the pubs; he was not looking for a pint either. There was some Red Leb circulating round Forfar, and wanted some. We started at the Granite Bar in Castle Street, peering in through the door, looking around and leaving as quickly as we arrived.

"The cunts not here, he must be at the Vollies, he can't be anywhere else because he is banned from any other pub in the town."

Chunks needed more cannabis just in case his Gold Leb ran out. He needed it to ward off aliens; they would not drain his blood if he was stoned out of his skull. That was what he believed, and there was no way you could tell him different. None of us had seen an alien Chunks said, so we were not qualified to dispute it. Chunks reckoned that the aliens almost beamed him up once when he was twelve years old when he was cycling along the path up Bummie hill. Balmashanner, locally called Bummie, stands high up the hill overlooking Forfar next to the disused stone quarry.

"Right, let's go in here, but not the bar, we will go to the lounge he will be sitting there. Mention nothing about drugs, leave the talking to me."

"Hi Chunks, I might have known you would sniff me out. How much do you want?"

Stuart was sitting with a glass of water just to be sociable. The real reason he did not need alcohol was that he was stoned out of his mind. He was a thin strange looking man around thirty years old, but he looked a lot older than that, and was wearing a long black grubby looking ex-military trench coat. He had short spikey hair, which was flat on one side, probably from sleeping on it. He sat there saying nothing for ages, eyeing me up and down, then looked at Chunky.

"Give me a half ounce Stuart before you sell it all, Peedie are you wanting a quarter?"

"Aye, give me a quarter, and I will get a stone later when I get back home."

I paid Stuart the money and slipped the Leb in my wallet and asked Chunks and Stuart if they fancied a lager. Nobody wanted one, so Chunks and I left the Vollies and headed up to Gallowshade. An old double bed mattress was lying in someone's front garden accompanied by a rusty cooker. Graffiti had been sprayed or painted on the front of one of the balconied flats. 'Shade rule, ya bass', and someone sprayed it on the window shutters on Eggo's shop in Glenogle Terrace.

We arrived at Chunks house and went inside.

"Mum, where is your handbag? I've got some hash for you to keep for me."

"It's on my shoulder where it usually is, you know that I can't leave it lying around or some cunt dips my purse."

His mum was a big built happy looking woman, and a single parent to Chunks and his younger brother. Any time the police managed to get a search warrant to search Chunks house, they could only search Chunks room, so his hash was safe in his mum's handbag, plus his brother could not steal it. She even slept with her bag and took it to the toilet with her. She never took it off. This was a rough area of Forfar, gangs were dotted around the town, and this was the Young Mental Shade gang area and she did not trust an opportunist gang member sneaking in and taking her money, but she trusted her sons even less.

"I am away to have a shower mum, where is a clean shirt?"

"Look Chunks I am not your slave, look for a shirt yourself, you lazy bastard."

Chunks clumped upstairs to the bathroom; every step stamped on in an act of defiance towards his mother. He soon appeared back downstairs and into the living room, and he was stark naked. He came over and sat beside me with not a care in the world.

"What have I told you about coming in here

with no clothes on, and we have a visitor, plus the fucking curtains are open? I don't want the police here because you are flashing your arse at everyone. Go and get dressed."

Chunks headed back to his room and appeared back fully clothed this time. He got a quarter of his hash from his mum's handbag, and we headed back towards my house. We got as far as the primary school, and some men from Kirriemuir accosted us. They all had the same style of jerseys with YMK knitted onto the back.

"Young mental K rule, get to fuck off this pavement and cross to the other side you Forfar bastards."

One of them took a swing at Chunks, and he immediately retaliated. There were four of them and only the two of us. One of them grabbed at my jacket and tore the stitching. He spat on my face, and that pressed a button in me I never knew I had. I went into an instant rage and lashed out repeatedly. Before I knew it two of them were lying on the ground, out cold, and Chunks was kicking the head of the last one. I kept kicking the mouthy one in the groin until he stopped talking, stamping on his twitching leg without giving a shit.

"Peedie for fuck's sake leave him alone, you will kill him!"

"Chunks he fucking deserved that, and so did the other two; they will not bother me again if they know what is good for them. That tall one will have a sore face tomorrow, and he will have to sit down to piss."

It always scared me to fight before that and always avoided trouble if I could. But now I had bother thrust at me, without having time to think, and I had battered three of the ones who had attacked us. I had found out by chance I could look after myself. We left them lying groaning on the pavement and headed to where we were going before getting attacked.

We arrived at the end of my street and I was aware of several people standing outside my house. I hoped that it was no more trouble because my knuckles were still bleeding, probably because they had been pounding teeth down someone's throat only ten minutes ago.

"Where is Mamie? I have been banging on her door for the last fifteen minutes."

"She has moved out, this is Peedie's house now."

Chunks introduced them to me, Killer Kez, Fred, and Chick. They had come up for a smoke with Mamie, so I honoured them by obliging them by letting them in. Fred had an LP with him. The Dark Side of the Moon, by Pink Floyd He put it on to the turntable and sat down. He opened a cigar case and slid out a joint nearly as thick as my pinkie. He lit it and a cloud of smoke plumed up above him and spread slowly in small spirals across the ceiling. Another joint was lit at the opposite side of the room by Chick, and soon they were getting passed around the room. After only ten minutes my mind was lost and numb to reality. The music was strange, a mind-altering set of notes was playing through my head. We sat still without talking to each other because we did not have to. The music was our stimulation and escape. I listened to the track called Time, ticking and ticking until an alarm went off. My head rushed with euphoria, I gave every note its own level in my head, and it was the best thing I had ever heard. Every song had its own brain mangling music and ended with the track Eclipse. By this time, I felt like I was talking through my ears, and my legs were lifting up by themselves.

The joints were getting built, then passed round and smoked at an alarming rate, surely my brain could not cope with this much longer. The souls of my feet felt like they were emitting a cold vapour, a minty polo cold, invisible to everyone except me. I had taken my shoes and socks off to stop the invisible polo mint vapour from ruining my new desert boots. Someone put another LP on to play, and we sat there listening to every single note, then a song came on called Comfortably Numb. My brain felt it was about to implode. I had to hold on to my ears to hold my head from caving in, but nobody was noticing my plight. I was feeling sick and had to run to the toilet. I just made it to the sink and everything I had eaten appeared in front of me in a stinking pile. The water from the tap was not getting rid of the vomit, something was blocking the plug hole. I stirred it round with my finger, fishing bits of pineapple out, setting them on top of the sink in a row.

"Are you alright Peedie, you have whitied with the amount of hash you have smoked. You are not used to it yet. What are you doing with that pineapple on the sink?"

With no warning, Chunks picked up all the bits of pineapple and ate them. I almost vomited again on the spot.

"It would be a shame to waste good food, kids in Africa would kill for a bit of pineapple. He pulled down his trousers and sat on the toilet. That was enough for me. I wiped my face and left the room.

"Stay and talk to me. I am having a shit, stay and talk to me I'm lonely. Come back, I am lonely. Come back, please come back."

I went back to the living room to a round of applause from everyone.

"Peedie has had his first whitey, fucking classic."

Fred handed me a joint, and I took a deep draw. I did not feel sick anymore, so I started all over again. I slipped back into the stone I was in before, in seconds, and soon I was in my Narnia again.

CHAPTER 4

My previous night had gone well despite my visit to the toilet to be sick. I had wakened up with no ill effects, and no lingering hangover like I got with a drink. Everyone was away home early, and Chunks had to sign on at the dole office. Today I was going to Kirriemuir to get the rest of my things from my parents' house.

The bus drew up at the stance and I paid for a single ticket because I would get a taxi back to Forfar. There would be too much to take on the bus. After what seemed an eternity, we arrived in Kirriemuir. I got off the bus at the road end and walked up the hill to the house. Mum was in the kitchen when I went in; she was busy doing the washing.

"What are you doing here, Peedie? Your dad is not at home."

"I have come for the rest of my things. Are they still in my room?"

"No, your dad put them in the shed when you left, and he has taken the key in his pocket to work. He will be home at five thirty, that's if he doesn't go for a pint first."

I decided to wait on him rather than make a separate trip back later. This was deliberate because he will get a twisted satisfaction from it;

a sense of conquest and superiority. He will get a strange enjoyment out of me having to beg for the key to the shed, he will have his usual condescending attitude, playing on my emotions to manipulate me for his personal amusement. I tried to get in using a bit of wire, but gave up in case I broke the lock, then I would not get anything. He would want to see an emotional outburst from me, he would want me to get upset, so that it would wind him up, then he would have an excuse to punch me, not that he had ever needed one before. I went back into the house and waited in the kitchen where mum was.

"Why do you have to wind him up coming here like this?"

"Mum there are some things I need, especially my working stuff."

"I could try to sneak the key out of his pocket when he is sleeping, you know fine well what he is like. Then you could come back tomorrow when he is at work. It will be us that suffers when you leave."

I sat at the kitchen table, trying to fathom out why dad had put my things in the shed when I left because he never knew that I was not coming back to stay. But I could never fathom out why he did anything, he had to make a deliberate scene, or he was not happy. It was no use if it was not satisfying his mental sadistic needs, or feeding his ego.

He arrived home at his usual time. He fumbled

about at the back door, taking his dirty boots off, then he turned around and saw me sitting at the table.

"What the fuck are you doing here you bastard? I hope you have not been annoying your mother."

"I am here for my things out of the shed, I need some of it because I am going back to work tomorrow."

"Now you fucking ask, after I have taken my boots off. Well, I'm not putting them back on again, you can fuck off."

"If you give me the key, I will get the things myself."

"You can wait till I have had my tea, then I will think about it again. I am not spoiling my tea, especially for a fucking poofter like you. You can just hang about in case I change my mind."

"Do you want something to eat Peedie, I cooked extra since you were here."

"Don't you dare feed that cunt, he gets fuck all in this house? He does not live here anymore, so he can starve."

James appeared for his meal and sat at the table. I headed to sit in the living room to wait for dad opening the shed.

"Where the fuck do you think you are going? Wait at the back door like the visitor you are. The living room is for welcome visitors, and you are not fucking welcome. Get out of my house or you will wear this plate of hot mince across your face."

I did not dare pass him to get to the back door, because that is what he wanted. He would use an excuse just to swing at punch at me, then hit full blast for ruining his meal. The front door was open, so I headed out and round to the back door and sat waiting on him coming out. I waited for around three hours on him coming outside.

"What are you sitting here for?"

"You said that I had to wait outside because you were having your tea."

"All you had to do was beg me, you could not have wanted your stuff that badly."

He slid the key in the shed lock, not looking at what he was doing, but staring directly at me with that smug arrogant look. I dared not look him in the eyes or that would have been fatal. He would have accused me of defying him and deliberately asking for a punch in the face. Nobody could look him in the eyes when he talked to them, at home, nor in the pub. He finally turned his gaze into the open shed, not moving nor shifting his arms off either side of the door frame.

"What shite in here is yours? Make sure you take any of my stuff, or I will break your gay neck for you."

He went back into the house for a fag and left me to put my things in bin bags. All my clothes were strewn across the concrete floor. I had to shake every item of clothing to get the slaters and earwigs off. Some items had slug trails on them and they all felt damp. My work boots were at opposite ends of the shed, so they were obviously thrown in at random with the clothing, and my record collection which I cherished more than my parents. I would have to wash everything when I got home, but at least I had them now. None of my LP records seemed to be damaged, so I stacked them up and set them flat in a bag.

Everything packed now I headed to the phone box to book a taxi back to Forfar, there would be no chance dad would give me a lift, back to sanity, back to where I felt free of fear and ridicule. I went back to the house and carried my belongings one bag at a time, trying not to burst them. I hoped that they would fit in the taxi boot because I would not leave any behind.

The taxi reversed towards the pile of bags, my whole life was in them, everything I owned. Twenty-one years on this earth and this was my life so far, summed up in a sorry damp musty pile on the pavement. The driver got out and opened the car boot.

"Have you been chucked out, then laddie, has your father thrown you out? Put some bags in the boot, and I will put the rest in the back seat."

It did not take long to pack everything in, so I got into the passenger seat beside the driver. He drove away, and nobody from my family, even bothered to come and wave me off, or even wave me good riddance. My mother would get grilled for letting me into the house, she would get questioned like she was in a court of law. He would ask, again and again, to see if she would change her story, trying to trick her into admitting that she was in the wrong. Then all hell would break loose because she must have been lying to him.

"What have you done to upset him? It must have been bad to have been thrown out on to the street."

"Being alive, that's all, just being born."

I told the driver my father's name, and he immediately understood what I was talking about.

"He is a mean son of a bitch your father, just a fucking bully. I have seen him in the pubs, he is untouchable. Nobody dares talk out of turn to him, and if they do, I have seen what can happen to them. I have seen him crush a man's hand for picking up his pint by mistake, and he ended up with two broken fingers. The police were never involved either, nobody would have dared to grass him up."

Forfar was getting nearer, we passed through the village of Padanaram, and over the railway bridge. We passed the Zoar Inn and turned left past the Sheriff Court, then down North Street. He stopped the taxi at my door and helped me carry my bags into the house.

"How much do I owe you?"

"You can buy me a pint the next time I see you

in the pub. I was in Kirriemuir dropping a fare off, and I was coming to Forfar to pick somebody up, plus, I hate your fucking cunt of a father. Someday somebody will take him out into the countryside and kick the living daylights out of him, or shoot the cunt. He will not always be as able as he is now."

I thanked him, and he drove off towards the town centre. He had just given me a bit of faith in humanity, a glimmer of hope for the future.

Nobody was getting to stay tonight because I had to go back to work, and I was getting picked up at seven o'clock in the morning. I washed my clothes and getting some sort of order to my pile of belongings. I was hungry and tired and totally disgusted with my mother. She never once came outside to speak to me when I had been packing my things in the shed, nor had she waved me off when the taxi was right outside the living room window. I had seen her standing back just out of sight as we drove away; I saw her spectacles reflecting light from the window. She was as bad as he was for letting this happen.

I made something to eat and sat down to eat it, listening to Pink Floyd. The music sounded a lot different not being stoned, but I could still remember what it was like. That was when I decided to try my hand at building my first joint. My first attempt was a disaster, and my second one was not much better, but it stayed stuck together this time. I sat admiring my handiwork for a moment, then carefully picked my joint up and lit it. A lump of smouldering hash dropped out and burned a small hole in my T-shirt. I had wondered what the smell was, but it had not registered that it was me burning. Next time I would have to crumble the hash a bit smaller. I sat relaxing, glad I was home, glad I had all my belongings with me at last. I took my time smoking my joint, savouring every lungful I inhaled. This was the first time I had properly felt at home since I moved to Forfar.

My alarm woke me at six am, I sprang out of bed and got dressed. I had an hour before I was getting picked up, but I did not want to have to rush at the last minute. I made myself a cup of coffee and filled my flask with tea. I sat and wondered where I would be working today, it could be anywhere. Tree surgery was big business and paid well.

The works van drew up farther down the street, so I headed down to meet it. Billy never knew my house number, but he knew it would not be in the big flash ones farther up at the top of the road. I opened the door and climbed in. The smell of diesel and petrol filled my nostrils with disgust. This was me back to earth with a bump, back to work, back to carrying a heavy chainsaw for eight hours a day. Lifting heavy hardwood tree limbs, or burning the scrap wood and leaves when we tidied the sites. It is hard work, backbreaking and sometimes soul destroying, but the money is good.

"Where are we heading today Billy? I hope it isn't far on my first day back."

"It's all right for you Peedie, I still haven't had time off yet, we have a lot of jobs outstanding. Our first job is in Fettercairn, a row of six tall Sitka Spruce to come down between two houses, with wooden fences and two phone lines and a greenhouse thrown in for good measure. Plus, we have to remove the branches from the site today, as it is a public right of way."

With being stuck behind tractors we took over forty minutes to get to Fettercairn. I saw the trees before I saw the houses on either side. They must be nearly forty-foot-tall, and wider than a 45-gallon drum at ground level. The pavement had been fenced off by the homeowner the night before, and he had also removed the glass from the greenhouse. He had a big trailer parked up the road ready to take branches away for us. Billy reversed as far back as he could get so we could unload the gear. I slid on my climbing harness and leg spurs, clipped on my chainsaw and headed up the branches trailing a safety rope behind me.

The rope was slung over a heavy branch and thrown down to Billy on the ground. I started up the saw and started sawing the branches a small bit at a time, so they would not cause any damage when they landed, slowly working my way down to the base of the tree. Poor Billy was moaning already as he was having to keep clearing the cuttings away as I cut them off. Sweat was running off me, a pair of thick black safety trousers, a hard hat, and the fact I had been off work for a while, plus smoking hash, all added up to the heat I was emitting from my body. Finally, I reached the ground, unclipped my saw and safety rope from my harness, and helped clear the ground around the first tree. Billy stepped out the distance he thought the felled tree would land and asked me to do the same, we always did that just to make sure we agreed. The very top of the tree had only eight feet of ground between two fences and a shed to land on, and it was my job to land it in that spot. I scraped a mark on the pathway where the tree had to land and set a traffic cone on the mark. I started the big Stihl chainsaw, which had a three-foot-long bar and chain, and made my first cut into the front of the tree, carefully cutting at the precise angle, then I cut the rest of the wedge out. My heart was pumping by now, this had to be perfect, and there was no room for mistakes here. I went forward to the traffic cone to double check my angle, as there would be no going back when I cut through from the back.

Happy with my wedge, Billy gave me the thumbs up that the area was clear and safe, so I started to cut from the back of the trunk, deliberately leaving a three-inch hinge for the controlled fall the tree had to make. I stopped for a second to check that the hinge was even on both sides, and I kept cutting until I saw the cut get wider. The tree was falling, slowly at first, then picking up speed before it landed with a crash right on top of the cone, flattening it to the ground spraying a cloud of spruce needles into the air. A dog started barking nearby, it must have been startled by the loud snapping crash the tree made landing on the path.

"I taught you well Peedie, but you have fucked my traffic cone."

"All skill Billy, don't try to take the credit for my tree felling skills, you know I am the best or you would not let me do it otherwise."

"Come on, then let's have a cuppy and something to eat. I know I deserve one, anyway."

I followed Billy to the van laughing to myself. The first tree was down, the rest would be easy now. We had something to eat and a drink. But did not sit long as we wanted the job finished. We both cut the trunk into logs for the homeowner, and he threw them over the fence into his garden. The thickest part had to be cut into smaller chunks as they were too heavy to lift. We did the same to the remaining five, and were soon on our way home, tired but pleased with our days' work, and the amount of cash we had been paid. The majority of our work was paid cash, sometimes cheque. When it was a cheque, we used to cash it in the Ogilvy Arms Hotel or Vissochis Chip shop in Kirriemuir. Money never went near a bank, nor paid any tax to the taxman. We did a specialist job, and we asked for good rates of pay for doing it. There were few people who had our skills, so we travelled far and wide reaping the rewards.

CHAPTER 5

I must have fallen asleep on the drive home. Billy was shouting for me to wake up, and I woke in a daze. I remember passing through Edzell, and nothing else. A familiar person was waiting for me as I stepped from the van. Chunks had been looking for me. He had forgotten that I was going to work. He had a rucksack on his back, and I thought nothing of it until he turned his back on me. He had cut a hole the size of a mug in the flap, and a hen's head was sticking through it, looking around like it was normal.

"Do you like Matilda? I have taken her out for some fresh air. She likes a walk around town because it makes her happy, then she lays an egg just for me."

"Why do you have a hen in your bag? I have never in my life, seen anything like it."

"She does not like her collar and lead. She gets tired legs, and the fucking dogs try to chase her."

There was no answer to that remark. The more I saw Chunks the weirder he seemed, sometimes he acted strange, and said nonsensical things, and he was different, to say the least. His appearance unnerved people who did not know him, and he could pick up on that. He put on a show for them just to prove to them they were

43

right to be unnerved. He would get down to the ground and crawl on his hands and knees, nodding his head as he went around in a circle, humming a nonsensical tune as he crawled, then he would stand up and carry on as if nothing had happened. He had piercing blue eyes and a wide genuine smile which he used to his advantage if he was wanting something.

"Where have you been Peedie? Matilda is thirsty. Poor girl, have you no shame leaving her out here in the burning hot sun?"

I unlocked the door and went inside, followed by Chunks and Matilda. Chunks took the rucksack off his back and set it on the floor, undid the buckles on the top, and lifted the ridiculous hen from the bag. He set her down on the carpet, and she just stood there. She was tame and not put off by me being near. Chunks thrust his arm to the bottom of the rucksack and pulled out Matilda's bowl, then filled it with water and set it down on the floor. She dipped her beak into the water and lifted her head to swallow it. Chunks sat down and rolled a joint, an enormous joint. I was needing a good stone after the day I had. My muscles were still aching after climbing up trees, and I chafed my skin after scraping on branches. Sitka Spruce needles are hard and sharp and show no mercy on bare skin.

"Give me a loan of your lighter Peedie, my one is fucked."

"Come on Chunks, make another joint with

my hash for a change, and put plenty in."

Chunks lit a joint and handed one to me, then lit one for himself. He had made another two from my hash and was using them first. Matilda just sat looking around the room, her head was moving like it was in slow motion, jerking in small movements as it went. I was used to Hatty the hen when James was younger, she laid eggs in the house. I inhaled a long draw of my joint and sat right back on the sofa. This is fabulous. My mind was wandering, thinking about my priorities and my life. Chunks was starting to nod his head slowly, taking a draw of his joint, and then nodding again. His eyes were closed, but it looked like he was looking around the room. He was humming a tune I did not recognize, then he stopped dead, and stood up and headed to the stereo. LPs were getting sorted into a pile on each side of the stereo on the floor.

"What are you doing Chunks? Just put on something trippy, I have got Deep Purple, Pink Floyd dark side of the moon, Animals, and The Wall."

"I am looking for a good sleeve to skin up on, and a good one to listen to as well. You just can't rush good stoner music; it has to be right."

He finally put my Pink Floyd the Wall on to play. We settled down and concentrated on the music. The notes meant more and more to me as I got to know the tracks. Strange feelings were rising up from my feet, I liked how that felt, the minty air hissing silently in jets from the hundreds of small holes in the soles of my feet. I imagined it must look like a steam iron, shooting hot jets of steam from the plate, but mine was cold and refreshing. I took my socks off and just sat there melting into the fabric of the sofa, slowly relaxing into a self-induced paralysis of my brain, one which I could snap out of in a second if I needed to, and go straight back into as quick.

"Somebody is at the door Peedie. Do you want to let them in?"

"Only if they have hash."

We both laughed and could not stop. Chunks answered the door, but only opened it enough to see who was there.

"It's only Fred and Brian, come in, you two, and skin up for fuck's sake."

"Peedie, I have never met you yet. I am from London and a cousin of Fred's. Can we stay here tonight? Fred's mum is threatening to burn his hash in the fire if he comes back home with it."

"Yes, of course, you and Fred can stay Brian."

"You all might as well know that I am gay, always have been, always will be. But don't worry, I would shag none of you, none of you are my type."

We all burst out laughing, Brian was mincing around the living room like an idiot, putting on an exaggerated walk like he was on a catwalk. He would liven the place up. Soon the joints were getting handed round the room, not in any order, from person to person, sometimes I ended holding two. I was floating, but did not get worried this time. My mind could control my descent if I floated near the ceiling. I could hover at will if I wanted, I could float like a balloon. Matilda rose to her feet and walked. She fell over on to her side and tried to get up, but she could not stand upright.

"Chunks, Matilda is having a job getting up. There must be something wrong with her legs."

"Peedie she is stoned out her skull. She likes a good toke, a blast of hash keeps her normal, and she will be fine when it wears off. A happy hen lays happy eggs."

That was it for everybody. We all laughed at poor Matilda. She was just sitting on the floor, turning her head almost right round in a circle, then slowly back again. I imagined what she was thinking, in her stoned state, and what her feet were feeling as she could not walk. We dare not look at each other or we were laughing. My ears felt like they were moving around and extending out like a funnel. I was hearing strange noises in my head and could not fathom where they were coming from. I knew that people were watching me, staring at my ears, which were now protruding at an alarming distance from my head. I tried to get them back to normal, but they were past saving. The noises were coming in quickly, swirling round my ear lobes several times, then shooting down my funnel ears and landing in the centre of my brain with a muffled bang. The sounds changed repeatedly, I could not stop them, and it was good.

I woke with a fright; someone was banging furiously on my door.

"Come on, Peedie you have slept in. Hurry up. We have a long way to drive today."

It was Billy, and he did not sound happy. I was still dressed from the night before, so I put my boots on and headed out to the van. I left everyone sleeping; they would wonder where I was when they woke up. I was getting lectured about sleeping in, but I did not care. The job was the last thing I was thinking about just now. My friends were still sleeping, and I was in this bloody van, thirsty and still tired, but I did not feel rough.

Billy woke me up when we arrived at the job, he was nagging at me, moaning that my mind was not focused. We had an important job today cutting down a large elm tree in a school playground that was dying of Dutch elm disease. There was not a lot of room for it to land, so I had to be on the ball. There was a bike shelter on one side and a school prefab building on the other. The windows had temporary wooden boards on them to stop flying debris from the tree. The school was closed for a holiday so it had to be completed today. I pulled myself together and looked for the best way to fell the tree.

Billy was getting edgy; crowds were gathering at the chain-link fence outside the school. They had come to watch the tree coming down. It is not something you see every day. Children were shouting with glee as the chainsaw started up and then when I started to cut my wedge into the front of the tree. If this went wrong, we had an audience, everyone would see us. Billy was worried, I could see it in his face. The tree was heavier on one side and Billy was worried that when it fell, it would pull to that side. I had accounted for that, and I was leaving a bigger hinge on the opposite side. I cut through the trunk slowly from the back, stopping several times to check my progress. The tree started to fall slowly, emitting a deafening crack, then it crashed to the round. I jumped out of the way as the trunk shot about eight feet in the air and landed back down with a thud. Everything around was intact with no damage anywhere. There were rounds of applause coming from the watching crowd as we headed to the van for a drink. Billy looked different now. He was relaxed that the tree was on the ground. All we had to do now was cut it into pieces and clear it up.

Several hours later, we had completed the task, and we headed homeward. It was a long drive to Forfar, so I leaned back and shut my eyes, hoping that I would fall asleep to make the journey seem shorter.

We arrived in Forfar faster than I imagined we

would. I never properly fell asleep, but nodded off at times. Billy dropped me off and headed home himself.

My door was not locked as it should have been. Everyone was supposed to be out by now; all they had to do was pull the door behind them. I went in and removed my boots, then headed to the living room. There was nobody in sight; they had gone away and not locked the door. That would be the last time that happened; they would not be trusted again. I filled the kettle and sat down to roll a well-earned joint, lacing it heavily with Red Leb for better effect. I ignited my joint and inhaled, holding my breath as long as I could. This was what I had been waiting for all day. My mind had been craving for happiness, since I was rudely awakened for work in the morning. I made myself a coffee and sat back down. There was a low groaning sound coming from somewhere in the house, but I could not pinpoint it.

The noise was getting louder, and I suddenly realised where it was coming from. A man was lying behind a sofa near to where I was sitting. I had not noticed him before now, and it shocked me that he was there. He was trying to speak, but he did not seem to be able to move his mouth. Saliva was running out of his mouth as he tried to tell me something, then I saw it. A syringe was dangling from his arm, just below a red leather belt. I tried to get him to get up, but he seemed limp and unable to move on his own accord.

I ran outside and up to the phone box, dialed 999, and told them to hurry, then ran back home. He now had froth around his mouth, and his eyes were dark and lifeless. He was still trying to speak when the ambulance arrived, they lifted him into a wheeled chair and out to the waiting ambulance. The medics lifted him onto the bed and waited for a doctor to arrive. He was given an injection and turned on his side in the recovery position. A doctor appeared from a side street farther along. He examined the man, shone a torch in his eyes, and slowly shook his head.

"What we have is a severe drug overdose, who found him?"

"I found him lying in my living room like that when I got home from work. I don't know who he is nor where he lives"

He was in a bad way, the doctor had given him some fluids and a quick check over, then the ambulance medic shut the doors, and sped off with all blue lights flashing, and the siren drowning my voice out. The police had arrived on the scene and were not believing that I never knew him, nor that I never let him into my house. I explained to them where I had been all day, and that I had left Chunks in charge and still asleep.

"Did you supply the drugs to him? We only want to know what he has taken. That will help the hospital when he arrives for treatment."

"Look, I have told you already, I don't even know who he is. He had a syringe in his arm when I found him."

I gave them a statement, repeating what they had already been told over and over again.

"Look, son, if this man dies, you could be held solely accountable, and there would be an inquest. You could get charged for allowing drugs to be taken on your property whether you were present or not."

Finally, the police left me and I started to panic. I hoped the man would be alright, more for the fact I would be implicated than whether he died or not. Luckily, I had hidden my hash from sight before they came. I had enough to deal with now, without getting charged with possession of cannabis.

Chunks suddenly appeared in my doorway as if from nowhere. He had been hiding out of view until the police had left my house

"Peedie, we never knew who he was, he said he was a pal of Mamie, so we let him in. We were all out our heads when we left yours, so we never knew he was still there."

"I could be in trouble because of this if he dies, shit has just got real."

"I just wanted to check you were ok Peedie. I will come and see you tomorrow when you get back from work."

CHAPTER 6

I had decided before I went to bed, I would not go to work the next morning. Billy was furiously banging on my door and shouting through the letter-box, but I ignored him. I could not work with what happened still fresh in my mind. After what seemed an eternity, Billy left, I could hear him cursing as he went away, he would be furious with me because he had a job booked, one which needed us both, but I did not care. I rolled myself a small joint, just enough to sort my brain out, but not enough to get stoned. The kettle boiled, and I made myself a coffee, slowly smoking the joint, savouring every breath of luxurious life-giving cannabis. This was better than working any day. I sat there chilling, any decided that I would go to the police station to ask about the man I found, and hopefully, they could tell me if he was alright, then I could relax.

There was nobody at the reception desk when I entered the station, so I rang the bell. A policewoman appeared from a room just behind reception. I explained why I was here, and she disappeared back where she had come from. I sat down on the row of seats behind me and waited. What would I do if she came back and said he was dead, would I be charged with murder, my mind was racing around and getting worse? I had cannabis in my pocket; I had forgotten that they would find that when they charged me for murdering him.

"Excuse me, sir, can you come over here a minute?"

I was miles away, the policewoman was back at the reception, and I had not even noticed.

"I have good news for you. The man is alright. He came around from his overdose and discharged himself from the hospital. I can't tell you his name or any medical details, but he was alright when he left the hospital."

The relief I felt was like nothing I had experienced before. A sense of calm entered me. This was the news I was needing, and I was free of prosecution. I went back home and sat down on the sofa, remembering who was lying behind it last night. If he signed himself out, he must have been normal enough to walk out of a hospital.

My hash was almost finished and there was none left to buy in Forfar. Chunks told me he would take me to Dundee to get some decent smoke. I was meeting him at the High Street bus stance in an hour's time. There was time for another joint before I went to meet Chunks, so I rolled a big one to set me up for the trip. I walked to the stance, but Chunks was not there yet. My mind was numb, but also very alert. I could control my thoughts at random. A rucksack appeared before my face, and the familiar head and neck of Matilda were sticking out the top. He was taking her on a sightseeing tour of Dundee. Chunks was crazy in public, he exaggerated everything he did. We sat on the wall watching everyone's reaction to Matilda, but nobody mentioned that they had seen her. The sight of Chunks probably put them off. He was wearing a scruffy black duffle coat which was covered in white fluff. His jeans were flared at the bottom, and he was wearing brown leather Jesus sandals. He sat slowly nodding his head backwards and forwards, making his long hair sway. The bus appeared at the stance. We barged past some people so that we could get the back seat, Chunks liked to sit at an exit door just in case aliens boarded the bus, then he could escape.

It took forty-five minutes to get to Dundee, and we got off at the Seagate bus station. I did not know my way around here and felt uneasy that I was here with only Chunks for the company. We walked for about thirty minutes and arrived at a door between two shops. Chunks opened it and we headed inside. The smell of rancid urine hit me the second I walked in. The close was dimly lit with rubbish strewn all over the place. We walked up a flight of stairs edging past someone lying on the steps. Even in the dim light, I could see that he had wet himself and a still running trickle of urine was heading down the steps. Never in my life had seen a door like the one on this flat, someone lined it with a sheet of steel, bolted in place across the entire area, with a small steel covered hatch built in at eye level. Chunks knocked loudly on the metal-covered door and the hatch opened. An eye appeared at the opening, suspiciously looking us up and down.

"What do you want here?"

"We are here to see big Charlie."

"Do you have ID? You could be the coppers, or any cunt looking for bother."

"Tell Charlie I have my ID in my rucksack. He will know who I am, tell him, Matilda."

The flap slammed shut, and eventually, the man appeared back at the door, had a peep through the flap and opened the six heavy door bolts on the inside of the door. I counted them as they clunked metal against metal. The door opened, and we were summoned into the hallway.

"Right you two you are getting searched for wires, we don't want any cunt sending stuff to coppers outside or anything fucking dodgy going on."

The big man who had eyed us through the flap frisked us both, then lifted our tops just to make sure. He was massive, a giant of a man standing at least six foot six with arms thicker than my thighs He signaled to follow him through, not talking this time, just using his finger. The living room had around a dozen people sitting around the room, every one of them smoking a joint.

Big Charlie spotted Chunks through the haze of smoke and asked him how Matilda was getting on. This was bizarre, we were in a drug barons flat, and they were all sitting at a large table talking about the health of a fucking hen. I sat down beside someone on a sofa, and he immediately handed me a joint. I inhaled a generous lung full of smoke; this differed from anything I had smoked before. I handed the joint back, only to be given another one. There was a single bed in the corner of the living room which caught my eye. A man was lying on it, writhing about slowly, emitting a low groan now and again. He turned around to look into the room, and I recognised him immediately. It was the man who had been in my living room with the needle sticking out of his arm. Charlie introduced the man as the Guinea pig. He was the one who tested drugs, especially new ones, to check the potency, the bigger the state the Guinea pig got into, the higher the price was. No wonder he managed to recover and sign himself out of the hospital, he must have a high tolerance for drugs.

"What are you wanting today, Chunks? I have Red and Gold Leb, ruggers, acid tabs, speed, cannabis oil, and anything else you fancy. My brother works at the docks and brings me goodies to sell every week. The boats are always bringing drugs in, and no cunt is any the wiser what is going on.

"I want six separate quarters of Gold Leb, twenty green ruggers, a couple of acid tabs, and, no that's it, that's everything."

Charlie emptied a cloth bag of wrapped drugs on the table, and spread them around like playing cards.

"Right Chunks, pick out your six quarters from this lot. You can weigh any one you like on my scales, and I won't rip you off."

There must have been over forty parceled up hash quarters on that table, and Chunks sorted through them and slid six of them to one side near Charlie who was watching everything that was happening.

"Right Chunks, here are the ruggers, and the two Purple Heart acid tabs, do not take the two of them at one time. The guinea pig was out of his nut for three days after downing two. He was well out of it."

"Peedie I thought you were needing hash you cunt, that's why you came with me."

"Give me a half ounce of that Gold Leb, and four of the Purple Heart acid tabs, I have never tried acid before."

This was like a corner shop, we handed Charlie our money and then we were given our drugs, but only after all the other drugs had been removed from the table and back in his pockets.

"If you are coming back here for hash, don't come on a Tuesday because that is when I sign on at the dole and take my mother shopping."

The wad of cash Charlie had in his hand was so big that he could not get it to fold in half, so he had to split it into two bundles. He told us he only signed on to be normal, he did not need the money, and he was the only one driving to sign on in a shiny black BMW car. Nobody would dare cross Charlie, everybody in the town knew him and what would happen to them if they did.

We thanked Charlie and asked him to let us out the front door. The bolts on the door were as thick as my finger, and there was a metal bar set into a slot on either side of the door frame. Nobody would break that door down in a hurry. The door opened and the stench of rancid urine hit my nostrils. The man on the stairs had left before we came out into the close, but he had left a pile of vomit on the stair where he had been lying. We got to the bottom of the stairs and the entrance door. Chunks barred my exit with his arm without saying anything. He opened the door and peered outside, and Matilda started screeching and squawking loudly. I nearly shit myself; it was like an alarm had gone off.

"The coast is clear Peedie, let's get to fuck away from here."

"What was all the noise Matilda was making about?"

"Matilda has laid an egg, she always makes a racket, and how would you like something that size coming out your arse? You would be fucking roaring too."

The air was fresh out here, not like the smoke engulfed flat, or the urine stench close. We headed back towards the Seagate to catch a bus, walking fast like we were trying to get away from something. The pace slowed down once we were out of the area, Charlie had warned us not to stop anywhere, or talk to anybody in case they attacked and robbed us of our drugs and money.

The bus station was busy, people were scurrying about trying to find the bus they were travelling on. There were about eight different stances, all going to different places. We found our stance right at the end, and a bus was there.

"Forfar via Murroes, Peedie that's our bus, and it is leaving in twenty minutes. We better split up, you sit on that bench over there, and I will sit here. We don't want to attract attention to ourselves carrying all these drugs."

I went over and sat beside an older woman who was reading a book. People were pointing at Chunks and Matilda, who was now out of the rucksack on to his knee. He did not want to draw attention to us, and there he was, showing off Matilda, and holding her egg proudly in the air. He was acting like a proud father whose child had walked its first steps, or said its first words He was definitely crazy in public, he was eccentric and very intelligent under that charade he acted out to strangers. Mothers pulled their children who were looking at Matilda away from

Chunks They had no reason to, other than that he looked like a tramp wearing his shabby duffle coat and because of his Rasputin like appearance

The bus doors opened and we paid the driver and went to sit at the back of the bus, right beside the emergency exit as usual. I watched as everyone came into the bus. Nobody came near where we were sitting, we must have looked intimidating. Chunks with his long greasy hair and beard, and me with my bushy beard and permed long hair down to my shoulders. We were like the plague to everyone on the bus, but we did not care. The driver started the engine and reversed the bus away from the stance. We were on our way home to Forfar at last. People got on and off at different stops along the way, and none of the ones getting on came to sit near us. Just as we were getting into Forfar at the stop beside the Guide dog centre, the bus stopped again. Chunks grabbed the emergency door handle and pulled me with him towards the open door. I just followed him still in shock as to what had happened.

"Run, for fuck's sake run, D.S. Adams and a copper have just got on the bus. Just keep running and don't stop."

We ran up a gravelled pathway and up a hill past the guide dog kennels for what seemed an eternity. My lungs felt like they would burst through my chest. Chunks was the same, we could not run any further. We looked back towards where we had run from, the bus was away and they had not followed us. DS Adams could not have kept up with us anyway. We walked fast, keeping a lookout for anyone following us and eyed anyone we encountered with suspicion, even if they were just walking their dog, we trusted nobody. We ended up Bummie, headed down another path and ended up in Easterbank, cut through there and headed for my house. Chunks stopped suddenly and about turned and headed for the cemetery behind Easterbank.

"Come on Peedie we will have to stash our drugs here somewhere. I have had a bad vision, and I trust my instincts."

We both found suitable stash places. Mine was in behind a stone in the drystone wall, Chunks hid his further along in a large empty carton, and buried it under a pile of leaves beside the wall. Nobody had seen us hiding our stuff, so we sauntered back through Easterbank again. Two dodgy looking men were sitting on a bench when we neared my house, and they both got to their feet the minute we arrived. DS Adams was one of them, and a constable.

"You two were a bit fast getting off the bus, you must have something to hide."

"No, we were trying to save some money on the bus fare by getting off earlier."

"Chunks you are a character aren't you, always the fucking lippy one. Stand and face that car, put your arms apart and lean on the roof, now spread your legs, you are both getting searched."

"What about Matilda, she needs a drink?"

"Never mind the fucking hen, Chunks, I know you pair have got drugs on you. We had a tip off that you were on the Dundee bus loaded with drugs. You ought to pick your friends better."

After he was certain we had nothing on us, he promised us he would get us one way or another. He was annoyed, frustrated that Chunks was cleverer than him, he had foreseen that there would be trouble, and so he had decided to stash our drugs. DS Adams was due off shift in the next half hour. All the cops would be at changeover at the station, now was as good a time as any to return to retrieve our goodies from the cemetery. We reached the gates of the cemetery and walked to where we had hidden everything. A woman was tending a grave just thirty yards away, but we decided to just collect our drugs quickly and leave. It would have been foolish waiting for her leaving, and attracting attention to ourselves by hanging around.

CHAPTER 7

Back in the house at last, back to my home. My dad would be upset if he heard that I enjoyed living here. I just could not get him out of my mind. Chunks had recommended an exorcism, and I think he was right. Dad was inside me; he had possessed my mind. Everything I did now, was unconsciously done the way he would do it. I was seeking something that could not be changed. Since I had been given electro-convulsive therapy years ago, my thoughts were different. I seemed to be incapable of giving affection to anyone. I had never had positive affection as a child, so did not know what it involved. I'd had girlfriends before, but they did not understand me, and I could not explain, as I did not know why I was empty like this. I was depressed and broken, my mind had decided that it no longer wanted me to be happy, and it was out of control. Dad was winning, and it was impossible to eradicate the hold he had on me.

"Come on Peedie get with it you arse, get an acid tab down your neck, that will sort you out good and proper. That will get that cunt of a father of yours forgotten about for a while."

"I might as well Chunks, what have I got to lose?"

I picked up one of the purple hearts and swallowed it with some coke, and waited, and waited. Thirty minutes later, I was still feeling like I had taken nothing.

"This stuff is shite Chunks. I'm getting fuck all from this tab, are you?"

"No, fuck all either, let's take another one. Fucking rip off bastard that Charlie is, and there is fuck all we can do about it."

We looked at each other, eyeing each other up and down to see if we looked different, but we were not. That was the decision made; another tab was getting swallowed. I did not even hesitate to swallow my other acid tab and never gave it another thought. We decided to go for a walk to see if that would speed up our acid trip.

We stopped to watch the diggers who were moving sand in the deep quarry below us, loading large dumper trucks. It was dark where we were standing, but the quarry was floodlit. A bright, clear sparkly light emitted from the large hole in the ground. We leaned on the fence for hours watching the antics of the hurrying dumper drivers who were like ants below us. Chunks hung his coat on the fence because he was feeling too warm wearing it. He decided that he would come back for it later in the evening on our way back home.

The hedge was in our way, we could not find a way round it, and there was no opening to let us through. It felt sponge like, not hard as it should, twigs were melting off and dripping to the ground below me with swirling motions as it cascaded to the waxen ground below, and we were trapped by its existence. We felt our way along the spongy hedge for ages until we found a way through it. My feet were not touching the ground now, and Chunks held on to my shirt so I did not float away. I was moving along without moving my legs. I looked down to see that my legs had disappeared.

The street lights looked fluffy with beams emitting from every angle, like a firework display of intensity, covered in gems of dripping sparkles and rainbow tinted patterns. The sight of the town lights in the distance was magical, all of them merging into a vast galaxy of swirling geometric beauty before us like stars blossoming and swirling into each other. We had found our way to the cemetery. I watched as the writing on the headstones melted before my eyes and trickled in geometric patterns to the ground below, then splash back up to reform in a non-sensical order and trickle back down again. The grass had a strange elastic texture, stretchy and soft. We lay on the grass on our backs watching the plastic waxy stars in the multi-coloured sky above us. We were in a magical pretend world, and it was slowly starting to fade.

"Listen Peedie, someone is coming."

Chunks startled me when he talked, I did not expect it. His voice sounded almost normal now, not synthetic like before.

"Let's hide here. I can see a young couple coming up the path holding hands."

We hid behind the gravestones and waited silently on them passing us. The footsteps were getting nearer and nearer. Then the couple was opposite us, right where we were hiding. I wanted to cough, but had to stifle it.

"Hey, min have you got a light!"

Chunks had shouted out from behind the gravestone and sprung to his feet. The man ran and left his girlfriend standing. She ran after him and left one of her high heels behind. We laughed and laughed for ages. A single question from behind a grave had terminated the romance. She never returned for her shoe while we were there, nor did he.

Daylight had appeared without us noticing. We had found a wooden shelter to sit into watch the light show, which was only in our heads. It had been spectacular alright, and we had both watched the same show. Feeling as it should be was returning to my limbs, leaving the artificial foam like effect behind. My legs still had a floating feeling in them, but at least they were where they should have been.

"Chunks we should get back home now; time must be wearing on. We have not been in since Saturday night."

Chunks slowly got to his feet, stretching his arms above his head. The sleeves of his jumper and his jeans were filthy, and so was mine. God only knows what we had been doing to get in that state.

"What day is it Peedie?"

"Fuck knows Chunks, we left on Saturday night, so it is Sunday, I think.

We headed for the South Street shop to get a drink and something to eat before going home. Frank, the owner who was serving someone else, could not stop staring at us. Yes, we looked a state alright, our clothing was filthy, and it was only seven a.m. I asked Frank if he had any Sunday Sports left.

"I have put them back to the suppliers. If it is something in the paper you were looking for, I have yesterday's one upstairs

I looked at the newspapers on display; the first one I noticed was the Dundee Courier, with Monday's date on it. We had lost a whole day somewhere, and I cannot think where. Thirst quenched, we headed back home.

"There is my jacket. I forgot I left it hanging there when we were watching the diggers in the quarry."

"Chunks there is no fucking quarry there. That was somebody's garden we were looking at, but it was so real. My mind is getting totally fucked up and confused now."

The acid tabs had made me rethink my life and what was going on in my fragile mind. Feelings of worthlessness were churning round in my head, dark feelings of despair and depression were taking over, and I could not shake the feeling off. It felt like I was when I lived at home. I was depressed with life. Worthlessness had been drummed into me for so long I did not really know what normal felt like.

We arrived at my house and I unlocked the door and went inside. There was an envelope lying on the floor with my name on it. I ripped it open and read it twice to make sure I was understanding what had been written. The letter was from Billy, and he had paid me off for repeatedly not turning up for work. I knew that I had missed a few days, but he had made the decision. At least he had paid me for the work I had already done. I counted the cash and slid it into my wallet. Chunks was pleased as it meant that I would be home all day.

"You will have to sign on at the dole office so you can get your rent paid and money for hash. You can't live without that, it is one of life's necessities, the staple diet for your brain."

"Skin up Chunks I have no fucking work tomorrow, make mine a large one."

I lit my joint and took a long, slow, relaxed draw. This was what I had been needing. My mood changed almost immediately.

There was someone banging loudly on the window. I stood up slowly and opened the curtains a bit. It was Fred and Brian, and someone else I did not know. Chunks went to the door and let them in.

"Peedie, meet Rachael, she is a good pal of mine."

Rachael sat down on the sofa next to me. Without saying a word, she picked up the LP record sleeve from the coffee table and skinned up. She was thin, almost anorexic in appearance. Her cheeks seemed to be sucked in, and her skin had a strange yellowish tinge to it. Her long spindly fingers rolled a joint, then another three.

"I won't share my joint with you because I have Hepatitis C. Don't worry, you won't catch it, and I always hog my joint just in case."

I had not heard of this illness, she was telling me about. She was a hard drug user, injecting herself between her fingers and toes as her other veins were no use now. She was a sorry looking state with her gaunt appearance and long black greasy hair. The joints were flowing round the room at a pace I had never seen. Soon we all stoned out our faces, laughing uncontrollably at everything and anything.

"Come on Rachael, show Peedie your party piece."

"Fuck off Fred I don't have any knickers on!"

"That will make it easier for you then won't it."

Rachael got to her feet and set an empty vodka bottle in the middle of the floor. She lifted her skirt and sat down on the bottle neck, gripped it tightly with her vagina and lifted it clear of the floor. She walked slowly across the floor still clutching the bottle and dropped it in the bin.

The whole place erupted in laughter, and I could hardly breathe, my chest was aching. Tears were running down my face in torrents. I was cured of my depression. Work could fuck off, for now, it was not good for my black moods. This was real life, away from my father and his violent outbursts, away from his drunken threats and bullying. None of my new friends were violent or threatening. They treated me with respect and gave me hash if I had none.

Rachael got up from the sofa and headed towards the door and left without saying a word.

"What is wrong with her?"

"Fuck all Peedie, she is fucking rattling for heroin, she is away to score some up the Dundee Road. Never leave money or anything lying around when she is here. She's a robbing bastard, and she is banned out of most of the shops in Forfar for stealing."

The smoke in the living room was getting Matilda stoned again. She was sitting on the back on the sofa beside Chunks. Her head and neck were swaying slightly side to side, only just managing to hold her head upright. Her beak was opening and closing like she was trying to speak to us, but no sound was coming out. She was out of her face again, and so were we.

CHAPTER 8

Life was repetitive now, every day comprised getting stoned, or looking for hash. The only thing which had changed was that I had to sign on at the dole once every two weeks, and even that was a chore. My circle of friends had grown, and they were all drug users. We tramped the streets going from one house to another, smoking joints in every one we visited. I needed more and more hash to have an effect on me now. My life was slipping from normality. I could not get my acid trip out of my mind. I could vividly remember all the things I had seen like they had been real, but my mind could not find the real answers it was looking for. My thoughts kept returning to that cupboard, that hook I had been hanging on, the bath full of cold water, and that sick, evil laugh I heard when I was submerged and struggling to survive, thrashing about under the surface. I could still see his smirking evil face as I looked up from my watery torture chamber.

I relived and replayed those events over and over again, never finding answers. How could someone who commanded respect and unconditional loyalty have treated me like that? He is still the same now as he was then, belittling and mentally abusing me to the point that I am going insane, losing the will to exist anymore. I could not stop it happening to me, years of abuse and mental control have become part of who I am, like a part of my genetic makeup. It was inside me flowing through my body like a virus out of control, like a parasite tunneling through every corner of my brain, multiplying and reproducing at an alarming rate, and I could not stop it. This life was no longer mine; he still owned me, so I bought myself four acid tabs and swallowed them all. I would die in an acid trip; I had lost the will to live. I sat wondering what it would be like dying, but I did not care.

Feelings of excitement filled my mind, and pulsating vibrations were swirling around my head, then I saw a vivid solid yellow flash of colour, followed by red, then blue, all colours exploding with a muffled bang in front of me. I heard someone talking to me, but could not understand them. I slipped into a deep dark hole, dropping out of reach. I was shouting, but nobody could hear me; I was trapped with no way out.

"Can you hear me? Come on, waken up, you are in a hospital."

A bright light was getting shone into my eyes, and I was being talked to by a voice I did not recognise. My throat was on fire, and I was thirsty. I tried to get up, but I was getting held down.

"Try to stay still. We had to empty your stomach with a pump when you came in. Your throat will be sore for a while, try not to talk too much."

I half emerged from the dark hole of unconsciousness again. I could hear voices drifting away from me into the distance.

"You are alright. Don't panic, the tube in your hand is there to help you."

"Where am I? What is happening to me?"

"You have been here for two days; you had taken a drug overdose. Luckily for you that your friend told us what you had taken, so we could act quickly. We probably saved your life when you were first admitted. I did not think you would pull through with the number of drugs you had taken. LSD is a very unpredictable drug to take."

I woke up and scanned my surroundings. Two nurses were making up a bed, two beds along from me. They did not talk to each other, but they were in unison as they tucked the sheets in, both instinctively knowing exactly what to do. A row of beds was along each side of the ward, and most of the beds were occupied. An old man in the next bed was eyeing me up and down suspiciously as I struggled to sit up. Then he smiled at me, with a smile that was so genuine, so real I trusted him immediately. I looked across at him sitting in his bed, and he winked at me.

"However bad it gets son; it is not worth killing yourself over. You are worth more than that. Whatever you are thinking now, it will get better. It may take weeks or even years, but you will get back on track."

Deep in my mind, despite the blackness which was rooted in every nerve in my body, there was a tiny part of me that believed that he could be right. I don't think I will get out of this depression very easily. It has been burning in the recesses of my brain. Flashbacks of my torturous childhood keep flooding back for no reason. It had taken me until I was fourteen years old before I could put my head under water, because of my submersion in a bath of cold water when I was only four. When one thing is overcome in my life, another childhood bad memory surfaces as fresh in my mind as if it had just happened yesterday.

I could not undress, dance, sing in front of anyone or look anyone in the eye, nor admit anything to anyone whether I knew them or not. My lack of confidence was because of years of ridicule, bullying, and violence at the hands of my father. I knew why I was like this, but I was trapped by my past, engulfed in memories which I could not eradicate. My head felt like it would burst, so much was running through my thoughts. It felt like someone had hit my skull with something heavy, compressed to half its size, then released quickly at force. I think I was still suffering from the after effects of the acid trip, which was cut short by hospital staff, and which still lost me from normality for two days.

I had woken up wearing a hospital gown in a hospital bed, but did not know who undressed me, nor even how I got here.

"Do you fancy something to eat? The food trolley is coming around in a few minutes, and you have eaten nothing since you arrived here."

"I am not hungry; I am still feeling a bit dizzy."

"If you eat something, it will probably make you feel a bit better, you don't have to eat a lot, just try a bit to see how you get on."

The trolley stopped at my bed, and a nurse came over to me and set a tray down on the over-bed table. She smiled, then playfully ruffled my hair. She did not talk to me, but she did not have to as her happy face said it all. I thought she must be about the same age as my mother, and she never smiled like that. She was humming a song I did not recognise as she flitted happily from one bed to another serving up the hospital delights. As I had ordered nothing in advance, I had to take what was left. The stew on my plate had started to dry at the edges, and a small dome of sticky looking mashed potato sat solemnly beside some dry looking cabbage. I took a small forkful of stew and lifted it to my mouth. The smell of the food filled my nostrils, but not with appetising aromas, only disgust. I was in pain and my sore head would not go away despite what the nurse had told me. I did not feel hungry, but ate about half of the offerings on the plate. I lay back against the propped-up pillows and watched as my new smiling friend next to me finished his meal.

"Well, at least you ate something laddie, you won't grow if you don't eat. People are like plants. If you don't feed and water them, they die. You will feel better soon, try not to think about things too much."

Despite his best intentions, I could not concentrate on the present moment, because I could not let go of my past. My past was not in the past, the past and the present were one thing, combined and magnified to a point where I could not separate them. My black moods were part of me, part of everything I did in life. Momentary bouts of happiness were always short lived, then would come crashing back down to reality, with an invisible force that was controlled by my father. He was always there in the recesses of my mind, lingering around just to leap out and spoil things when they were just getting better.

The lunchtime plates and cutlery were gathered up taken away. Visitors began appearing on the ward, but I would not get any. I had nobody who cared enough if I was alive or dead. My smiling friend was beaming from ear to ear as his visitor came bounding down the ward to see him. She must have only been about six years old, and she was followed by a smiling woman not far behind.

"Peedie, this is my daughter and granddaughter."

I said hello to them and watched as they all embraced and kissed each other. The girl climbed on to his bed and snuggled into him, never taking her eyes off me.

"Grandad, what is wrong with that man? Why is he in the hospital?"

"Oh, he is just in to get fixed up a bit. He just needs a rest here until he can go back home."

The visitors had all left except my new friend's family. They sat chatting away and smiling at each other most of the afternoon, occasionally turning around to talk to me. I wished that I could have had a dad like him, my life would have been different, and I probably would not be sitting in a hospital bed after trying to kill myself. I could not even do that right. Dad would have loved that; he would cast that up as his party piece over and over again. I could actually hear him saying it in my mind. "Fucking pansy bastard could not even kill himself with a drug overdose, the useless cunt, the worthless arsehole."

When I was told over and over again that I had false memories, that I was too needy, that I was wrong, gay, difficult, an instigator or trouble making pansy, and repeatedly told that I was a crazy lunatic, not right in the head, what impact has that had on my self-image? What about my mental health and self-esteem? Or I deserved whatever happened to me such as beatings, punishment, or public humiliation, I was told that I couldn't take a joke and that I was too sensitive, and that was the bastards excuse for his own behaviour, which in other words meant that it was all my fault.

"Well, it has been nice meeting you Peedie. We will see you tomorrow if you are still here. You look after my dad Sandy for me. Bye, everybody."

Sandy had never told me his name, and I never asked him. He was looking very sad, not his usual smiley face.

"What is wrong Sandy?"

"Today might be the last time I see my family. I never told you before that I have terminal cancer, because I have been very ill for a long time, and I will die here. I want you to take charge of your life and stop trying to kill yourself. Peedie I would do anything to live long enough to watch my granddaughter grow up. There is no time to waste for me; every minute I live is a bonus to me. I am on very strong painkillers and they are not doing me any good. When they let you out of here, change your friends, and your drug habits, they will never do you any good, only regret and harm will come out of it if you don't."

"Sandy, I will move out of my flat as soon as I get somewhere else. I have never felt comfortable since I found a junkie dying behind my sofa. I cannot go back home as dad hates me and does not care if I am alive or dead."

"Good for you Peedie, you will look back at your life and find out your so-called friends were just using you for a safe place to party for free."

"Thanks for the advice Sandy, I will definitely give my life a makeover when I get back home."

"Peedie I am going for a lie down, all these visitors all afternoon must have tired me out, please get the nurse to waken me up when the food trolley comes around, I have ordered something good for tea."

"Yes, I will Sandy, have a good sleep. I am going to have a shower, and the nurse has brought me a towel and soap, because I brought nothing in. See you at teatime."

The nurse came to show me where the showers were. She had to go with me as I had not been out of bed since they admitted me. I sat with my legs hanging out of the bed, finally setting my feet on the cold linoleum floor. My head was spinning a bit as I stood up, so I sat back down.

"Do you want a wheelchair? You don't have to walk if you don't feel ready."

I politely refused her offer; I would not be humiliated getting pushed along to have a shower. Everybody would stare at me and think that I was feeble and useless. I would walk even if I took all day. The nurse linked arms with me and off we went slowly to the showers.

"Right you, be careful. I am not coming in to wash you. Just press this bell when you are ready to come back to the ward."

That felt like it was the best shower, I had ever had. I held my head back and let the water rinse the shampoo from my hair. My head was not so sore now, and I had managed to keep my food down. I was seeing a psychiatrist in the morning, hoping to get some order in my scrambled mind. My life had to change; I could not carry on like before. I did not know what was real anymore, and what fantasy was. The dressing gown and clean pyjamas I had been given smelled clinical. I dried myself and got dressed, and just sat on the wooden bench looking around me.

"Have you fallen down the plug hole Peedie?"

"It's all right, I am fine. I am just coming."

"Do you fancy going to the lounge to watch television for a while, it will get you out of bed, and you won't be so bored either?"

I felt a bit more relaxed now. I was watching television, but was not taking anything in. Sandy was right, most of the people coming to my house only come for a smoke They do not come to visit me, but tag along with the rest of the regulars. I sat wishing that I had some hash now, something to get my brain back to normal. The painkillers they had given me did nothing for my headache except make it less pulsating.

"Come on, Peedie you have fallen asleep."

The nurse had come to look for me as the meals were coming around the wards. We walked back to the ward to my bed. They pulled round the curtains around Sandy's bed, but I thought nothing of it because they were always closed when he fell asleep. My nurse went back up the ward to tend to someone further up. She flitted from bed to bed, writing on the boards at the bottom of each bed, then she eventually reappeared back at me.

"Peedie I have something to tell you, Sandy passed away in his sleep half an hour ago. He knew that he did not have long, that is why we let his family stay here all afternoon. They knew he did not have long to go. It was a shock to us he went so quickly, but at least he will be at peace and not in pain anymore. If you want to move to another bed until we take him away, I would understand. The doctor has to see him and issue a death certificate, then he will be taken to the hospital mortuary."

I could not believe it. Sandy was so happy despite being in pain. He was giving me advice about my life when he was in the process of dying himself. My life was a mess, and I had tried to kill myself with an overdose. I suddenly felt selfish and uncaring. Sandy had everything to live for, and now his granddaughter would not have him around to watch her grow into a woman. My mind turned to how his family would be feeling right now; they would all be upset. If it was me lying in a hospital bed like Sandy now was, my family would not care. I was a burden to them, a thorn in their side, a waste of space, a nutcase, I was called all these things and more, but I would not be missed by any of them.

CHAPTER 9

I was released from the hospital at last after getting handed a bottle of anti-depressants and a letter to give my GP. Sandy had been taken away from his loving family, and I was still fighting my demons, but I was alive.

My house looked dark and dingy after my time spent in a bright hospital. The place had lost the sparkle I thought it had before. Full ashtrays were dotted around the room, making the place smell foul. They were emptied, and the air was freshened by opening the windows. I made myself a cup of coffee and sat listening to my song Comfortably Numb. I had missed that song, missed what it meant to me, but it sounded different without drugs, it had lost the clarity of the music notes and the different things it did to my brain. There was no option but to skin up a joint, and I needed one. My mood had not lifted, and they told me that the antidepressants could take a few weeks to start working. That was too long for me; I needed lifting immediately. I lit my creation and took a long draw; the effect was almost instant. By the time I had smoked it all I felt better, my brain had been kick-started into normality. My home seemed different, like I was just visiting, like I was at my parent's house.

That was not the best feeling to have in my present mental state; I was not coping as well as I thought it would. The hash had made me feel paranoid. I shut the curtains so that nobody could look at me through the windows. I turned the volume down on the stereo and listened. Someone was knocking on the door. I went to see who it was.

"Who is it?"

"It's me Zafoid Beeblebrox, from the Shade, open up and let me in Peedie."

I opened the door and saw Chunks standing there with a smug face.

"Look at my new coat. Are you fucking jealous yet?

"Chunks it's an old woman's coat. Why are you wearing that for fuck's sake?"

"It's not an old woman's coat. It's mine you arse, and I bought it from the charity shop, feel the furry collar Peedie."

The coat looked like a type of rough tweed, brownish flecked zig-zag patterns from top to bottom with a brown furry collar. It looked absolutely ridiculous, but it suited him. He twirled round to show me the back, and twirled back smiling.

"Admit it, you love it, don't you?"

"Chunks get in the house before someone sees me talking to you with that coat on, I would be black affronted."

We both burst out laughing and headed inside

and sat down on the sofa.

Chunks had cheered me up. He rolled a joint and handed it to me. I looked at it with glee and lit it, and inhaled the golden leb smoke. I was buzzing from head to toe, I was content and happy.

More people arrived at the door to welcome me home, and they were carrying several crates of lager, and two bottles of vodka.

The music was pumping out through the windows and into the street. Not another joint was smoked that night. It was one of the best nights I had spent with people for ages.

"Where did you get all the drink?

"Peedie we stole it from the back of the Vollies when the delivery was getting put inside, the gate was unlocked so we just grabbed what we could. There is nothing better than a free drink. There are traffic lights at the Vollies, and another set just up from here, they are digging up an old gas main, so there was so much noise and traffic queuing nobody noticed us"

Fred handed me another lager and one to Chunks and Danny. Danny was about six-foot-tall and as thin as a rake; he was sitting laughing at everybody for no reason other as he had just smoked too much hash. He opened his lager and took a drink and handed the rest to Fiona his girlfriend. The atmosphere was good, and I was happy for now, my life tonight was perfect.

Everybody was staying at the house tonight,

so I locked the door and went to bed. I must have been tired or drunk as I fell asleep quickly.

I was rudely awakened in the morning by frantic banging on my door. The banging got louder, so I sat up in bed trying to focus. The first thing I saw was traffic lights in the bedroom changing colour in front of me. I sat there confused at what was playing out live in front of my eyes, trying to comprehend what I was seeing.

"Come on, open up, it's the police."

Chunks had wakened up as well, and he was laughing. I went to the door to ask what the problem was.

"Traffic lights have been reported missing by the road contractors. We just followed the cable to your door; the lights had to have been in your house as the cable went under your door."

"Look, I knew nothing about it. I was pissed last night. Some cunt else must have done it for a laugh."

The policeman was trying to be serious, but he started to smirk. Chunks and I tilted the lights to get them out through the bedroom door and managed to get them out the front door with no damage.

"Take them back to where they were and we will say no more about it. No, wait, don't go when it's red, you have to wait on the green."

He laughed and so did everyone else. Chunks and me carrying a set of working traffic lights up the street, you just could not make it up. We set the lights beside the pile of sandbags where they were borrowed from, turned around and sheepishly went back inside and closed the door. We went into the living room and sat down, then we saw it, Danny and Fiona having sexual intercourse on the sofa opposite. Chunks rose to his feet, walked over to them and tapped Danny on the shoulder, and who was still in his passionate embrace, and asked him if he had a light for his joint. Only Chunks could have done that, he just did not care as he had no shame. We laughed and could not stop. Danny and Fiona covered themselves up and sat upright.

"You bastard Chunks I was nearly coming, you fucked that up. My lighter was in my fucking jeans pocket and I was not wearing them. You fucking arse."

Danny joined in the laughter, even he could see the funny side. It was like a scene from a movie and we had just watched it unfold in my living room. That was just what my life felt like, a movie, and I had the leading role. I went from one scene to another and never got to play myself. This was what had been my problem all my life so far. Having to act as I did in front of dad, being his object of ridicule, and having to bottle up any emotions I had for fear of being punched and tortured for being a pansy, a gay useless good for nothing. I had to choose my replies to dad carefully for fear of what would happen. You could never read what he was thinking when he started on me, it depended on the amount of drink he had consumed, or if he had fallen out with someone at the pub, or if I had looked at him the wrong way. There was no right way to look at him. I was alive and breathing and that was enough.

Everyone left and went their separate ways, and they left me on my own contemplating what I would do next. My life was becoming a mess, and I needed money. Life on the dole was grim and almost all my money was getting spent on drugs. Smoking joints had also got me addicted to nicotine. I decided there and then I would change things one way or another. I opened a lager and switched on the television to get some background noise in the flat as it was too quiet and I was not used to that. Before long, I had drunk seven cans of lager without noticing, and it did not stop there.

I woke later in the day and it was dark outside. I had missed the daylight hours. I got dressed and opened another lager to sort my brain out, then headed out to look for Chunks. His mum opened the door, still wearing curlers in her hair. She was smiling from ear to ear.

"I think he is down at the Victoria bar, that's where I am going once, I get myself dressed. There is a band playing there tonight, plus I have a date with a friend if you know what I mean."

The Victoria was busy and the country music was loud. Four band members were set up in the far corner, blasting out songs to the audience of followers. I did not see Chunks at first as he had been sitting down at a table with his aunt and younger brother.

"Do you want a pint Peedie, my brother is paying?"

"Aye, go on, then you have twisted my arm."

We both squeezed our way through the crowd and got the attention of one of the barmaids. Someone served chunks our drinks, and we turned around to head to the table. Somebody banged into me, and a splash of my lager landed on someone's trousers. He was huge and furious with me; I had not seen a face filled with rage like that since I had been at home.

"You fucking poofter look what you have done, you better buy me a drink to show how sorry you are."

"Peedie just buy him a drink for fuck's sake, he will kill you, and nobody ever messes with him."

I ignored Chunks, I saw red, a flash of rage as I had never felt before. For a split second I saw my father sitting there, how could he dare call me poofter? I grabbed his shirt and pulled him off the bar stool. My fists were pummeling his face, which was now bleeding. Someone tried to stop me and they got hit as well. I stood up and kicked him, and did not stop until he stopped moving. I stood looking down at him, and how pathetic he looked lying there. I picked up his pint of lager and poured it over his head. People had moved away from me, nobody said anything.

The music had stopped and the pub was silent. My knuckles were cut and bleeding after hitting his teeth, and I had splashes of blood on my shoes and jeans. I scowled at anyone who dared look at me, even Chunks who was staring in disbelief at what he had witnessed. Without saying a word to anyone I calmly walked out the pub door and headed back home. The man could have been dead for all I knew, but I did not care, nobody called me that name, never.

Word got around what I had done to the man in the pub, and they looked at me in a new light now. People were terrified of that man, and I had battered him senseless. Some had wanted to beat him up, but he had a reputation of being a hard man, so he got away with things for years. He never came after me either when I thought he would, and when I met him in The Masons bar a week later, he ignored me like I was not there. I looked for trouble now, I looked for an excuse to fight with anybody who crossed me, or looked at me in the wrong way. I had turned into my father and had not noticed.

CHAPTER 10

Life in Forfar was getting out of hand, it was not possible for me to go out to any bar without somebody trying to be the big man to prove that they could fight me. It was getting boring now, and I was sick of proving them wrong. Chunks had got into the wrong crowd and was taking hard drugs, injecting himself with anything that could go through a syringe needle. I had lost a good friend. I deliberately distanced myself from him as I was worried that he could tempt me to try heroin as he rated it as the highest of highs, the stone of a lifetime. But I had seen first-hand what it could do to your body and mind, and for once I did not want to try it.

A loud knock at the door startled me. I got to my feet quickly and grabbed the baseball bat from behind the front door if it was going to be trouble; I was ready. I opened the door slowly and could not believe who was standing there. It was my father and my mother.

"Peedie come home until you sort yourself out. We have heard about you and the state you are in with drink and drugs. You will get yourself killed at this rate."

I could not believe that I had agreed, so I packed up my belongings and went to live back at home. I did not have much to pack as the flat was fully furnished, so I put my things in the car boot and posted the key with a note through the shop letter-box. He would be glad now that music would not be pulsating through my wall into his shop next door. I had lost count of the times he had warned me about my noise when the shop was open.

We sat in silence in the car as we travelled the five miles to Kirriemuir, and my thoughts turned to what I was to become. I had no sooner gone into the house when I met David, who was grinning from ear to ear.

"I am glad you have come home Peedie, I have missed our laughs. You are sharing my bedroom. Come on, I will give you a hand with your stuff."

Things unpacked and put in some order, we headed down to the kitchen. Mum was cooking stew and dumplings. I had forgotten what real food smelt like and I sat with my mouth watering at the thought of eating it.

"Peedie I am glad you are home; I have been worried sick about you. I have heard many stories about you getting into bother, and about all the drugs."

"Mum, I have been fine; everybody is just exaggerating about the drugs. People have said I was on heroin, but that is one drug I have never touched."

"If you are looking for something to do to get some money, Bruce at The Ogilvy is looking for a bouncer, and its cash in hand as well. Go up and see him later. Your gran has put a good word in for you. She is the cook there now."

David and I headed to The Ogilvy and met Bruce the owner.

"I don't know about hiring you, I have heard about you and you're fighting. I want somebody who will stop fighting, not start it."

"If you give me a chance, Bruce, just for this weekend to see how it goes."

"You will only ever get one chance, and no wages if you start trouble. Be here at eight o'clock sharp, and I will tell the other staff you are starting."

The place filled up fast; there was barely room to move. I stood leaning against the wall, eyeing everybody up and down. I was wearing a black T-shirt, like Bruce had asked me to, my muscle-bound arms bulging out of the sleeves. I must have looked menacing standing there. I was the only bouncer for over three hundred revelers, and as I did my walk round checking the toilets and dance hall, I encountered hardly any trouble all night. Chucking out time came around quickly, and I herded everyone outside without incident. Bruce appeared with my wages and handed them over with a smile.

"You can work here from now on. I have never had a night where there has been no trouble at all."

"There was some trouble, but I sorted it

quickly before it escalated. I had to throw one person out because he was trying to vandalise the toilets."

David appeared from downstairs to walk me down the road to the house. We headed out the steel fire exit stairs and headed for Dewar Rhinds the baker. He served hot food through an open window on the gable end of the bakery. That is where most people went after the pub. Half way along the street, I heard my name getting called

"Hey, Peedie let's see how hard you are, now you are not in the pub, you fucking so called hard man. You think you are the big man because you threw me out."

We both ignored the name calling and walked calmly onwards. Suddenly, a hand grabbed my T-shirt, and I heard it rip. I turned around fast and kicked him right in the stomach, then kicked him twice in the face as he bent forward. He fell to the ground in a crumpled heap, shouting abuse at me. I stamped on his legs repeatedly as he lay there, but he still would not stop giving me abuse, so I jumped on his head and knocked him out cold. A crowd was gathering by that time, but nobody uttered a word to me.

"Fuck off you lot. If you know what is good for you, you saw fuck all. "

They cleared the area and headed back towards the Ogilvy. If anybody called the police, they would charge me with attempted murder.

"Come on, David, let's go home before the police get here."

"No Peedie wait a minute, aren't you forgetting something? That cunt you just battered was carrying a bag of hot pies, we better eat them before they get cold."

"He won't be eating them either with that sore face. Check they are not squashed."

The laughter started between us, and we laughed all the way home. We munched on our hot mince pies, which were kindly donated by the victim. I loved inflicting pain on someone who was annoying me, loved rendering them unconscious so they could not tell what happened when the police and ambulance arrived. That bought time to get away from the scene before someone took them to the hospital. I never checked to see if they were dead or alive before I left them lying there. I did not have a conscience; I thrived on the power it gave me.

When we opened the door to the living room, mum was still up. She was waiting for dad getting home from the pub.

"What the hell have you been doing, where did you get all the blood from? Get yourself changed and stick that lot in the washing machine, trainers as well."

I did as she asked and headed upstairs to bed. I was shattered after being on my feet for six hours in The Ogilvy. I lay there laughing to myself at what I imagined his mashed-up face would look like in the morning, and if he had wondered where his pies were. David had fallen asleep and was snoring lightly, with a snort in between breaths. The next thing I knew was the police were at the door, and dad was arguing with them.

"My boys have never left the house tonight since they came in from working at the pub, then they went straight to bed, so fuck off from my door."

"We have an arrest warrant for Peedie, so we have to take him in for questioning. "

"At five o'clock in the fucking morning, getting every cunt in the house and all the neighbours up out of their beds. You could have come at seven or eight, but then you would not get a kick out of it you black bastards. You have an arrest warrant, but you don't have a warrant to come in my house."

"We are not leaving without him and tell him to come downstairs wearing what he had on last night when he was bouncing at the pub."

I went to the door and stepped outside to my unwelcome guests.

"Remember, tell them fuck all, and admit nothing, you never left the house after your work. We are all witnesses to that, remember, say fuck all to the black bastards, fucking filth."

I went into the back seat in the police car without a struggle, after all, I had nothing to hide, I had done nothing to feel guilty about, and I had witnesses to prove it. We arrived at the police station and they led me into a room with a table and four chairs in it. An officer sat me down at one side, and he and another officer sat opposite me. The questions were getting thrown at me relentlessly, never halting, they were trying to get me to slip up with my story. The victim had sustained a cracked skull and two broken ribs apparently, and my suggestion he had slipped on a pie did not go down well. They asked me to remove my clothing and shoes and put them in a clear plastic bag. I got dressed in my white paper disposable boiler suit and was led to the cells to rethink my answers. Nothing would make me admit what had happened, I did nothing, and I was innocent. Nobody came back to see me until seven am. I had sat there on that thin mattress all that time, then an officer just let me go home.

"Where are my clothes? I can't walk down the street wearing this shite, every cunt will know that they have banged me up for the night."

"Look, sonny, your clothes are getting kept for forensics, and if they find what they are looking for, you will get charged with grievous bodily harm. We are confident you did it and confident we will link your clothing to the scene."

I went home wearing my new paper suit, getting cheek from several workmen who came out of the paper shop around the corner, and strange looks from anyone driving past me. I went straight upstairs and climbed into my bed. It had been a long night, working in the pub, then in the cop shop all night, but at least I had not been charged. I even slept in my paper overalls as I was too exhausted to take them off.

"Are you getting up today? You have been sleeping all day, and its nearly teatime. Your dad is away to work, and he will be back home soon."

Mum was trying to get me out of bed. She wanted to find out what had happened to me, and if the cops had charged me. I told her over and over they had not had evidence to charge me yet, and they would not find any. I had convinced my brain I was innocent.

"Where are your bloody clothes you were wearing when you left here last night, surely they can't need them? Plus, I have washed and dried the blood from the ones you had been wearing, so they have the wrong clothes."

"Look mother, I will get them back if they can't tie them up with what happened. I thought that was the whole point of you washing the blood-stained ones in the first place."

David was worried in case they questioned him about what had happened, and in case any witnesses came forward. I knew none would give a statement, none of them would be that stupid. We went upstairs to discuss what was to be done if they questioned David. I knew he would not talk even if they caught him off guard, his mouth was as tight as a duck's arse, and that is watertight. David was close to me and reliable. He would lie for me instinctively, denying he knew anything. He was used to lying all his life; he often had to think on his feet to save a beating, as I always had to. After any question or accusation, regardless of how small it was, I automatically denied it.

Mum was shouting for us to come downstairs for our tea. We had sealed our pact so we scurried down to the table. Dad was already eating, only glancing over at me as I sat down at the table. We all ate with nobody saying a word, but that was normal in our house, eating was a necessity, not a social occasion. It had never been a pleasant experience at mealtimes, but at least dad could not force me to eat vomit now. Mum sat staring at me out the corner of her eye, only shifting her gaze to look over to dad. I do not know what she was thinking, and she never said. She was deep in thought only just managing to get her fork to pick up food from her plate.

Dad got up from his seat at the table and picked up his fags from the worktop and sat back down. He lit one, and blew the smoke all the way down the table, then flicked his ash onto the carpet.

"What about the black bastard coppers then? I take it you have not been charged yet, admit fuck all, even if you did it."

"I never told them anything dad, even though they kept me all night."

"Stay out of trouble, and if you can't, don't get fucking caught. If you have to kick the shite of somebody, do it up a close or somewhere no cunt can see you, not near the fucking bakers. You are more of a man now, you have found your fists, at last, never back down, and never stop hitting until you hear a bone breaking. A broken nose can stop the biggest of men until you can get the boot into his balls."

David and I went up to the Ogilvy for a game of pool and a pint, I could not drink as I had to do my job at the disco later on. I needed a clear head working in the heat of that place. Bruce turned the heating up so that people would get thirsty and drink more alcohol.

My stint in the pub bouncing, was quiet for a while until a mob came in to cause trouble. One of them started on David for no reason. I warned him to calm down or get out. He smashed a bottle and swung it round at me, cutting my T-shirt as he did. I swung him round using his outstretched arm and grabbed him from behind so he could not move his arms. The bottle was still clutched tightly in his hand. David kicked the bottle from his grasp, sending it flying in the air, landing with a smash in the corner of the dance floor. He was trying to kick me with his heels, so I pushed him almost running towards the fire exit stairs. I shoved him all the way down, and he landed in a crumpled heap on the last few steps. I followed him down and stamped on his fingers as hard as I could. He would not be punching me tonight or any time soon. The rest of his mates said nothing, and left by the stairs, and never came back in. The rest of the night was trouble free, even the walk home at closing time.

I was rudely awakened at five thirty am, dad was telling me to get up. The police were at the door for me again and want me to go to the station with them. I put my clothes on and went downstairs to be faced with the same officers from last night.

"We still need to ask a few questions about the assault. There are a couple of things we need to clarify."

"You black bastards, why do you not come at a civilized fucking time to question my son, especially as he has done fuck all, always the middle of the fucking night. I have work in the morning you black arseholes."

I said nothing and just went with them; there would be no point struggling or refusing to go. I wanted it over with and cleared up. The two officers led me to a side room and sat me down. They left me there on my own for over an hour and a half, then they entered the room and said I was free to go. They laughed at me; they had arrested me for a laugh just to fill in time until the end of the night shift.

Dad had still not left for work when I got home. When I told him what had happened, he went ballistic? He went outside and started the car and took off at speed. I never saw him for over an hour.

"That pair of coppers will not be back here annoying you again. I have been to the police inspector's house. He was still sleeping when I banged on his door, but he listened to what I was saying."

Dad went to work, he would be late, but he did not care; he had got the result he had wanted. Two hours later, the same two police officers knocked on the door. They were accompanied by the inspector. Mum answered the door and shouted abuse at them for coming back again.

"It's alright, nobody is getting arrested, and these officers have something to say to you Peedie."

One of them started to talk, softly at first.

"I am sorry for what we did to you last night. We do not think it funny at all, and it will never happen again."

"Sorry, could you speak up as I never heard a word you said?"

Mum was at it; she had heard it all clearly. She made that man repeat it three times before she felt happy that she had humiliated him enough, then she asked the other one to apologise as well. When she thought that she had accomplished total humiliation, she was happy. The inspector stood smirking at the officers as they recited their apologies. They would not be getting me out of bed anytime soon.

CHAPTER 11

Life settled down for a while, but my drinking did not. I never got charged for the assaults, and the police left me alone, for now at least. David had got a loan of a large frame tent with two bedrooms and a living area. For no reason other than he met someone from Edzell, he wanted us to go there for a holiday, away from Kirriemuir. We were getting a lift there later in the day by a friend of Bruce from the pub who had a van.

We got dropped off beside the Edzell Castle road end. I unceremoniously dumped our camping gear over the dry-stone dyke into the field opposite. David jumped over first and I followed behind. This part of the field was a wasteland with gorse and whin bushes growing in random clumps covering a large area. We found a clearing large enough for our tent, so we erected it. None of us had built it before, so it took a long time to get it finished, plus I had a hangover which did not help. Our holiday accommodation was bright orange, with a blue roof. Despite the semi cover of the bushes, our tent stuck out like a sore thumb, there would be no hiding place for us if things went wrong here.

"Come on, David. Let's go for a fucking pint. I am gagging for one now, and parched like an

Arabs' sandal."

"At least we got the tent up before it pissed down, mum reckoned we would get soaked today, she felt it in her bones she said."

"The sun is splitting the pavements David; her bones are liars."

We laughed at our own sick jokes walking the mile into Edzell with David farting in music like tones at random moments along the way. He was still like that from when he was young, when he could emit volumes of shrieking smelly vile air from his arse on demand. We both still found it extremely funny; we acted like schoolchildren, at the slightest fart.

The Panmure was the first pub we went into. I had entered first just in case there was bother. All heads turned around to look at us, eyeing us up and down as like they had seen no one come into their local bar before. I ordered two pints of lager and sat down at the bar.

"I will pay for those pints Gavin; those guys look like they need a drink."

The man spoke with an American accent, and so did several others in the bar. I thanked him and found out they all worked at the Edzell Military Air force Base. The pints were going down well and soon I was chilled out. We stayed for a few more pints, then headed for the chip shop for something to eat. Two white pudding suppers, and six pickled eggs between us, we sat on a bench at the Muir and watched the world go by.

This holiday would be good.

Darkness was falling, so we headed to our tent. We never brought a torch or any form of lighting, mainly because we did not think we would need one. It was a long road in that light, and everything around us felt creepy. Several times we had turned around on the road as we thought we were being followed. The cottages we passed were in darkness; dogs were barking furiously at us as we noisily walked past. The farmstead was the worst to pass with the dark open barn doors filled with darkness staring back at us. Our footsteps seemed to echo as we made our way along the road. When we reached our field, we looked to our right and saw the silhouette of the castle ruins towering over the trees. The silence now was deafening, our minds were in overdrive as we listened to every slight noise, wondering what it could be, filtering out real noises, from imaginary ones in our minds. Finally, we reached the fence and stood on the second wire from the bottom, which sent a high pitched a squeal into the surrounding darkness, then stepping over it and setting down on the other side. I lit my lighter to find the zipper on the door. David crashed in a heap beside me after he tripped over a guy rope, muttering with disgust at the primitive arrangements.

We sorted our sleeping bags out and slid awkwardly into them, cocooned in a nylon padded tube for warmth. The lager had had its effect on me, so I had to go outside to relieve myself. It felt that the stream of processed lager flow would never stop. Back inside to struggle into my sleeping bag and a certain lack of comfort, I settled down for the night and fell into a semi-drunken slumber.

In the morning we both seemed to waken up at the same time, a deep cough coming from outside the tent had startled us.

"Who the fuck is outside, I have got a big stick and I am not scared to use it. The six of us will come out and kick the shite out of you."

David was panicking now. Another cough came from right outside our tent. We could see a silhouette standing outside nearly touching the canvas, heavy breathing was as close now as we could almost feel it on our face. That was it for me, I stood up and pulled the zip up around the door and dived outside, and just stood there in utter disbelief as a young calf was standing looking back at me. It looked lost and alone, not another cow was to be seen anywhere, and this one was too young to be out on its own. It had saliva dripping from its mouth, and it kept flicking its tongue up each nostril in turn. It seemed tame and did not seem to fear us. It walked around the area near our tent, never wandering far before returning to watch us.

"Hey, lads, grab a hold of that calf till I come over to get it."

The farmer walked over towards us grinning

from ear to ear. The calf had been missing all night from the farm sheds and its mother had been noisily looking for it. He put it round his shoulder like a scarf and held on to its legs.

"Could you come and open the gate for me lads and close it again when I get out? Thanks again for keeping her safe."

The farmer was a thinly built, soft-spoken man who wore gold coloured glasses. He waved to us as he drove off in his Landover. We never actually looked after the calf, more like it homed in on us because we were there.

We were hungry now and had brought nothing to eat with us on our trip. We headed off to Edzell to look for food, any food as long as it was edible, we would not mind. The road looked a lot different in the daylight than it did last night in the dark. It was a beautiful part of the countryside with the castle as an added bonus. It was sunny and warm on our faces as we walked into the village. We stopped at the public toilets on the Muir on the way in, which had a vase of flowers adorning the vanity unit in the corner. I had never seen public toilets so cared for in my life. The ones in Kirriemuir smelt foul and had all manner of obscene vulgarities inscribed in a different handwriting all over the walls and even the ceiling.

The café was open, a large converted church like building with pool tables at the rear. A small man peered through the smoke-filled air. The light was dim, comprising a single bulb hanging over the fryer behind him. An old lady smiled at us and asked us what we wanted. She looked frail and thin and was dressed in old style clothing, which was more suited to a film set than a place of business. Her hair was pure white, set on top of a thin wrinkled face. We ordered two bacon rolls each because she did not have sausage as advertised as she told us, Davie, her husband had not been to the shops yet. He looked like he should be in a care home shuffling along slowly only just managing to bring our coffee over to us. We had watched him make the coffee using a standard house kettle which he filled from the taps on the sink. The ceiling was very high and dark with the smoky air just lingering in the roof space looking for an exit. The roll was the best thing I had eaten since we arrived here and we just sat in silence looking around us.

A group of youths appeared jostling at the counter trying to get attention to get served.

"Come on, Mary. Get a move on, show us your knickers."

"Hurry up, Mary, or it will be tomorrow we get served."

The verbal abuse carried on relentlessly as Mary shuffled back and forth behind the counter, spreading margarine on the rolls lined up in front of her. She looked like she was getting annoyed.

"Davie, Davie those lads are taking the piss

out of me."

"Come on lads put the piss back in Mary."

Davies retort was funny. He was taking the piss with his reply to her, and she did not seem to notice. Nor did he seem phased with the youths who were still joking around with her as they were getting served.

"Stay up at the tables here lads, the tables at the back beside the pool tables are not open yet."

The chairs and tables were old like something from the 1940s with a waxy red faded tablecloth adorning each one. Mary was walking between the rows of empty tables, giving the illusion that she was wiping the table tops. She was going through the motions of what she had probably done for decades, now more of a habit than for hygiene.

Belly's full we left the café and headed back up the road towards our tent. We looked back towards the village and saw the youths emerging from the café. They seemed to watch us as we disappeared out of sight. The tent stood out against the green grass and bushes, there would be no chance we could miss finding it. The zip slid up easier than it had when we first erected it, and we entered the lounge area and stood looking around us. We had nothing to cook on, sit on, nor any lights. What had seemed a fabulous idea was now looking less glamourous? This was not what we had imagined, and we had no way of getting home.

"Hey, you two in the tent, can we come over to see you?"

I peered over to the road, shielding my eyes from the sun and there stood the three youths from the café.

"Yes, come over if you are not looking for any bother, because we can't be arsed with that shite."

"No, we would not start shite with you, we thought you looked like a fucking nutter when we saw you in Smokey Joes café."

They jumped over the fence and weaved through the bushes towards us. One of them had a carrier bag full of beer cans. He dipped his hand in and pulled a can out and handed one to me.

"I am Lenny, and they are my pals Bob and Tam. We are just being nosey, my dad said that he had seen a big tent in the trees and wondered who it was."

"I am called Peedie, and this is David, my brother, we are from Kirriemuir, just staying for a change of scenery."

We all sat in the sun and drank the whole bag of beer between us, and soon I was needing more. We were invited to the village for a drink. It did not seem to take long to get to the village, we were getting used to walking the road. Bob led us halfway along the main street and turned left down a small hill beside a garage. When we reached the bottom, a fantastic wire rope suspension foot bridge was directly in front of us. Tam ran half way across the bridge and swung it from side to side. David followed him and joined in, the bridge looked as if it would disintegrate and fall down.

"This is what locals call the shaking bridge, it is not good to go across when you are pissed, and I live over the other side."

Bob and the rest of us crossed over the bridge, the sandstone rocks jutting out from the fast-flowing river were erupting a white foam spray as the swirling brown water cascaded over them. We walked about fifty yards and a large house appeared in a clearing in the trees, with a residential caravan parked beside it.

"This is where I stay because my sisters all have a bedroom each and there is not enough room for me. It means I can come and go when I want, and no cunt is any the wiser. Come into my bachelor pad and sit down."

Bob was not house proud; that was the first thing I noticed. There was dirty clothing and a variety of dirty dishes lying in small untidy piles around the furniture. He opened the fridge and took a can of lager out for everyone. It was the only thing in his fridge; he had crammed lager into every space, making the shelves sag slightly in the middle. Bob put his stereo on and blasted out a Nazareth song I had not heard for ages, he played it repeatedly until the tune was playing in my head when he finally changed the song.

Even although my new friends were the same age as David, they seemed to be decent lads, and I had not punched their heads in yet, so that was a bonus. We stayed there drinking all day until it was getting dark outside.

"Come on, David. We better be getting back to our canvas luxury dwelling before we can't see on the shaking bridge; it is bad enough in the daylight."

"You can both crash here if you want, there are plenty of spare beds, and we still have time to nip to the chip shop for something to eat before it shuts if you want."

"Yes, Bob, we will stay here if it's OK. I am too pissed now to walk the distance to the tent now, anyway."

We all headed for the bridge led by Tam and Lenny. I lost count of the times I tripped on the rough track before we even reached the bridge. I was not used to the path like they all were. The bridge was making loud eerie squealing noises as the wire holding it from swaying too much was rubbing on the steel rings which held it in place. It was hard to walk with us all going over at the same time because we were carrying on and drunk. The chip shop had closed early, so we headed back to the caravan, back to our home for tonight.

"Let's do a séance Bob, we have not done one for ages."

"Lenny. Fuck off, you know Tam freaks out if

we do that."

"Fuck off Bob I do not, more like you freak out at your own shadow you prick."

Lenny took the Ouija board out of the box and set it out on the coffee table. He put the lights out and lit a small pillar candle. I had often heard of the boards but I had never seen one before. It had a row of numbers from one to ten, the alphabet letters from A to Z, and the words yes and no printed on it. We all put our finger on the glass except David, who had to be persuaded that he would not die instantly if he touched it. Lenny started asking questions.

"Are there any spirits here with us tonight?"

"Yes, I have vodka in the cupboard."

"Tam stop being a fanny, be serious or you can wait outside till we are done."

"Are there any spirits who would like to talk to us?"

The glass moved slowly at first, then slid quickly to yes on the board.

"Are you male or female?"

The glass moved effortlessly and spelled out male. This was freaking me out already.

"Do you know anyone in this room?"

The glass hovered for a few seconds, then slid over to B, then to O, then back to B.

"Stop fucking about you bastards, I fucking have to live here, stop winding me up or else you can all fuck off "

We were not winding Bob up. If I had not seen

it with my own eyes, I would not have believed it. Poor Bob was freaking out now, I could see he was not enjoying this as much as we all were.

"How did you die?"

The glass did not move at first, then spelled out: I fell off my horse.

Lenny burst into hysterical laughter and took his finger off the glass.

"What a way to die, what a fucking tosser, I bet he was pissed."

Lenny had only just finished what he was saying, and he fell backwards with force, screaming like someone had burned him, then he got up and ran outside. He dropped to the ground and curled into a ball still shouting and screaming.

"Get off, you bastard, leave me alone."

Bob ran out and grabbed Lenny and shook him.

"Lenny, come on man, it's only a fucking game, there is fuck all happening to you.

He pulled Lenny to his feet, and he was visibly shaking. Bob helped him into the caravan and sat him down across from me. He looked around at us all looking at him, then he lifted up his T-shirt. A mark like a whiplash, had suddenly appeared across his chest and his arm.

"The bastard was hitting me because I laughed at him. I saw the whip he was lashing me with coming at me."

"What an imagination Lenny you stupid cunt, a ghost from an Ouija board can't hurt you.

Your mark must have been made when you ran screaming like a girl."

"Peedie you were not lashed with a horseman's whip like I was. It happened to me not you; it would be different if someone had whipped you to near death."

Everybody laughed at Lenny; he was being dramatic as usual. He was still declaring his affliction and pointing at the weal on his chest, which had got larger than when he first showed it to us. Without warning, the walls of the caravan started to shake along the door wall. We all felt it, then the banging started, and it got louder and louder.

"We are all going to die. I fucking told you not to laugh, you bunch of arseholes we are all doomed."

The noise stopped and Lenny grinned at us. We all sat looking around the room speechless, then we heard it.

"Come on, you cunts in there, keep the bloody noise down. We are all trying to sleep in the house. Do you know what time it is? I banged on your bloody door for ages before you answered me, now pipe down the lot of you."

"It's Bob's mum, she was the one who was banging, not the fucking horseman. Lenny, you are a prick."

"I don't give a shit, if you cunts don't believe me, I felt that fucking whip hit me."

We all went to bed after downing another two

cans each. I was wakened up in the middle of the night with rain hitting the aluminium roof. I pulled the sleeping bag over my head to try to muffle the noise. I seemed to be the only one awake. My mind was awake and alert now, the effects of the lager had left me. I felt alone and vulnerable in this place even though we were all here. It reminded me of being at home when I was young, alone and vulnerable, even though there were nine of us in our house. With my evil dad standing listening just outside my door, waiting and hoping for me to make any noise so he had an excuse to hurt me with his fists. I was feeling low; my mood had gone back to where it had been before. Feelings of fear and dread were engulfing me, seeping into me and running through my veins. Flashbacks of my childhood came rushing into my mind. I could hear dad breathing outside the door, his whisky smelling breath coming through the slight gap in the door. He never left that doorway all night, and I never slept for fear of what would happen.

CHAPTER 12

David was the first to waken and get out of bed. He went to the toilet, with his every footstep vibrating the thin caravan floor. I could hear the splash of urine hitting the toilet bowl water, it ran and ran for what seemed an eternity, and then the usual morning squeaky long drawn out fart emerged.

"For fuck's sake that is fucking stinking David, I can smell it from the living room."

"Well, Bob, it's better out than in. That's what I say."

Soon we were all awake, David had made sure of that, he never crept about when he got out of bed, and the thin walls dividing the rooms did not help. Lenny was still showing off his whiplash scar, still maintaining that a demon had attacked him. It had gone from a horseman to a demon overnight, and no doubt it would expand when he recited his demise to everyone he met.

"Peedie we will have to go back to the tent for clean clothes, my jeans are filthy."

"Yes, we will head off now then, I am heading to the shop for a bottle of coke, and I am as dry as an Arabs sandal."

We bid our farewells, promising to meet up later in the day. The bridge looked amazing in daylight as we crossed over to the village, it did not seem so shaky either, but maybe it was because we were sober.

A herd of cows met us as we left the village, they were running frantically along towards us, and we saw our farmer behind them.

"Stop them before they get to you, put your arms out to your sides and shout."

We knew what to do instinctively as we had been brought up on farms. David went to one side and me the other. We managed to turn them round towards the farmer. He stayed in front of them all the way up the road to the farm and turned them through an open gate.

"Thank you so much for helping, a dog spooked them farther up, and I lost control. Normally they just saunter down to the gate and go in by themselves."

"How is the camping trip going then?"

"We never stayed there last night so I hope our tent is still in one piece. We love this place and wished we could live here."

"Well, I have an empty cottage you can rent, it is in a bit of a mess, but if you want it you can have it, it is five pounds a week rent. Come to the farmhouse at twelve o'clock and I will show it to you if I can find the key. I have to go to Brechin just now for some shopping but will be back in time to show you round."

The tent was still erect and standing out from the greenery around it, but I had already made the decision it would not be slept in again. I had decided the cottage was getting rented by me, and I had not set eyes on it yet. I could not go back home after this holiday; I would end up back in Sunnyside Psychiatric Hospital. Dad had infiltrated my thoughts and I had not clapped eyes on him since we left. He had brainwashed me into thinking I was useless and a burden on society, and now I could not change that. I wished that he had killed me years ago in one of his violent rages directed at me all my early life, then I would not be in this dark unhappy place. I needed help, professional help, but was scared to go. I did not want to be sent to that hospital to get Electro Convulsive Therapy again.

The farmer was home when I knocked on the farmhouse door. He came out with the key for the cottage, dangling from a key ring in his hand. He was smiling at us with such a genuine, gentle face; he was definitely a gentleman. The cottage was located right in the middle of the farmyard beside sandstone-built sheds with large wooded painted doors. A black small wooden gate set into a stone wall was the opening into the garden behind the cottage. There was a track to other farm buildings on the other side. The farmer fumbled with the key, but could not get it to open the lock, so he handed it to me. It seemed to open easily for me, and I opened the door and went inside.

"I will leave the two of you to have a look. Just

come to the house to tell me if you want the cottage, and take your time."

The hallway stank of dogs, a foul musty smell filled the entire house. The kitchen was directly opposite the front door and the bathroom to the left of that. This place was grim alright, even the living room had balls of dog hair blowing around like tumbleweed. This cottage had not seen a paintbrush in years. The two bedrooms still had carpets on the floors, which were black and shiny in places with ingrained filth. The kitchen had a sink unit and nothing else. Someone had neglected this house for years by the look of it.

I decided there and then I would rent the cottage. I would live in hell before I went back home. The farmer was happy to have me as a tenant and told me he did not want any rent until I had done the place up. David and I both spent the afternoon sweeping and clearing out the rancid smelling carpets. I lit the fire so we could get hot water for cleaning and headed to the village to buy cleaning products and something to eat. I decided on washing powder for cleaning as it would double up for washing clothes. The water was heating up by the time I had returned and David had finished scraping the last of the underlay from the wooden floors. The cleaning seemed to take a long time before it felt habitable, but between us we got it done.

"Well, that's it clean Peedie, but what are we

going to sleep on? There is fuck all in this shit-hole."

"I will get stuff to furnish it when I can, but first I think we should go and bring the tent here while it is still dry."

It took three trips to bring our tent and belongings to the cottage. I unrolled the tent and set it out like a mattress; this would be better than sleeping on the floor. With a sleeping bag on top, it would be reasonably comfortable. I had moved in with nothing but a tent, a kettle and a couple of pans and some plates, cups, and cutlery, but it was home. I filled the kettle and set it on top of the burning wood on the fire so that we could get a cup of something hot. This was the way I heated up our soup. I was camping indoors until I could get some furniture.

David went to the village and reappeared over two hours later in a van. The driver got out and so did Tam and Bob.

"Dinna say we are no good to you Peedie, my dad is throwing out this couch and two chairs, and David said you could use them."

Bob was looking like the cat who got the cream. He was pleased that he had helped me out. I had somewhere to sit now in comfort. I thanked Bob and his dad, I felt humbled when he refused any payment. He drove away, waving out his window, leaving Bob and Tam at the house.

"Later we are all going down to the posh bit in the village and start knocking on doors, and

Lenny will be coming with us."

"What are we going to do that for?"

"Peedie you have fuck all in your house, the rich cunts will have plenty of stuff in their garages and outhouses."

We arrived at the first house in the street, and Lenny knocked on the door. After a few minutes, an older woman came shuffling to the door.

"Hello, Lenny, how are you getting on? I have not seen your mum for ages. How can I help you gents?"

Lenny gave her a sob story about me. I could have burst into tears if I had not known it was lies. He laid it on thick that I had nothing.

"Come around to the side door and I will see you there, I may have some bits and bobs from the house you can have, and maybe something in the garage as well."

Lenny was handed the garage key, so he opened the padlock and handed her the key back. He opened the wooden door, and it creaked all the way round. I could not believe there were a cooker and a fridge and a twin tub washing machine in her garage and I was given it as a gift, along with bedding, curtains, and towels. None of the things were the most modern, but they were fabulous to me. Bob's dad delivered the stuff to my cottage for nothing. It was a company works van, so the fuel was free. We continued our begging spree all along the street, staring into open garages to see if there was anything useful, we could ask for. Tam borrowed a wheel barrow to collect all the things which had been given to me, and we made four separate trips to the village before we had collected it all.

Over the weeks which followed I was given everything else, I needed to live in my new home. I decorated the rooms as I could afford paint, and soon the whole place looked fabulous. It was lonely living here, even though I had friends around me. My mind was switched off from certain things in life and affection towards anyone was nonexistent. Nobody got close to me because I did not know how to let them near me and did not totally trust their motives. I shut my brain off from reality and life because my childhood had trained me to be like that.

My night out at the Panmure Arms was worth the hangover in the morning. Someone had offered me a labourer's job on a water pipeline starting on Monday morning. This might lift me out of the black hole my mind had sunk into.

The van was parked across from the pub when I reached the village, because the ganger lived there, and had unlocked the doors so that everyone could go in and sit down. The van filled up, and the ganger came out of his house.

"Where the fuck is Jimmy? He has two minutes and we leave without him; the drunken bastard is always late on a fucking Monday."

Nobody replied, and the van drove off towards Dundee, where we would be working. He had left Jimmy behind to teach him a lesson. My first job when we arrived was to stand and watch a digger backfilling the pipe track in case any large stones landed on the steel water pipe which had been laid and tested.

I tried my hand at dry stone walling and was a natural at it, so got to reinstate all the walls that the pipeline had been dug through. I was content with my job, and the wages were good. The drink was easily obtained now I had the cash to spend. Friday nights could not come quick enough, and I always asked to be dropped off at the pub before I went home. This was a disaster for me as I could not stop drinking until the pub closed, and I had to be physically removed at the end of the night.

"Come on, Peedie there is a party at the staff quarters at the Panmure Arms after the pubs shut."

Bob had come to meet me, as he knew that I had to be persuaded to go home after closing time. We headed to the cottage so I could get washed and changed out of my work clothes, then headed back to the staff quarters party. When we arrived, nobody would let us in the door. Somebody was hanging out the upstairs window giving us abuse and ridiculing me because I was not getting in. That was when I lost my temper.

I woke up in my bed the next morning with an

axe beside me in bed. The shaft was covered in blood, and my knuckles were cut on both hands. My mind jumped into shock; panic set in, I must have killed somebody. I recovered enough to go to the village and was met by Lenny outside Smokey Joes.

"You had better not go any further, you are in serious shit for what you did last night."

"What have I done, Lenny? You are freaking me out now."

"When you never got into the party, you just flipped out. We all thought you had given in and just went home, but you appeared back at the door with a three-foot-long axe and started chopping at the door like a crazed lunatic. People were jumping from the first-floor windows to escape in case you got in."

"Lenny, I can't remember anything from last night. Did I kill anybody or hit them with the axe?"

"You almost got somebody who was standing behind the door, the axe head came through the door panel after you had chopped at it for ages, you just would not listen to anyone, you did not appear to be sane anymore, and nobody had ever seen lunatic behaviour like that before. You were oblivious to everything around you, and you had smashed several car headlights on the way here, and Smokey Joe's window as well."

"For fuck's sake, why have I not been arrested yet? Surely somebody phoned the police."

"Nobody phoned, because the owner did not want you charged. Fuck knows why because I have been banned for less."

Luckily, the blood was from my own hands and not from a murder victim, but it could easily have been different. I did not remember being there, nor walking the mile home for the axe, then the mile back, nor smashing car lights and the shop window. No matter how hard I tried to recall the previous evening, I could not remember anything. There was a big gap in my memory, which I could not fill in. I was lost in my own head, and this was not what I wanted to happen. I was getting like my father, a psycho-pathic violent bully.

I turned around and went back home, and back to bed, I felt ill and nauseous, I was con-fused and yet agitated that my memory of what had happened had vanished. I had fallen asleep, but was woken up by a loud knocking on the front door. The axe had already been hidden up my chimney, set on a ledge farther up out of sight, so I nervously opened my door expecting the police, but it was not.

"So, you are the one that hacked at my pub door with an axe. You must be one fucked up person to have done that. I will not be calling the police if you come and fix the damage."

"I don't understand that. Why did you not call the police?"

"Because I was young once, and have been in

the same place you are now. I will pay for the materials and you can repair it at the weekend.

Do not let me down, I am giving you a chance to do right for yourself."

He went back in his car and left me standing in total disbelief as to what had just happened.

CHAPTER 13

I went to fix the damage I had caused on Saturday morning after checking that it was alright to make a noise at that time. Job completed to the owner's satisfaction he asked me to follow him to the hotel corridor upstairs.

"How much would you charge to paint all this corridor if I supply the paint?"

"I don't think it would be right for me to get paid for it after what I did to your pub before."

"Right then if you can't think of a price, I will pay you eighty pounds cash when you have finished it, which will keep you out of mischief this weekend at least."

I enjoyed painting in the hotel, the chef provided and cooked all my meals, and I got a couple of free pints at the end of my shift. Life started to change for me for the better. I still drank alcohol but not in the vast quantities I used to. I met Fiona a girl from Aberdeen who liked me for who I was. She seemed to be infatuated with me and followed me everywhere I went. No matter which bar I went to, she would turn up and find me like a sniffer dog.

This relationship was getting serious for her, but not for me. She was full on, and obsessed with me and I only wanted to take things slowly.

I came home from work to find she had broken into my house, and she was wearing my clothes. Fiona was a stalker and I could not get rid of her. All she wanted was somewhere to stay, and I was the chosen victim because I had a house. It was not me she wanted, anyone would have done, but I was a soft touch and let her stay. She stayed in bed most of the day when I was at work and I could not get her to leave. I listened to all her lies about her demise and felt sorry for her; she had conned me. Money started to go missing from my wallet, small amounts at first, but then it got more and more. I did not grudge her money for essentials, but when fifty pounds went astray; I had had enough. I told her to be away from my house before I came home from work, and never to return, but she was still there when I got home, lying naked in the bed

I went for a pint to calm, down but met Jenny on my way there. She was more like a man than a woman, always dressed in men's clothing and boots, with short cropped hair.

"Peedie you are looking miserable today, what is eating your arse?"

"Jenny, it's Fiona. I don't want to be with her any more, but I can't get her to leave."

"I have seen her go back and forth to your house often when you are at work, so she does leave the house. If you want, I will have a word with her tomorrow when you are at work. I will see what she has to say for herself."

I agreed with Jenny going to speak to Fiona. Maybe she would have more luck than me. I arrived home that night to an empty house, and Fiona seemed to be gone. My clothes she used to wear were lying on the bed, and everything she owned was nowhere to be seen.

Jenny arrived at my door, smiling from ear to ear.

"Well Fiona has left and definitely won't be coming back; you can be sure of that."

"How did you manage that Jenny? I have tried for weeks to ditch her."

"It was easy. I just walked right into the bedroom and pointed my loaded shotgun at her, told her to remove your clothing and to put hers on. I made sure she only packed her stuff, then she left without complaining, it is easy if you know how. I drove her to the bus stop and watched her leave on a bus to Brechin, she won't come back because I warned her that I would shoot her on sight."

Jenny meant it as well, she was deadly serious. We became good friends after that and I used to do odd jobs for her if she needed help.

Locals used to fear her because of her appearance, but I could see through that disguise, and could see a frail woman who needed help. She had never married and only had her Jack Russell dogs in her life. I built high fences to keep her dogs in to make life easier for her and never took a penny in return.

Freedom from Fiona was a relief, and I started to live again. It was strange coming home from work to an empty house and sleeping on my own again.

"Do you fancy a change of scenery this weekend Peedie, I am going to have a night out in Brechin for a change?"

"Aye, Bob, I fancy that. I am sick of the pubs in this shithole anyway, and David is away to Kirriemuir for the weekend."

The bus was on time and we paid for our tickets and sat at the back. I had never walked about in Brechin before, but had been driven through it when I was younger. The pubs here had a different atmosphere than Edzell; people looked at me like I had two heads. We ordered a pint each and sat at the bar on the high stools at the end. We were getting stared at now by several men about my age, then one of them approached me.

"You had better move from that bar stool if you know what is good for you. That is some cunts stool."

"Look, you can fuck off and sit back beside your friends. I am not moving for you or anybody else, so get out of my face."

He went back to the table, he came from, and sat down. They were talking loudly amongst themselves, but nobody had challenged me for what I had said. Bob finished his pint first, then I finished mine.

"Wait a minute Bob, I will have to go for a piss first before I go, and you can wait for me outside if you are worried about waiting on your own"

Bob went outside, and I went to the toilets, followed by two of the arseholes from the table. One of them grabbed me by the shirt and pointed in my face with his finger, while the other one took a swing at me which landed on my chest. That was it for me, I grabbed his finger and bent it back until I heard it snap. I grabbed his hair and smashed his face on to the sink several times with force, then did the same to the other one. One of them definitely had a broken nose, his blood was pouring out of it all over his clothes. I gave them both a hard kick just for good measure and left them lying there. Then I just calmly walked out of the toilets, past their friends and out of the pub. I had no remorse doing it either, I was immune to compassion, and I had no morals.

Bob and I headed for the next bar and sat down. We had only been there five minutes when we were interrupted by one of the men from the last pub.

"You had better watch your back you bastard, they have taken my mate to the hospital because of you, and you should see his fucking face."

"Look fuck off or you will get the same as him, and so will anybody else who fancies trying."

"Come on, Peedie let's leave here before we get bothered. I don't fancy waking up in traction in the hospital, getting fed with a tube. This has gone far enough now let's go."

"Fuck them all Bob, they won't bother us now. We will just enjoy our night and ignore them."

We went from pub to pub and got no trouble, plenty of evil looks, but none of the locals dared say anything. I don't know what was getting said about me, but it worked. I ordered a taxi to get home and sat waiting beside Bob on a low wall eating a fish supper until it arrived.

The driver asked questions all the way to Edzell, he had heard about my antics in the pub because he was the one who drove the man to the hospital to get his nose looked at. I was glad to get out of that taxi as I was feeling queasy after travelling. Bob had fallen asleep, so I woke him up and half carried him out of the car, the drink and fresh air had caught up with him. I paid the driver, and he reversed away from the house and turned his taxi round in the farm steading, stopping as if to get a good look at me in his headlights. Bob was throwing up in the toilet so I had to go outside to piss, the lager I had consumed all night had to go somewhere and I could not wait. I stood looking up at the night sky looking at the stars glimmering above me, having to refocus several times as I stood swaying from side to side. My bladder empty I went back inside to see Bob asleep already on the sofa with his mouth hanging open. I poured myself a pint glass of water and drank all of it and went to bed.

It was like a scene from a movie, when I was rudely wakened in the morning. I heard raised voices and loud banging on the front door. Someone was trying to force the bedroom window open, and was shouting threats to me. I peered out the living room curtains, and saw two cars parked outside my garden gate, and at least seven irate men, one of whom I recognised from the pub.

"Come out here you bastard, because if you don't, we are coming through your fucking door. You battered my brother, and now you will pay big time."

The door was getting battered with something heavy, it would not last much longer, so I went to the small cupboard beside the front door and took out my 12-bore shotgun barrel, and slowly slid it out through the letter-box.

"The next bastard who bangs on my door gets fucking shot, now fuck off the lot of you before I come outside."

"Run for fuck's sake the nutter has got a gun, and he has it pointed at me through the letter-box."

I heard the mad scramble to get back in their cars, and the gravel pinging everywhere as the wheels spun as they took off. The barrel was the only part of the gun I had in the house, it was in the cupboard when I moved in, but it had the desired effect, better than I had hoped for. They would not visit me at my house again.

CHAPTER 14

It had been quiet for ages and not much was happening in Edzell apart from getting drunk every weekend in the pubs. Bob and I were going to have a night out in Brechin again and hopefully, this one would be less of an issue than the last one. We were in our third bar of the evening when I was approached by a huge man called Hoss. He whistled and the next thing I knew was getting knocked to the ground by at least ten people. I curled up as small as I could, but was still injured badly and rendered unconscious. Luckily for me, a lot of my injuries had been inflicted when I was out cold.

I woke up in Stracathro Hospital, sore and bruised all over. Luckily, they had not done much damage to my face, but I had several cracked ribs, and some skin missing on my elbows. The nurse offered me a drink and helped me to sit up. I was in agony, but wanted to go home.

"You would be better staying at least until tomorrow morning until you have seen a doctor before you leave, you were unconscious when you were admitted, and you could have a concussion."

The nurse's advice went unheeded, and I

signed myself out of the hospital. I got dressed, in my now dry blood-stained clothing, and headed for the bus stop. I was having trouble breathing, and lifting my arms because of my ribs, but I managed to get on the bus and sit down. The bus stopped in Brechin to pick up passengers, and I got off. There was unfinished business to take care of today, and it could not wait any longer. I headed back to the bar where I had been attacked, and spotted Hoss sitting in the corner on a bar stool surrounded by some of his friends. I did not hesitate for a second, and barged past everybody, and sat down next to him at the bar.

"Right Hoss, you are buying since I never got to finish mine when I was here last time, and mine is a pint of lager."

Everyone looked at Hoss, then looked at me. They were looking for the signal to attack me again, but I did not care.

"You have got some balls coming here, but I've got to hand it to you for your style. Dougie, get this man a pint of lager on me."

That was my days of trouble over in Brechin, so I could drink in any bar in the town without fear of getting attacked. My nerve to go back in the same bar and sit beside Hoss was the hot topic all the way back to Edzell. There had been thirteen people who attacked me that night so that had helped me a bit. With so many of them surrounding me, there was not enough room for

137

them all to hit me at once. They all respected me now and would never bother me again as long as I was friends with Hoss. I had the freedom of the city and was untouchable, and I used it to my advantage in every bar I visited.

Although I enjoyed female attention, it was low on my list of things I needed. I had become self-sufficient and relied on nobody. I could fend for myself. That was probably because of me being brought up the way I was. Nobody helped me then, nor cared for me. I had learned to survive on my own since I was very young. Since I had removed Fiona from my life and my mind there had been nobody else, I had gotten close to. I judged anyone who tried to get close to before we could get to know each other. I could trust no one because I thought they must have an ulterior motive. This was a serious psychological problem that had been instilled in me just by being brought up with my siblings. I could trust none of them with anything, they would promise me things, then turn Judas when my parents came home.

Many times, in my life I have been dropped, crushed and ground into the dirt, by the closest people in my life, and the circumstances which came my way. I have been made to feel worthless, and this has made me feel depressed to try suicide, several times. My mood was now low, dark and utterly depressing, and I have no will to carry on with life as it exists now.

I had lost count of the times my father told me to be a man. To be a man in his eyes was to fight, to have no empathy, and to never, ever cry. The result was the depression, anxiety, and violence which was weighing heavily on me and my chance of happiness and life. My work was an escape for eight hours a day, but evenings, nights, and weekends were when I had time to sit and over analyse everything in my life. The drink was my only escape from the reality which was dragging me down into the depths of gloom, and it was spiralling out of control. I had friends, but I never let them see the real me, never revealed what was under my armour. That would not be manly to reveal the way I was feeling.

Real men never gave in, never showed their true colours. Dad had browbeaten that into me over the years. He never showed affection to me all my life; the only attention I got was violence and bullying. I was singled out and made to be the one in the wrong, so he felt better about himself. His ego was the most important thing in his life; nothing came before it. He thrived on making me the scapegoat for anything that went wrong, even when I was not around when it happened. I had been his punch bag, his stress relief, and his way out of being responsible for his actions. I soon realised that if I expected nothing from anyone, I would never be disappointed.

I was momentarily dragged from my morbid thoughts by a knock at the door. I got up and switched on the light. I had been sitting in semi darkness and had not noticed. Lenny and Tam were standing waiting on me.

"We could see your shape lying on the sofa even although it was nearly dark, we thought you had topped yourself because you were not moving or reacting to us at the door."

"For fuck's sake Lenny I was just chilling out for a while. I have no drink or fuck all left."

"That's what we are here to see you about. Some of my mates want to have a party at your house, and they will provide all the drinks. We have told them all about you."

"If you have told them everything about me, and they still want to come, they must be mad. When do they want to come here?"

"Tomorrow night if that is ok, they were going to go to Bob's caravan, but it is too small, plus it is a fucking shit hole now."

"Tell them any time after nine am tomorrow is OK with me."

I headed down to the village with Lenny and Tam for a pint at the Glenesk Hotel. Lenny's mum Wilma was serving at the bar and he always got free pints sneaked to him when nobody was looking. Sometimes he handed his mum the money, and she handed the lot back as his change. That would be the perfect mother, one who plied you with pints of lager for free, a dream came true.

I had never bothered to walk this far to visit

this pub because it was right at the other end of the village, plus it would be too far to stagger home when I was pissed. The place was busy, mostly with gamekeepers judging by their tweed and plus fours attire. Lenny's mum was clever. When the gamekeepers bought a large round, she overcharged them by three pints every time, and they were that far gone they never noticed. We drank the whole night for free, with even the odd bag of crisps and roasted peanuts thrown in.

"Right lads, it's time you went home. I've got a hunky man waiting for me when I get home, so come everybody drink up please."

"Mum, stop embarrassing me. It's only our dad at home, and he is a fat mess."

"Well, he's my hunky man, Lenny, and you are my little cutie boy."

"Come on, Peedie and Tam. This woman is not my mother, let's get out of here."

Wilma was full of fun; my mother would not laugh and joke as she did. Lenny was a very lucky person to have someone like that. He was totally oblivious to it and took it for granted because it had always been that way.

We all headed up the street towards the chip shop and met Bob and some of his friends. He had been in the Panmure drinking, and playing pool.

"Who fancies going for a swim in the river? We are going down now, so hurry up so we can all go in together. The streetlights only lit the path so far down to the bridge, then it was almost dark. The water was deep and slow moving under the bridge, between the large sandstone rocks, which formed a natural dam before it frothed up as it cascaded through the gaps.

"What are you cunts wearing when you go in?"

"Peedie get with it, we always skinny dip, we never wear anything in the water."

Lenny just dived in and went right under the water and resurfaced farther along, then everyone else did the same. I stupidly went in slowly as I did not know the water, nor where the rocks were. That was the biggest mistake I made that night. The water was freezing cold as it crept higher and higher up my body. I ducked under as the water reached my chest and stayed under as long as I could to get acclimatized to the temperature. This was fantastic, invigorating, and something I had never done before, and something I would definitely do again. After ten minutes, we got used to the semi darkness and climbed out of the water and jumped from rock to rock.

"My knob has shrunk to fuck all in this cold water, it has sucked right in."

"Lenny, you never had a knob, to begin with, you cunt."

"Well, it's better than having a vagina like you Bob."

Everybody was laughing so loud that they heard us from the village. Tams two sisters had come down to see what all the laughter was about, and Tam spotted them.

"Fuck off home, you perverts, staring at all the penises you two."

"Tam, we can't see them as they are too small and we don't have binoculars."

"At least we don't have a huge fanny as slack as yours, men have to tie a plank across their arse so they don't fall in when they are humping you."

The banter between them as brother and sister was something I had never witnessed before. Body parts and sex were taboo in our house as children, and would never be mentioned as adults, even in a joking manner. I had never seen my sisters naked, and they had never seen me. But here was Tam parading about in front of his two sisters like it was normal.

"Come on in you two, there's room for another few swimmers in here."

His sisters both got undressed and were soon naked. They both stood on the big rock beside where I had just been swimming. I stood there with my eyes transfixed on what was standing over me. Their bodies were silhouetted against the street lights in the distance behind them, just an amazing sight, standing there like it was an everyday occurrence. One of them jumped in, followed by the other, both disappearing under the water. Then I felt it, a hand grabbed my testicles, and another hand grabbed my arm and pulled me under. I did not struggle for fear of excruciating pain and just went with it. She let me go and we both surfaced at the same time laughing like school children.

"I should have warned you about my sisters, they both like underwater fishing for cock."

"We enjoy hunting for it out of the water as well Tam, and we are coming to the party tomorrow night at Peedie's house."

Lenny was larking about shoving us back into the water as soon as we got out. Bob tried to grab his leg from where he was standing below him in the water, and Lenny jumped across to the large rock opposite but did not quite make it. He lost his footing on the sandstone and slid into the gap between them. He went under the fast-flowing spout of water and disappeared from view. He emerged further down at the shallow stony bit, and he was screaming loudly. Bob was first to get to him, then me, we could see even in this dim light that his skin down his right side and down part of his leg had been scraped badly. We helped him out to the riverbank and helped him get his boxer shorts on before we took him up to get help. The rest of us got dressed without drying ourselves. The naked swimming gala was over for tonight.

Lenny's mum was shocked at the state of him; he had scrapes all down his side and his thigh. "I have filled a warm bath for you to make sure your skin is clean so it does not get infected. Just pat your wound and don't rub it dry."

"Mum it looks worse than it is, yes it's sore, but I am not dying, nor am I going to a fucking doctor, nor am I as stupid as rub it with a towel."

We saw that he was alright, so we headed to our respective houses and planned to meet up the next day to plan the party of all parties.

CHAPTER 15

I met Lenny in the afternoon and he had just come from the hospital after getting a non-stick dressing on a deeper part of his wound. He had woken up sore and his wound had stuck to the bedsheet, pulling the scab with it.

"Are you still coming to the party at mine tonight Lenny?"

"Fucking right I am Peedie, and I am bringing my sisters Gwen and Sylvia with me, so you better keep your zipper padlocked."

"I never even got introduced to them last night Lenny, they just sort of appeared."

"Gwen introduced herself to you in the water though, plus you were too busy ogling their tits to ask their names."

We went to Smokey Joes for a roll and a coffee, reminiscing about our half drunken antics from the night before. Mary complained she was having to all the work as Davie was not feeling well. She was definitely in a bad mood today, slamming the cups down on the counter as she was getting our order ready, and my usual soft yolk fried egg roll was more like a Frisbee it was so hard, and fringed with a crispy brown edge.

Gwen appeared and sat down beside us and said nothing at first, and just sat looking at us.

She had a smirk on her face and a twinkle in her eye, and I could see she was full of mischief. She was not as tall as I remembered from last night, and she had blonde hair which looked dyed.

"Oh, it's you Peedie, I did not recognise you with your clothes on, you look different today."

"I could say the same about you then couldn't I, you weren't wearing very much either, were you?"

We laughed, but were interrupted by Mary.

"If you are not ordering anything Gwen, you had better get out, I have enough to do without having to listen to you sitting chatting up men like a hooker."

"I least I can get a man if I want one, you dried up old prune, you wouldn't know what a good time was if I handed you it on a plate, you jealous old cow."

Mary looked startled, but never replied to Gwen's outburst, and she just carried on like nothing had been said. She never lifted her head as she washed the dishes in the sink behind the counter; she looked miles away. I wondered why they were both still working such long hours at their age and dwindling health. This old converted church, even its present dilapidated condition would be worth a small fortune if they sold up, and so would the ground it sat on.

We finished our coffee and Gwen took the empty plates and cups to the counter for Mary. She never apologised for her unsavoury outburst, but clearing our table was her way of saying sorry. Gwen came across as brash and uncaring, but there was a different side to her appearing through her armour. Her sister Sylvia was the polar opposite and let Gwen do all the talking for her, probably something they had done since childhood. My family never talked to each other, but instead talked about each other. It was every one for themselves in our house, and take no prisoners. They all had the art of shifting blame in my direction to save themselves. They thought it was wholly acceptable to see me getting beaten to a pulp for something they had done, then offer to help wipe the blood off my face and body.

The bus stopped at the stance further down, and David got off, followed by a lady friend I had not seen before. She was tall and quite thin with long brown hair. Her jeans looked like someone had painted them on they were that tight, finished off with a short T-shirt and a red pair of high heel shoes which she seemed to be having a problem walking in.

"This is Mags, Mags this is my brother Peedie."

"You have come on the right day David; we are having a big party at mine tonight. All the drink is getting supplied by somebody else. We don't have to buy fuck all."

"Right, that's it decided then. We will stay in Edzell tonight and go back to your mums in Brechin tomorrow afternoon. Her bedroom walls are too thin for my liking. I bet she hears everything we do in your room.

"Thank fuck for that David. I am glad we are not going back home tonight; mum is getting on my tits just now about getting a place of my own."

We all started the mile walk to my house, stopping for a minute to talk to Jenny. Then continued slowly the rest of the way, taking up the full width of the road, and only moving when a car appeared. Gwen and Mags walked behind the rest of us, reminiscing about her swimming naked the night before. They seemed to know each other well, and they carried on catching up with all the Edzell gossip until we reached the house. Mags had a strange mannerism about her, and she came across as timid and hardly able to cope with life.

Mags sat down on the sofa beside me, but ignored me completely. She was talking to David sitting across from us, and was wondering where she would sleep tonight, even though it was not even six o'clock yet. It will be a long night for the rest of us once the drink gets flowing. Lenny informed us that the drink would get delivered around seven, and he promised that we would not be disappointed. All the drink was coming from the Gannochy Estate from the gamekeeper's final shoot party. The last shoot had been cancelled at the last minute, and Bob's mum has had the honour of getting rid of it from the marquee tent before it was taken down.

The transit van pulled up at the door at seven thirty with enough drink to stock a small bar. She had six boxes stacked behind the front seats, which we were not getting unloaded, but the rest was ours. I had never seen that much drink in one living room before. We would not run out tonight, that was certain.

I put ten packs of lager, four bottles of Vodka and a bottle of Gin in my bedroom to make sure it would not get stolen. What was left in the living room would still be too much to drink, but we would definitely try tonight?

I was the first to open a can and start drinking, followed by Gwen. She sat back down on the sofa opposite, never taking her eyes off me as she did. She was pulling at her skirt, lifting it up just enough to reveal that she had no knickers on. I tried not to look, but could not help it, especially as she was obviously putting on the show put for me. She slid her legs further apart and flicked her skirt up to reveal a mound of black pubic hair. That confirmed the dyed blonde hair; her curtains did not match her rug. This had the makings of being an interesting evening, and Gwen had just started her first can of lager.

More and more people arrived, most of them I had never seen before, some even had brought the drink with them just in case there was none. Bob sat down beside me and immediately noticed what Gwen was doing.

"Gwen, please stop fanning your skirt up and down, I can smell your minge from here. For fuck's sake cover it up and put it away".

"You would be lucky to smell my sweet vagina Bob, maybe you will if you grow a penis like a man, not the little boy you are."

Everyone was laughing at the two of them and their friendly banter. Most of my new friends had a closeness between them, which I had never witnessed before. If I had said that to a woman friend in Kirriemuir I would be slapped across the face for it.

Mags got to her feet and headed towards David's bedroom, and beckoned him to follow her through. I never saw her again that evening, but David reappeared twenty minutes later.

I think all the noise and new faces was probably too much for her to cope with all at once. David never went back through to check up on her again. He was too busy having a good time to notice the time, and so was everyone else. Lenny was sitting with his sore side towards the arm of the sofa to try to protect it, and his other side had a woman attached to it like a limpet. He was going over his experience in graphic detail, but adding arms and legs to it to impress his lady friend.

The drink was getting drunk at such a rate I had to go to the bedroom to restock the living room. Music was blasting from the stereo, reverberating off every eardrum in the house. Gwen was dancing around the floor on her own, gyrating her hips and rubbing her crotch, licking her lips and making eye contact with every male who had a pulse.

"Oh, for fuck's sake Gwen, sit on your arse woman before you fall down, and you are showing yourself up."

"Sylvia my fanny is chewing through my knickers looking for a man. My juices are flowing like a tap, oozing out and trickling down my legs. I will have a man tonight if it's the very last thing I do."

People were egging Gwen on, clapping to the music and laughing along with her. She was definitely the life and soul of the party and was the centre of attention. Nobody took offence to her raunchy actions and foul mouth. Gwen was Gwen, and she would not change for anyone.

People were heading for home, some on foot and some getting lifts from friends until there was only about twelve of us left in the house. It was three thirty am, so I went to my bed; I had drunk past my limit and did not want to go further. I left everyone and told them just to shut the door when they left, or stay overnight if they desired.

I half woke up to somebody slowly running their fingers up and down my legs, getting close to, but not touching my testicles. It aroused me, but did not react to the gentle caressing, which was sending ecstatic signals all over my body.

Gentle kissing on my legs was nearly sending me into orgasm, and the kissing did not stop until the lips gently nibbled my testicles. I stroked the long hair and held on gently as the lips slowly slid down my penis, stopping and starting, and moving slowly up and down. My fingers caressed her neck and down her shoulders and moved up to stubble. It was a fucking man; a man was sucking my penis, and I had not noticed. I did not let on that I had found out, and just let it happened until I exploded into an orgasmic spasm, ejaculating into the mouth which was giving me so much pleasure

The person slid down to the bottom of the bed where they had come from, stood up, and quietly left the room. I lay there in shock; I had let a man do something so pleasurable which I would never have allowed. It was the best orgasm I had ever had in my life. He was better at giving pleasure than any woman I had been with before. I lay there contented, but started feeling guilty. My dad must have been right all along. I must be gay to have let that happen; he would love to find this out. The pleasurable act had turned in to a nightmare. I was doubting my sexuality; my previous experiences with women were never as good as what had just happened.

I woke around eleven am and went to the toilet. The house was deadly silent and in a mess. I headed towards the living room door, which was slightly open, and the curtains were still closed. I switched on the light and looked around. Gwen was still here lying on the sofa, and several other people I could not remember from the party were dotted about the floor sound asleep. The noise of a tractor coming from outside woke everyone up. A stranger with long hair, sat up and stretched his arms in the air.

"God, I was in a mess; I can't remember anything from last night."

"Nor can I, I was well out of it, last night."

He had said he couldn't remember anything, but his eyes said differently. He must have been the one who had sent my mind and body into an orgasm, beyond anything I had experienced before. I had allowed it to happen, so it was my fault, I could have got up out of my bed and kicked the shit out of him for doing it the moment I realised it was a man. But I could not move from the pleasure zone I had entered, I had willingly stayed still and let his mouth pleasure me for what seemed an eternity, and I had wished that it would never stop. I looked at his hands, but could not imagine letting him touch me, this was so wrong, but also so good, my mind was working overtime and it was out of its comfort zone now. Memories flooded back of the verbal abuse that had been hurled at me in my youth. Pansy gay bastard, poofter; the words of hatred my father hurled at me starting ringing in my ears. Why hadn't I taken Gwen's offer of sex? Then this would never have happened. I would not be feeling violated like I was now? But I could say nothing to him because everybody would find out what I had consented to take place and had enjoyed so much.

He got to his feet and headed through to the kitchen and came back drinking a mug of water and sat down on the only space left on the sofa. He turned around to look at me and his gaze sent a shiver down my spine.

"Well, thanks for last night, it was a fab party, well what I can remember of it, anyway. If you are having another party tonight to finish off all this booze, I can come back if you want."

"No, there is no party tonight. I am having a quiet night on my own for a change."

"Right, I am going to head home to Brechin. I hope we can meet again sometime."

I had openly lied to him; there was no chance I was having a quiet night in with all this alcohol cluttering up my living space. I could not take the chance of him coming back in case he replayed last night's scenario. I was not taking any chances. He went to the front door and glanced back at me and our eyes met briefly. I jolted back to reality and moved my head round to look at something else.

"The offer is still open. If you want, we won't remember what happened the next morning again."

He left my house and thank fuck for that. He

was propositioning me and I had not punched his lights out. That's what would have happened in different circumstances. I would have left him for dead lying in a pool of his own blood. I was feeling sick, repulsed and felt unable to comprehend what just happened. This was alien to me, I felt my mood changing, and I could not control it.

Gwen looked at me with a suspicious look. I could see the wheels turning in her mind, and she was thinking there was something amiss.

"What was that cunt on about before he left, was he doing what I think he was doing? He was fucking hitting on you, wasn't he?"

"Don't be such a fucking arsehole Gwen, I would have kicked the shite out of him if he had, I hate gays, I fucking hate them."

If she had known the truth, I would have been horrified. I had discovered that there was no difference between oral sex with a man or a woman, but I could never admit it to anyone. This guilt would have to be kept bottled up in my mind forever and never revealed. I could never hate a gay person now, knowing what I knew.

"Oh, I know him, that's all, he was gay at school, and used to get bullied a lot, that's why I remember him."

"Well, he won't be fucking gay with me, I can assure you of that, my bum hole is as tight as a duck's arse, and that's watertight, it lets nothing in."

We laughed at what I had just said, it sounded ridiculous, and it was.

Gwen tidied up around the living room after everyone else had left to go to Smokey Joes and soon had a refuse sack full of empties. The kitchen was as bad, and even the bath itself had rubbish in it. Between us, it was soon ready for round two tonight.

CHAPTER 16

When we reached Smokey Joes everyone who had been at the party had been and gone. I ordered a chip roll and another for Gwen. Mary peeled the potatoes and set them side by side on the countertop. She picked them up one at a time and sliced them into chips, placing them into a small chip basket. She lowered the small basket into the massive industrial fryer, and waited, and waited, wiping surfaces randomly as she did. Chips cooked to her liking, she placed them on to the pre-sliced rolls.

"Do you want sauce on your rolls?"

"Thank you, Mary. Can we have brown sauce and red sauce please?"

"No, you can't, you can have one or the other, but not both, and this is not a charity either. Davy makes the rules, and I keep them."

"Well, how about half a squirt of each then? That would still be one squirt, Davy would approve of that."

"Okay, then you win this time, one half squirt of each and no more."

We could not eat our rolls for laughing, much to the annoyance of Mary, who could hardly hear the customers, but then she was hard of hearing anyway at the best of times. She shuffled over to our table, and gave the bare bits of tablecloth between the plates a wipe, moving my mug to wipe up a small drip of coffee. This was her way of trying to hurry people up to leave, she made them feel uncomfortable enough to gulp everything down and leave. Hopefully, Davie would be well enough to return to the shop soon to take the piss out of Mary, he had a sick, dry sense of humour which was to my liking, someone as sick as me was hard to find.

Lunch finished and feet rested we headed to the Panmure Arms for a hair of the dog. Gavin was behind the bar, as usual, I'm sure he slept there. He always wore an immaculate white shirt and tie, and black trousers and shoes. He looked like he was about retiring age, but did not act like it. The charade of his immaculate attire hid a funny man underneath. He looked out of place when he lifted his leg to fart, then when he dispersed the smell by waving his hands back and forth behind him.

"I heard you are one reason the pub was quiet last night Peedie because half the village youth were at your house."

"Aye Gavin, it was a fantastic night, lots of people and even more drink. Nothing smashed either, so all's good for tonight again, bring it on."

"A pint of lager for me Gavin, and whatever Gwen is having, and get something for yourself."

I picked up my cool pint and sucked the froth

off the top; it definitely tasted better from the pumps than a can. It hardly touched the sides of my throat before I had another one in my hand. Gwen was still on her first pint and lagging behind, but she did not have a thirst like mine.

Four pints was my limit before I had to go to the toilet, and I was bursting. I headed for the only cubicle and stood there; the relief was instant. I stood reading the graffiti on the wall in front of me, laughing to myself at the funny comments, zipped myself up and turned to leave. Written on the back of the thin chipboard door in black marker pen was 'Peedie is a poof' and that was like a red rag to a bull to me. I lifted the three-quarter door off its hinges, but lost my balance. The door fell over and hit the wall, so I picked it up and headed to the bar with it in my arms.

"Which arsehole wrote this on this fucking door? When I find out who it was, I will fucking kill them with it."

"Come on Peedie it might have been written for a laugh, go on for Christ's sake, and put the door down before you hurt somebody."

"Right Gwen, are you coming with me or what? Whoever wrote this is getting hunted out until I find them, fucking poof, I will give them poof."

I left the pub still carrying the toilet door and headed to the Glenisla Hotel. People were following me now, but I did not care; some cunt would pay for this shite. The door was the first thing the barman saw when I entered the bar, then I peered round it.

"I don't want to know Peedie, I see no door in my bar. What are you drinking?"

"A pint of lager please, and some answers. Some bastard has written this on the door about me, not man enough to say it to my face though."

"I know who it was."

"Where do they live, they are getting a visit very shortly?"

It was in Duriehill road, near the top, and I knew exactly where it was, so I headed up the street, with the door under my arm. The house door opened when I began kicking it, so it hit the wall behind it with a dull thud. An irate woman came to the door demanding to know what my problem was, so she got told what it was.

"Your fucking son wrote this shite on the door, and he will rub it off one way or another. He does not even know me, the little bastard that he is."

"Steven, get your arse out here, some cunt is at the door for you."

"Who is it?"

"It's that person you wrote about on the toilet door in the Panny, so you better get out here or he will come in and get you."

He appeared beside his mother looking terrified. I must have had my death stare on, because he admitted writing it straight away.

"It was only for a laugh. I don't even know you, but I have heard you are a nutcase, so I thought it would be funny."

"You had better get something to clean marker pen off, or I will use your fucking face to wipe it with. You accuse nobody of being a poof, not even if they are gay."

He appeared with a scourer and soapy water, and cleared the offensive words from the melamine door and did not stop until he completely removed it without a trace.

"Now get your fucking shoes on. You are carrying the door back to the Panny. I'm fucking sick of carrying it around. Get a move on if you know what is good for you."

"Mum, are you going to let him get away with this?"

"Just get your shoes on and take what comes to you, you will learn the hard way not to mess with people's heads. You get away with everything you do, you make my life hell, so get on with it and man up to your sins."

He picked the door up and followed me up the street grunting and groaning at the weight. We reached the Panny and I held the door open and he carried it inside.

"What the hell are you doing Peedie?"

"Gavin this is the bastard who wrote the shite on your door, and he is here to put it back on for you."

Gavin looked at me with total disbelief, and

just smiled and said nothing. I lined the door hinges up so it could get hooked back on, and he made it look so difficult but he managed to get the door reinstated.

"Right, you little shit, let's see if it shuts now it's back on its hinges, we can't have it falling off, can we?"

I swung the door round, having to push him to the side to get it closed. The lock worked and everything looked as good as new.

"Well, what about this gay thing you were writing then Steven darling? You must fancy me or something if you were thinking about me. Do you like my cute arse, or is it cock you want?"

I patted his arse and he stuttered something, but never managed to get it out. I had had my fun, so left him standing in the cubicle and went to the bar.

"A pint of lager please Gavin, sorry about earlier. Your door does not squeak now, so that's a bonus."

"Lucky for you nobody was needing a shit when you had the door on a tour of the village. You are definitely original; I will give you that."

Steven gingerly peered round the toilet door and slowly appeared into the bar. His light blue jeans had a huge wet patch on the front, he had pissed himself with fear, and my joking romantic advances had totally freaked him out. He scurried passed everyone at the bar and into the street, and I laughed until tears came running down my face.

The pub was filling up and Gavin was telling everybody about my antics with the toilet door. It was the talk of the village because some people had heard the story elsewhere before they came to the Panny, and had come to check to see if it was true. A group of youths came in and sat down at the other end of the bar, they were loud but not causing bother.

"Keep it down a bit, lads, you are a bit too noisy for me at this time of the night."

One of them was calling Betty, horrible names. She was a simple plain woman in her late thirties who kept herself to herself. She dressed in older style frumpy clothes which were twenty years out of fashion. I could see she was getting angry with them.

"Sweaty Betty, Sweaty Betty, Sweaty Betty."

"Right lads that's enough, it's not Sweaty Betty. It is perspiring Elizabeth."

I spat out a mouthful of lager on the floor when I heard it, and the whole place erupted in hysterical laughter. Gavin was funny, and he just spat out random comments periodically that were hilarious, and this was his best one yet. The more I thought about that sentence the funnier it seemed. Poor Betty sat back down to her drink thinking Gavin had chastised the youths, missing the piss take altogether.

CHAPTER 17

I woke up in the morning with a head so sore it felt like it would implode. It scared me to even move as the room was spinning slowly when I shut my eyes. My arm touched something when I stretched out, and it moved.

"Peedie you were a fucking mess last night."

"For fuck's sake, Gwen, what the hell are you doing here in my bed?"

"You asked me to that's why, you wondered if I could give a good blow job, so I obliged, and I am still waiting for my answer, because once you come all over me, you rolled round and fell asleep."

Memories of the wild night were starting to come back to me now, and the amazing sex we had together.

"Shut up and go back to sleep woman. I will tell you after the next time you do it. I can't make up my mind yet.

We stayed in bed nearly all day and Gwen got the answer she was looking for at last, she was good at it.

The emersion had heated the water, as I could not be arsed lighting the fire to heat it. I filled the bath and climbed in and lay on my back. This was bliss and relaxing after the hectic night before.

"Open the door Peedie, I need to pee."

"It's not locked Gwen so just come in, but no looking."

Gwen came in and sat down on the toilet. She was stark naked, but she had no shame with her body. She stood up to leave, but instead climbed in the bath beside me.

"Come on make some room, and you can sit at the tap end. It's a lady's place at this end."

We just got washed and got out, no sex or touching. We were like an old married couple, comfortable with each other. But we were not even a couple, more like friends with benefits.

David had wakened and got out of bed and was waiting patiently at the bathroom door when we emerged.

"Thank fuck for that, I am nearly pissing myself, plus I am getting the bus to Kirriemuir soon. I will be back tomorrow or the next day."

"You could have gone outside you cunt, it's all right for men they don't have to sit down."

"Gwen fuck off, the neighbours kids were playing in their garden. I don't want to be arrested for being a flasher."

"You would be alright David; they would not see your tiny knob from a yard away."

The banter continued for ages, David was giving Gwen as good as he got from her. I opened a can of lager for myself and one for Gwen.

"Get your lips round that, that will sort you

out, the hair of the fucking dog."

"Look min I don't want a can at this time of fucking day. I've not even had fuck all to eat yet, you daft cunt."

"I will just drink them both then, problem solved."

I went to the bedroom to get dressed and sort my hair out. It was sticking up because of my night of sweaty passion.

I was joined by Gwen, who was trying to find some of her clothes that had been hastily discarded in her drunken amorous state. I left her to it and went to finish my second can, and Gwen appeared topless beside me and David, who did not know where to look.

"What have you done with my fucking bra? I'm sure I had one on when I left my house last night, and if it's not here where is it?" What's the matter David, have you not seen boobies before, don't be shy, you can ogle them if you want?"

"Just put one of my T-shirts on for fuck's sake, and stop going near the window. The kids are playing in the garden a few feet away."

Gwen went right up to the window and pressed her bare breasts against the glass for a laugh. When she stepped back and moved away, we could clearly see the imprints complete with nipple marks on the glass.

She just did not care what she did. Finally, she chose a T-shirt of mine and finished getting dressed. She wanted to go to Edzell to look for her bra, which had mysteriously disappeared from her body between the pub and my house. We walked slowly because we were still a bit delicate after our night out and the vast quantities of lager we had consumed.

"There it fucking is, my bra. How the fuck did it get on to Jenny's door handle?"

"I remember now, you were swinging it around your head like a propeller, shouting for Jenny to come out and wear something feminine instead of her man clothes. She came out and told you to fuck off."

She quietly opened the garden gate and sneaked to the door, grabbed her neon burnt retina pink bra from the door handle and ran for it, leaving me standing there like a plonker.

I ran to catch up with Gwen. We were laughing like two school children at what had just happened. It was so ridiculous it was funny. She lifted her T-shirt and put the bra on but had to move to the side of the road to let a car pass. Gwen lifted her T-shirt above her head, revealing her bare chest to the elderly male driver.

"That will give the old cunt something to tell his wife about when he goes home, that will have kick started his heart for the rest of the day. Now fix the clasp at the back of my bra. I can't get my fingers to work."

Bra fixed and breasts finally contained in their proper place, we went to the café farther along the road for something to eat. Mary at Smokey

Joes would have taken too long to make us something to eat, and we wanted food now. Gwen ordered a black pudding roll with a fried egg on it as well, and I had the same. We sat there in silence for a while, just eating and drinking and watching the world go by.

"Peedie do you remember your party when you got a blow job?"

"For fuck's sake, Gwen. I am eating a roll."

"When you let a man suck you off and you enjoyed it, well it was me who sent him through to do it to you for a laugh. I told him you were gay as fuck and gagging for it."

I could not answer her; I was dumbstruck. She has known all someone had violated me in my bed, and it was her who orchestrated the whole thing. If I had done that to a woman I would have been arrested. But I could not report it and make it public. What if Gwen tells somebody, and it gets broadcasted, then my life will be ruined? Then my father would find out and he would think he had been proved right all along, then he could deride and wound me with his hateful comments. He would wait until he had an audience big enough to suit his ego, then he would strike. He would point and laugh as he said it, this would be his finest hour, his stage would be set to to call me a gay poofter, a faggot, a pansy bastard, and all the things he had called me as a child would now be endorsed and validated in his mind. The power he would get from this would be immeasurable; he would be in a place of power so great I could no longer ignore him.

"Peedie for fuck's sake talk to me, you have gone quiet and now I am worried. I didn't mean for you to get so upset."

"My only worry is if this gets made public; if you tell somebody."

"Fuck off, I would tell no one you daft cunt. Telling people that I told someone to do that to you, would make me look depraved, and anyway, why would I say anything, anyway."

I sat for ages just surveying everybody doing what they do, and I wondered what their lives were like, and if their heads were almost bursting like mine. I hated myself, and the guilt from that night was starting to engulf me, and drag me back to that dark place in my head. I hated that despondent place, but was powerless to stop myself slipping back into it. My life was a charade, and I was acting out all the scenarios to whichever audience was in attendance at the time. I could not let them see the real me, the broken, worthless person I had turned back into again.

"Come on, Gwen. The pub is open now. Let's go and have a pint. I need to sort my head out."

Gavin was standing behind the bar when we went in, smiling from ear to ear as usual. I asked for a pint of lager each and sat at the bar. A drink was my salvation, my escape from my burdens and reality. I needed it to function, and I needed it every day just to carry on as normal

"Who's paying for this drink, then, this is not a charity?"

"Sorry, Gavin. I was miles away."

I handed Gavin my money, and he looked me in the eye and I instinctively dropped my head, nobody looked me in the eyes, ever. Growing up, I never dared to look my parents in the eye, that was being defiant, disrespectable, and a reason for a beating.

"Your drinking is getting the better of you son. I have seen a big change in you since you came to live here."

Gavin was right, but I could not stop, the drink was keeping me sane and it was a reason to live, a reason to get out of bed in the morning.

"Come on, cheer up you dismal looking cunt, what's biting at your arse today?"

"Just ignore him, Bob, he is being a miserable beggar today. I gave him a blow job to die for last night, and this is how he bloody reacts."

Bob laughed, and so did I. His laugh was so infectious and could make any situation seem funny. He was a person who liked happiness and thrived to live life to the full, even when he had nothing himself. My life was not like his, he had a wonderful family who cared for him, not one who despised his very existence.

We finished our drinks and headed outside for fresh air and were joined by Sylvia.

"Gwen, you are needed at home for something. Mum is asking if you can pop in later."

"Yes, I need to get clean clothes anyway, my knickers are getting crusty."

"Too much information for me, Gwen, far too much."

"Right then you two I am heading home for a while; I will probably see you later if you are lucky."

The house looked dull and empty when I went in, and it was needing to be tidied up a bit. I put the kettle on and made myself a cup of coffee and turned on the television. There was nothing interesting to watch, but I left it on just to have some background noise and sat looking at the walls. This place was getting me down, and I needed cheering up fast. I was sick of life and there was no light at the end of the tunnel in sight.

The farmer had told me he would be away on holiday all week. I don't know why he told me that because it mattered nothing to my life. He was away lying in the sun in Portugal, and I was in this shithole. I had never really looked properly around the farm before, so went to explore. The sheds were the original ones dating back to when the farm was built, two storey sandstone with slate roofs. The doors were painted green and had large blisters on them caused by years of hot sun. They were filled with implements and things more suitable to a bygone era. Pitchforks were lined up on hooks on a wall, and old milking equipment was stacked in the corner. I made my way from one shed to another, wondering why all this stuff was still here, why keep stuff that was no longer useful. That's what I felt like now, useless and not vital in civilisation; life would go on whether I was in it or not. I sat down on a barrel and went into a trance, lost in my own deliberations and my misery, which consumed my every waking thought.

I could not carry on any more I had to get out of this agony. Nobody would miss me or notice I had gone. I was just a tiny particle of a vast universe, a paltry molecule of life and a lost cause beyond help.

There was a ladder just to my right, an old hand made wooden one which led to another level through a large square opening. I made my way slowly up the rungs one at a time until I reached the second floor and stood up. There was not enough light at the far end to see properly, but could just make out a pile of wooden crates and a rope. On closer inspection, the crates were empty except one which had some books inside it, which had yellowed and were dusty from probably years of being uncovered. The rope kept coming back to my attention; I picked it up and ran it through my fingers, looking at the twisted natural fibres which together made it complete.

My mind went into overdrive and my thoughts turned to my unhappy life, and I could see a way out at last. There was a beam above the hatch in the floor, and I bound the rope round it and the other end round my neck, and jumped through the hatch. The pain hit me immediately, the rope had broken, and I had struck the ladder on the way down. I lay there unable to get a breath; my chest was heaving and pains were shooting up from my leg, which was twisted underneath me.

This had gone so wrong, I was as useless as my father said I was, I could not even kill myself properly, I had even messed that up. It was getting dark in the shed and I could still see the hatch above me. My mind turned to my stupid attempt to end my life, and the broken rope still dangling above me. My neck was sore and felt like the skin was broken, and my head was pounding. I had to get out of here and back home to take stock of what had just happened. Pain shot up my leg as I pulled myself up using the rungs of the ladder to hold on to. I ripped my jeans and I could see that I had scraped the skin on my leg, exposing red sores, which were strangely not bleeding. I limped out the shed door and across to my house.

"Where the fuck have you been Peedie, I have been here for ages, and what the fuck has happened you?"

"This is not a good time to ask stupid questions, Gwen."

"But look at the fucking state of you. Something has happened."

"I walked around the corner of the farm on my way home and several people attacked me, let's just leave it at that"

My leg was in agony, but I tried to play it down. I looked in the mirror at the pathetic person I had become. I was empty of emotion and had lost the will to live and could not see an easy way out. I cleaned up my leg, which was not as bad as it first appeared to be, but my neck had bruised and had noticeable marks on it at one side where the rope had dug in before it snapped. Gwen could not find out the true reason I was in this state, I could never live it down, this was the lowest I had been since my days in Sunnyside Psychiatric Hospital.

"Are you going to be long in there Peedie? I am bursting for a pee."

"Aye, I'm just coming woman hold on for a minute and I will be out."

There was no way I could admit to anybody what I had tried to do. That I had been attacked by a gang would have to be played out to anyone who asked why I was bruised or had marks on my neck. I would probably have to replay this over and over again until everyone knew what I wanted them to know. I knew how to look after myself with my fists and was feared by many, but I was at a loss at how to get my life back on track. Gwen tried hard to cheer me up, but she saw only my expression. She could not see deep inside my head, which was a different place now, a scary dark and deep hole devoid of emotions. She tried to love me, but I could not return it because I did not know how to. Loving or accepting love was always overwhelming because I never had it in my childhood.

"Come on you silly cunt get the kettle on and cheer up for fuck's sake, it's not the end of the world."

"Gwen, I was just going to before you asked me. Look, I have the cups lined up ready."

It was the end of the world for me, I was at my wit's end and could not suffer this life I was living. I was acting out my life to suit each situation and depending on who I was speaking to at the time. Nobody could understand what was happening to me because I bottled up my true feelings because it would not have been manly to admit I was depressed. I was forced to act as if nothing was wrong my whole life so far so that I did not appear weak in front of my father. If I ever did, even for a second, he would jump at the chance to mock and humiliate me in front of everybody he could. I had hidden my emotions for so long now I could not find them buried deep within me.

CHAPTER 18

The news came as a complete shock to me, and it was not news I was happy about. Gwen and all her family were moving to Northumberland in a week's time. Her dad, who was a mechanic, was transferring to a higher earning job down there. Gwen reckoned that there would be a better chance of her getting a job there as Edzell was far too small a place. Apart from the odd seasonal jobs, there was nothing.

"I will really miss you, Gwen. I was getting really close to you."

"Fuck off you soppy cunt, you only liked me for one thing. You just keep your head down and stay out of bother and remember and make an appointment at the doctors for them, anti-depressant things you were telling me about."

I headed to Edzell holding hands with Gwen, something I had never done before. She squeezed my hand gently every so often, probably just to reassure me that everything would work out for me. Today would start differently, no pint in the pub to get my brain in order, nor a coffee in Smokey Joes. I planned to go for a long walk towards Edzell Base to have a look around. I had lived here for ages and had never really seen anything around it. Gwen said her usual goodbye, comprising sticking her middle finger in the air, then saying "spin on that you bastard" then emitting a deep belly laugh to finish off with. She was a character all right, just as everybody had told me, but I had made a good friend, and I would definitely miss having her around.

I never got on my walk as Bob turned up and insisted that I accompany him for a drink, and it would have been rude not to, plus he was buying which made my decision a lot easier. The doctor's appointment could wait until later in the week. I could not go in smelling of alcohol and have to sit listening to him ranting and raving about the wrongs and harms of the demon drink. He had told me so many times in the past that I could nearly recite his rant before he even talked.

After only four pints Bob decided that he had to head home and let his mum's dog out to do the toilet as she was at her work all day. I came outside with him and headed home for something to eat and have a bath to help clean my damaged leg. The bruising on my neck was going yellow in places and seemed to be spreading, but it did not feel as bad now at least. Gwen had already gone home to help with the packing to get ready for her new adventure so I would not have her company today, nor anyone else's. People had slowly drifted away from me after hearing all about my violent rages, which had been grossly exaggerated as they passed it from person to person. I needed no one in my life either as I had learned that I could rarely trust anybody, and they could never get close enough to get to know me.

The bath was bliss, painful to lie down in until my grazes got softened a bit in the soapy water. I must have drifted off as I woke up fighting for my life. I could see my father standing above me, shoving me under the water and holding me down. All my strength could not release his vice like grip from my neck, I was passing out.

I sat up panicking and looked around me, but he was not there and had never been there. The bath water had gone cold, and I had woken up from a nightmare which had repeated itself many times. This had all happened in my mind; it had not been real, but I could smell the after-shave which he always wore still lingering in the room. He was not with me in person, but he was etched in my subconscious, reappearing when I least expected him to. His hold on me was so deeply entrenched in my thoughts, he was always in the back of my mind in everything I did in my life. He had brainwashed me from such a young age that it became normal, part of life, and part of me.

My towel was damp with the splashing I must have made in my weird dream, but I dried myself after checking outside the bathroom door to check he was definitely not there. I was cold now after lying so long in the bath so made myself a cup of sugary tea and sat down. I piled some paper on the fire and topped it up with dry kindling and logs and set it alight. The fire was soon crackling and spitting hot sparks on to the floor, and I started to warm up. The flames were entrancing as I sat watching them flicker and dart around the chimney opening, puffing out little wisps of smoke into the room as the fire heated up and boiled the sap in the hardwood logs. Soon I was miles away in another moment in time, back to my grans happy home where I was safe from harm.

My front door opened and David appeared and sat down beside me. Neither of us talked, we did not have to. Years of living together in our frantic home as children had given us a subconscious type of communication. We could tell what each other were thinking and finish each other's sentences. There was a closeness between us which I did not have with anyone else, we could talk about anything, well almost everything. I could never reveal what had happened to me at the party, the sexual act that I would have to carry around in my mind until the day I died. I had decided that it was my fault and mine alone, I could have cried out to stop it going any further, but I had enjoyed it so much and let him carry on until the end. He was not the guilty one; I was.

The silence was broken when David farted loudly, still, none of us talked, only sniggering to ourselves.

"What a fucking smell David, Jesus that is rancid, go and fucking change you must have shit yourself."

"Peedie you can be just as bad if not worse than that, your farts are so bad they have a texture when you smell them."

"What are you doing tonight, David? I am going to Gwen's leaving party at the Glenesk Hotel, everybody is welcome to go."

"No, I'm meeting Mags tonight, she is coming on the bus from Brechin later, so you better put ear plugs in when you go to bed tonight, to drown out her howling and groaning all night."

"You fucking wish, she will moan at getting no sex you mean, that will be more like it. A two second hump will be all she will get tonight if any at all."

We could openly joke about our sex life or lack of it. We were not prudish when it came to those discussions, but I could not reveal the severity of my thoughts regarding my mental health as it was now, not to him nor anyone else. This was a burden I had to carry by myself. I could let nobody see what I had become. There was an image of me that had to be upheld, and I had to keep that side of my life intact and private, and my public persona could not be destroyed.

We got changed and headed the mile walk to the village. David stopped off at the Panny, and I walked to the opposite end of the village to

Gwen's party at the Glenesk. I could hear the noise about fifty yards from the hotel. The music was pumping from huge speakers at the back of the function suite. Gwen appeared from the throng of revellers wearing a pink helium-filled balloon tied to her bra strap, and a length of silver tinsel tied round her head. She was drunk; I had never seen her this far gone with a drink before. She was always outlandish and loud when she was sober; she did not need to drink.

"Come on, you fucker get yourself a drink, it's a free bar tonight, my dad is paying for his own, leaving party, the silly cunt will get a big bill for that, especially now you have turned up."

"Aye, I will have a whisky and a pint of lager then, then I won't have to go to the bar so often."

"When you get served come and sit over there in the corner with us, just look for my balloon floating above everyone's head."

I finally made it to the bar and got served, then pushed through the crowd of still queueing revellers towards the table, spilling splashes of lager over them as I squeezed through. Nobody noticed the wet splashes they now had, but I would not have cared either if they had. I would have thrown the whole pint over the first one who complained, then would force them to get me another one to replace it. My pride would not let me apologise to anyone. I was above that, and I could never show weakness.

"You took your time you cunt, now sit on

your arse, I have kept you a place. Shift your fat butt along a bit mum, we are sitting right on the edge of the seat."

"Gwen, stop being a cheeky cow. You are getting as lippy as Sylvia. Talking about Sylvia, where has she bloody disappeared to now?"

"I am sure I saw her when I came in. She was sitting on the wall further up with a lad of about sixteen."

"Gwen go and get us all a drink, tell the bar staff that I wanted it delivered to my table, here is the list, just write down what you want at the bottom."

The drinks appeared quickly; it was obviously a bonus if you were paying the bill. Pint after pint appeared for me at the table, and I tried to keep up with the flow but was falling behind. I felt sick; a queasy feeling was having an effect on me. I went outside for fresh air and stood there trying to focus, then it came, a jet of putrid vomit sprayed from my mouth with such a force it landed over three feet away, right down the front of a woman. She froze to the spot with a look of terror and astonishment as the vile smell filled her nostrils. She gagged as the vomit dripped from her coat and handbag on to her high heel shoe, and she looked like she was either going to, or coming from a wedding. Then she shouted abuse at me, shouting at the top of her voice for a more dramatic effect. It backfired on her immediately because a crowd had appeared to see what the problem and laughed at the mess, she was in. Her expression was priceless; it was fixed in a stare and she could not talk back to them.

"Better out than in Peedie, come on back in and finish your drink, you have at least four pints sitting there."

We both went back inside and left the pitiful woman standing there, trying to get her coat removed without touching my vomit gift to her.

"Gwen, did you see the state of her fucking face, and the vomit dripping off her fingers? She won't be picking her nose tonight. That has to rate as the best laugh ever. I never knew that my innards could hold so much liquid."

"Well, you have a lot more room now inside you. Get caught up with this lot before mum orders more."

"I think it was mixing it with the whisky that caused me to be sick Gwen. Usually I can hold a lot more than that."

"As soon as I have finished these three pints, I am heading up the road. I fucking hate goodbyes, Gwen."

"Yes, I am going home as well, but we can meet tomorrow before I head off. I think I have had too much to drink as I have to keep going for a piss every five minutes. My fanny is like Niagara Falls."

"Right then I will see you tomorrow then. I will try to remember to set my alarm."

"Bye, then Peedie, but you can fuck off if you want a goodbye snog with your vomit breath and lips."

CHAPTER 19

The street was unusually busy as I made my way home. A crowd of people was gathered farther up beside the Panny and some of them were shouting so I went over the road to get a closer look. There was a commotion behind a wall which I could not see, then a loud roar and David landed on the pavement six feet in front of me. I got him to his feet and he seemed to be alright even after his crash on to the tarmac.

"That bastard over there had his fucking hand up Mags's skirt, so I punched the pervert in the face."

"Right David fuck, him, whoever he is, I am going to kick the shit out of him."

"Come on then you hard man, you were hard enough to throw my brother over the wall, come and try me."

He came over the wall in one leap, he was like Man Mountain but I did not care. I kicked him in the groin with such a force he let out a pathetic squeal. The beast of a man stood still for a minute, then landed in a heap on the pavement. His head moved as my foot hit it, and he immediately said something to me

"The slag was gagging for it."

This was my excuse to lay into him with my

feet again, but he would not stop speaking."

"The slag wanted a real man so fuck off."

I saw red, a flash of temper exploded through me and I totally lost control. I jumped on top of him and kicked him so hard that he was rendered unconscious.

"Talk now you pervert bastard, go on I fucking dare you."

Nobody said a word to me nor intervened. It was like time had stood still, all the people who were screaming for me to stop were standing looking at him lying motionless, in total silence and shock. I gave him a kick in the ribs for good measure and he never moved, never uttered a word. I made myself scarce and walked back in the direction of the Glenesk, I needed time to think, and to work out what I was going to do. That man was lying unconscious on the pavement, but that was not what I wanted to happen, I had wanted him to feel every punch and every kick and stamp before he was knocked out, he had got off lightly.

A police car and an ambulance went rushing past with their sirens and lights on. They stopped further up at the Panny, and I watched from a distance as they tended the now conscious man. He was sitting up and leaning against the pub wall getting his face cleaned up. I could not see what damage I had caused, but I hoped his nose was broken, then he would remember me for longer, as it would also give him black eyes. The ambulance driver turned into a side road and headed back towards Brechin; I obviously never did enough damage as they never took him away with them.

Another police car came speeding past and slammed on its brakes. Two officers jumped out of the car and dived on top of someone in the middle of the road. Then I heard the shouting, and it was David who was doing it.

"Get off me, you black bastards you are fucking hurting me, get to fuck off me, you cunts."

They cuffed him and bundled him into the car, then they walked over to talk to the man who I battered senseless. A crowd gathered around the police, and I could see them all pointing in my direction. Without warning, they went back to the car and let David go free. He was not happy, but he should have been.

"You black bastards are lucky you let me go, I never did anything, you cunts."

"Don't push your luck sonny, we thought that you were your brother. If you know where he is, it would go in his favour, if we get him now."

"Like I would tell you, I was not born yesterday, if you want him, go and look for him, you will never find him."

They eventually drove up towards my house, then slowly past the Panny and the road past where I was sitting, and then left the village, the other car headed out the road in the direction of Edzell Base

I sat there for around thirty minutes and headed back to the Panny. The wedding reception was in full swing, and nobody was outside now. The music playing was Scottish and I could see them all dancing around. Somebody recognised me, so I moved out of sight around the corner, to the car park. A woman was first to appear out the door, followed by a youth wearing a kilt. She scanned the area outside, then went back in. Ten minutes later I saw my man come outside for a smoke, accompanied by someone else who I assumed to be his partner. I could not resist it and I shouted to him.

"You can still smoke, so your lips can't be fucking sore."

He dropped his cigarette and scuttled back inside, dragging his partner with him. The coward ran away, he was not being a big man now. He was looking out the window at me, smirking that I could not get in to get him. The pub reception door had been locked, but that did not phase me, I headed round to the kitchen back door and opened it, then pressed the fire alarm bell. The noise was deafening, reverberating through the entire building. Staff and wedding guests started to file out into the street, lining up in the car park. People were shouting and panicking about losing family members and friends, and the band members were still carrying their instruments and electronics out.

"There is the little shit who vomited all down

my coat earlier and thought that it was funny, the bastard."

She had spotted me standing in the crowd trying to blend in with the wedding guests so that I would not get noticed. I was trying to find the arsehole who I knocked out earlier, I had not finished with him yet. People started looking at me and I started to walk towards the road. I felt a hard thud on my back, turned around and saw a bottle lying on the ground. Another one whizzed over my head and smashed onto the pavement behind me. I lost control and ran towards the culprit. It was the man I knocked out earlier, and I went for him with such a force that he went flying backwards and fell over. He swung his leg and kicked me as he fell, so I kicked him in the stomach and landed another kick quickly after. Somebody grabbed me by the hair, trying to pull me back, I swung round and punched him in the face so hard that he let go, then he went for me again. Nobody pulled my hair, never, years of getting my hair nearly twisted off my scalp by my father had made me very defensive. His blood exploded from his nose as my fist hit it full on, he bent forward, clutching his face, with blood dripping through his fingers. More people started to join in against me, I was outnumbered and trapped between a high wall and a bus.

The aluminium sign on the boot on the bus was bolted on, but I managed to rip it completely off, it was about three foot by two foot in size. I lifted it up and swung it around like a sword, swinging it at everyone who dared step near me.

The crowd stayed a safe distance from me because they could see that I meant business. I was free of the corner and heading for the street, and I was hit in the head by a bottle thrown from the edge of the crowd. My balance was affected for a minute, and I could feel my blood running through my hair, that was it for me. Man, Mountain was the one who threw it, and that was his biggest mistake. I ran towards him using the bus sign as a shield and swung it at him landing it across his back. I was like a thing possessed, nothing could stop me now, and I was enraged to a point of no return.

He fell down to the ground and landed badly, with kick after kick, landing solidly on his head and body. There was no more movement from him, he was knocked out cold again, twice in one night. He should have learned the first time, the total arsehole, his night was ruined, and so were his blood-soaked clothes. A hand grabbed me from behind and I instinctively turned around and just stopped in time from hitting David with a punch

"Come on Peedie let's get to fuck out of here before you kill somebody."

"Come ahead whoever wants some of this shit, who wants a fucking broken nose like him?"

I was aware of the sirens and blue light before David was, and he was grabbed by a policeman, then another one cuffed him, they had him face down on the tarmac, pressing his face hard down. I saw red and tried to rescue him from their grasp. I leapt on top of them and swung a punch at an officer, hitting his face and knocking his hat off. Several other officers grabbed me and finally managed to get the cuffs on me with my arms at the front. I was bundled into one of the police cars while they dealt with the unconscious man in the car park. I started kicking and wrecking the inside of the car and realised that I could lock the doors to keep them out.

"Open the door, sir, if you know what is good for you."

"Fuck off you black bastards, you can get me a Ford Granada, then I will come out, now get to fuck away from the car."

I could see David in a car across the road from me, and he was sitting grinning at me, he actually thought that this was funny, he was smiling from ear to ear. I gave him a wave and smiled back and waved at him, he could not wave as his hands were behind his back.

"Open the bloody doors, just open them and it will make it go better for you in court."

"A Ford Granada or you can all fuck off; this car is shite."

David's police taxi, drove away, leaving me on my own, he was getting taken to the police station. Another car drew up beside me, a Granada, its lights and siren going full pelt. Two officers emerged and walked over to the car which I had made my refuge, and knocked on the window.

"Kind sir, here is your Granada you requested, kindly step out onto the pavement and have this one if you will."

I kept my word and did what I had been asked and walked over towards the Granada, and was immediately knocked to the ground by one of the first officers on the scene. He was being the big man in front of the ever-increasing crowd. He bundled me into the back of the car, deliberately banging my head off the door frame. He got into the driver's seat and waited on his colleague getting in beside him. I sat as calmly as I could in the seat behind him, leaning back in the seat like I did not care. He kept looking in his rear-view mirror at me, and I just ignored him. The car drove away slowly, getting a rapturous round of applause from everyone who had lined the streets to watch, they seemed elated that I was finally going away. The car started to pick up speed as it left the village through the archway, and kept a steady speed up along the long straight part of the road. They had forgotten about me in the back because I was sitting quietly, and had dropped their guard. I lifted my arms and swung them round with full force at the driver's head, hitting his skull with the handcuffs, then I hit him again.

The car came to a stop after hitting the verge and the officer in the passenger seat got out and pulled me from the car. He was radioing for assistance; immediate help was required. The male prisoner has assaulted the driver so badly that he can't drive. Badly assaulted my arse, he would not know a kicking if he saw it in a movie. It served the bastard right, he was rough with me when I was arrested, now we were quits, he got what was coming to him. He shoved my face down on to the grass verge and pressed his knee into my back. I was struggling to breath, and I could not move, but he would not release me even for a minute because he probably feared what might happen to him, and he would have been right.

A van drew up beside us after what seemed an eternity, and I was unceremoniously bundled into a caged section in the back. They took off knowing that I was safely locked up, and I listened to them all talking about me like I was not there. They were describing someone which was not me, they were talking about a crazed psychopath who knocked the same man unconscious twice and attacked everyone who approached him. Three police assaults, damage to police property, damage to a bus, willfully setting off the hotel fire alarm, resisting arrest, breach of the peace and putting people in a state of fear and alarm, they were describing my father not me, I had finally become him. He would be proud of me now, I was no longer the pansy he did not like, and I was the same as he was now. I was feared and respected wherever I went, I was now a proper man and I was proud.

The police station in Forfar was busy when we arrived. It was like a bustling shopping centre with officers going about everywhere I looked. I stood at the desk as I was told to and was charged with everything I had allegedly done, apart from the serious assault on the unconscious man, he was still in hospital getting checked up on and were waiting on the results of his examination before they charged me on that.

"You do not have to say anything, but it may harm your defence if you do not mention when questioned something which you may later rely on in court. Anything you say may be given in evidence. Do you understand?"

"The cunt deserved it, that's all I am saying; he should have shut up when I told him to."

I was put into a cell with a thin plastic covered mattress and a hairy brown blanket. My shoes and belt were removed, then lastly my handcuffs. My wrists were cut and bleeding from them being too tight, and probably with struggling to free myself and hitting with them.

"You black bastards look at my fucking wrists, look at the state of them."

I immediately lashed out at the officer who released me, and the next thing I knew I was surrounded by several officers. I was held down on the floor by three of them while the other two started hitting me in the stomach, and testicles. They finished and got to their feet and left me lying there in agony.

"Try anything again, you little bastard and you will get what is coming to you, you don't hit officers and get away with it."

"You won't get away with hitting me either, you black bastard pigs, I will get you charged with this."

"Charged with what, nothing happened to you? You must have been hurt when you were struggling, and I have a whole police station full of officers who will corroborate my statement, so shut your mouth if you know what is good for you."

He clanked the heavy dark green painted metal door shut, and peered through the metal flap as he did, smirking like he was enjoying the show. I ran towards him and he flinched back from the flap and slammed it shut. I kicked the metal door for ages, but felt no pain.

"Hey Peedie I am in the cell across from you, can you hear me?"

"Yes, David, did you hear me getting the shit punched out of me?"

"Yes, it was funny hearing you calling them every name under the sun. I have been here for ages, where have you been?"

"Oh, it took them a long time to get me here what with one thing and another. They had a problem with the cars and one of the drivers got injured, and they have blamed me as if I would?"

"What day is it Peedie?"

"It's still fucking Friday why?"

"I was told that we would be appearing in court on Monday, at Ten o'clock, which is going to be a fucking long time to be in this shit hole with the pigs going about. There is fuck all to do, and worse than that I have no fags."

I heard a knock on my cell door and an officer opened my hatch and told me to stop talking as other detainees were getting annoyed with us as they were trying to sleep. It did not seem relevant to the officer that they were the ones making the most noise opening and clanking shut the barred gate entrance door to the cell unit, and opening and shutting the hatches on our doors. A telephone kept ringing at the end of the corridor, I lost count of the times it rang without getting answered, and an officer walked about whistling the most ridiculous out of tune tone. I did not recognise, and they were asking us to be silent, they had a bloody cheek.

I lay on my back on the thin mattress under the hairy blanket, but I could not get comfortable no matter what I did. I started to bang on my door for someone to come.

"Right, laddie, what are you wanting, I am trying to do paperwork along at the end, this had better be good."

"Officer, all I want is a pillow because I can't

get to sleep without one. I tried rolling up my blanket and using that, but then I was too cold, so had to use it as a blanket again."

"Do you think that this is the savoy laddie, you don't get pillows in here, but I will give you an extra blanket if you want?"

"Yes, that would be fabulous officer, thank you very much."

"Well, if he is getting an extra blanket, can I have one, I am his brother, so I deserve one."

"Right then the two of you, I will go and get you one each if there is going to be no more noise and you go to sleep."

The blanket was passed through the flap, and I pulled it through. It was a heavier blanket than my first one so I used it for on top of me and folded the other one up for a pillow. I lay down and tried to recall everything which had happened earlier, which had led to my incarceration in here. There was graffiti etched all over the place, left by previous guests of the establishment. I don't know what they had used because everyone's property is taken from them before they get put in a cell.

I must have fallen asleep because I woke to the loudest alarm, I think I had ever heard. Officers were frantically checking the cells for a fire as the smoke alarms had been activated.

"It's all right everybody, I have found what has caused the alarm to go off. Where did you get a cigarette and something to light it with?"

"I had two fags and some matches stuffed down one of my socks, the custody officer never noticed them hidden there."

It was bloody David, the sneaky little cunt, only he could have done that. They searched him to see if he had any more tobacco products and left him without any doubt what he had just caused.

"Thanks to you the fire brigade will have to attend, because our alarm system is connected, and they won't be happy getting hauled out of bed for nothing. See what you have done, it was all going well until that alarm went off, now everybody is kicking off in the cells again."

The noise stopped eventually and it was calm until I woke up early the next morning. Everybody was getting asked what how they would like their eggs, fried, for the breakfast rolls, and what they would like in their tea. I had already been tipped off by a young officer what to ask for.

"I would like the yolk hard, and no sugar and milk in my tea please."

"Aye, and can I get the same as him then?"

David and I watched out the hatch on the door, it was funny seeing him at last after talking through a steel door. The guard was back dishing out the fried egg rolls and cups of tea. I heard the first door getting banged and a disgruntled moan coming from the cell.

"What to fuck is this, the egg is as hard as

rubber, and I never asked for black fucking tea either, you can take this lot fucking back because it is not what I asked for."

I took mine as it was passed through the hatch, and it was exactly what I wanted, the yolk was soft and there was at least three spoons of sugar and milk in my tea. David inspected his, and he got the same. I had been advised to ask for the opposite of what I wanted. The guard was an old man who only cleaned up and cooked meals for the custody cells, and he loathed his job with a passion. He moaned at having to clean up the spilled tea chucked back out from the first cell he passed it through. The mugs and plate were made of plastic, and post office red in colour. A plastic mug would not be my first choice when having a cup of tea, but this was the most appreciated tea I had ever had the good fortune to drink. It was Devine, luxurious and unadulterated bliss, sipping it in tiny bursts making every bit of it last as long as possible because I did not know when I would be getting a drink again. My egg roll was the same, only lacking salt, but I would not hold that against him. Half an hour later he came to collect the plates and mugs. I thanked him for giving us our breakfast, but he did not respond, and just went to the next cell to collect the rest.

"Oh my God, what a fucking smell, the stench is so bad I can hardly breathe in here, for fuck's sake I wish I had an opening window."

"What has happened David, what is going on in there?"

"I have just taken a dump in the toilet and the smell is so bad it is nearly choking me; it is fucking stinking."

The toilets were in the cell and made of stainless steel with the flush controlled from the corridor side. David had done a shit in it, but could not flush it, he was roaring on an officer to come and flush it, but none appeared. We laughed at his predicament, making it seem so comical, and still, nobody came.

"Peedie you would not laugh if you were in here, I will tell you, that shite is a curry special, filled with rice and morsels of sweetcorn, and garnished with flies who won't fuck off. Fuck knows how flies can get into a cell with no window and a closed door."

That was it for me, I started to laugh and could not stop, the thought of a swarm of flies diving down into the toilet bowl to inhabit his freshly deposited shite was funny, and I could not get the picture out of my mind.

"What is going on in here you pair?"

"It's David across there officer, he wants his toilet flushed, he says it stinks in his cell."

The officer peeped in the hatch and immediately sprang backwards.

"That just has to be the worst smell I have ever had in one of these cells in all the years I have worked here, that is so vile your insides must be decomposing."

He flushed all the toilets on both sides, then he took us out one at a time to get a wash and freshen up. David's turn came and the officer sprayed air freshener in his cell, a lovely fresh, flowery smell, I could smell the difference from my cell. So could David when he was locked back in it.

"Oh, that's better, it does not smell of shit anymore, but it does smell of mixed roses, with a hint of shite fused together in sweetly scented undertones."

Everyone in earshot started to laugh, and even the officer found it funny. It lightened my mood for a while, but it did not last for long. I sat in my solitary cell for too long without any stimulation, and I could not cope. Boredom started to submerge me deeper into my depression. I had too much time on my hands, and the up and coming court case was weighing heavy on my mind. I wondered if our father would appear in court to give us moral support, but at the same time, I knew he would not appear, nor give a shit what happened to me, and possibly David either. If I get jailed, I will be his hero, I will be a man, someone to look up to like he was to everyone who knew him. He was a man not to be messed with, and I would soon be like him. Time never seemed to pass, and what seemed like twenty-four hours after breakfast, sandwiches and a mug of tea were delivered through my hatch in the door.

"Officer what time is it.?

"Thirteen ten precisely, why do you need to know, you are not going anywhere?"

"Is that all, I have another day and a half to spend in here, can't we get out to run about for a while?"

"You should have thought about that, before you did whatever you did to end up in here. You cannot leave your cell unless a doctor asks to get you to a hospital or something like that. It would be more than my careers worth to let you out for anything, never mind a run about. My advice would be to just chill out and settle down until Monday morning. Then, depending what your sentence is, you will either come back here or get released."

Saturday was over, now it was time to try to get some sleep. David had stopped speaking to me because he had no fags, not my fault in any way, but he blamed me. I fell asleep through utter boredom, I think, but was woken in the middle of the night by screaming and loud banging. Another guest was getting admitted to the establishment against their will, as I had been, and they were not happy. Officers with raised voices seemed to be wrestling with the man, and also what sounded to be a drunk woman as well. They were wanting to be put in the same cell, but this was politely refused. They were finally separated, and put at different ends of the corridor.

They seemed to shout backwards and forwards relentlessly between the cells, driving
me closer to insanity. Her voice was shrill, and
sounded like an electric hammer drill on steel.
Her mouth never stopped, she talked inces-
santly, asking the same question over and over
again. Did he sleep with someone else or not? I
wished he would answer her, even lie if he had
to, but ignoring her at this time was not the answer. Sleep evaded me for the rest of the night,
and at last, it was Sunday, only twenty-four or
so hours to stay in here now. The customary
egg roll turned out to be a bacon and egg roll
today, with a choice of tea or coffee. There was
a different man doing the meals today, he was a
lot younger that the previous man we had, and
he was cheery with us, smiling as he served our
Sunday breakfast. I even managed to get an extra
coffee without any questions asked. The hatch
was closed again and I sat down trying not to
think of the rest of the day cooped up here, when
without warning my hatch dropped down. A
man with a black eye was peering through at me
with an inquisitive look on his face.

"Do you remember me, sonny?"

"No, I don't, should I remember you?"

"I'm the policeman you attacked in Edzell; my
name is Inspector Milne. I have just come to ask
if you want The Sunday Post, as I have finished
reading it."

"Look I'm sorry about hitting you, it was not meant to all turn out as it did. The newspaper would be nice to fill in time with."

The paper was handed through to me and I started to read it page by page, cover to cover, and even read every advertisement and then sports pages. I had only ever glanced at the paper before, only ever reading Oor Wullie, or The Broons before, then I read it over again. Time was not passing now and my fingers were black after reading the paper for so long. I wished that I had a pen to do the puzzles page, but that was something that I could possibly use as a weapon so a request for one would be futile. The police would not be worried about a slap with a rolled-up Sunday Post that's for sure. I lay down to try to sleep some time away, but was just settling down when I was asked to come out for a wash and freshen up. I washed the black newspaper ink from my fingers and put water in my hair to try to get the tangles out. Washing filled in five minutes of my time, and I was sent back to my suite to stay until Monday morning. It was going to be a long day and it was only about eleven o'clock.

Tea time came at long last and was a mug of tea, and a fish supper from Jacks Chip shop, because nobody was employed to cook for us on a Sunday night. That was probably the best meal that I had ever tasted. I peeled off a small flake of fish at a time and savoured every chip and crumb of the batter. I wiped the last few chips across the paper to get every grain of salt and drop of vinegar, then I licked the paper. That left me four pages greasy fingered of out of date newspaper to read, and I read every word.

It was a quieter evening as there were no more new admissions, and anyway, there were no empty cells. Every one of us started to relax into life in the cells and just sat it out quietly.

CHAPTER 20

We were all rudely awakened at six am. I know that it was that time because we were told by a grinning policeman that we had the court at ten am, and we had precisely four hours to get ready. Before that shout to get up, time had no meaning and the only way of telling roughly what time it might be, was if it was dark or light outside, because the cell lights never went off. We were already dressed, so only had shoes and a belt to put on, and breakfast time was still two hours away. Getting us up at that time was intentional, we had never been wakened so early before, and this was the worst morning to be sitting idle for me.

"You might as well get spruced up first for your court appearance since you are on your feet."

I followed the young officer to the sink at the end of the corridor. I washed as best as I could, but there was no way of disguising the stale, sweaty odour coming from my clothing. My long hair looked like a twisted mop head and was greasy.

"Is there a comb or a brush I can get a loan of, officer? I can't go to court looking like this."

"No, there isn't I'm afraid, you will just have

to go to court like the sack of shit you are, you people make me sick, expecting special privileges after what you have done, now get back to your cell."

He was trying to wind me up, trying to get a reaction from me so I would let him have it between the eyes, but I wanted out of this place. He was lucky, but it would have been different if we had met outside. My clothing was crumpled beyond even semi presentable, after wearing and sleeping in it since Friday, and there was dirt from the road and the grass verge ingrained in my jeans, and my T-shirt was ripped. I looked like a vagrant. They were keeping me looking like this to make me appear worse in front of the Judge.

The hopefully last breakfast was handed to me through the hatch, but I was not hungry. I forced my egg roll down me to try to stop me feeling queasy. My stomach was in knots, and I was at my wit's end wondering what would happen to me. David did not seem to care, or he was not showing it. Someone opened my cell door, letting a flood of fresh air fill the tiny space.

"Right Peedie don't just stand there, get your shoes on."

My shoes felt unnatural on my feet; they did not feel right after just wearing socks on the concrete tiled floors for so long. That was the first time I could see my fellow residents and neighbours as they were herded out to get their footwear on as well. We were a sorry looking bunch all right, and one of them was worse looking than me, wearing only a disposable white boiler suit which he had been tearing through boredom.

We were handcuffed as they led us through the barred entrance to the cells and led to the custody desk. They handed everyone except David and me their belongings which they all signed for.

"Why are we not getting ours, then?"

"You will get yours if you get released, but I sincerely doubt it. I think the two of you will be heading for Perth Prison, when the court hears what you have done, so keeping your things here will save us having to catalogue it again. It is sealed in a bag in a locked room, so nobody will steal it if that is what you are worried about. In the unlikely event, you are released you can come back here and get it."

We were the last to be led out a back door to a waiting police van, and we climbed in and sat down on the hard seats. Everyone else had gone in one large van, which we could see through the window, but we were getting taken separately.

We were getting treated like big time criminals, singled out to make us look bad. The fresh air was Devine, and I filled my lungs with it to full capacity, looking around me at the bright sky and greenery. My concrete home of the last few days had deprived me of that luxury in which I had taken for granted for so long.

The van stopped and started and weaved through the streets until it stopped at the court. The back door of the building was open, and we were led still handcuffed into a locked room to await our time slot in court. The officer looking after us seemed different from any of the rest we had had the misfortune to meet, apart from the Inspector who gave me the newspaper. I asked him how long they would keep us locked in here and what would happen in court, as I had only seen a court on television before.

"The custodies are up first, that's your lot, then it's everything else. Sheriff Kermack will be on today, and he is a tyrant, and hates custody cases. There is no point in sugar coating it; he just does. For goodness sake, don't look him in the eye, keep your head bowed and only look up if you are answering a question. Refer to him as Your Honour at all times, when he stands, you stand, when he sits you sit, unless you get sentenced that is."

David was laughing and joking with some of the others awaiting their fate, but I just could not stop thinking if my father and mother would be there to see what happens to us today.

"A booming voice shouted into the room, Coghill, Mr. Coghill."

An officer led him out of the room and he never appeared back. I sat wondering if he had been released or had been taken to another room. The officer appeared back and sat down without talking or even looking at us. He had changed from the happy, friendly man into a professional police man for the court appearances in front of the judge.

Name after name was called out, but not ours. There was about fifteen of us locked in that room before the court started; some people were from other police stations we had not met before. One of them who had been quiet the whole time started talking to me.

"Have you been up before? Kermack is a total nut case; he stands for no shit in his court, and don't laugh at his stupid wig, even if it's sitting squint on his head."

"No, this is my first time and I am bricking it; the pigs think I will be sent to Perth Prison."

"Perth Prison is OK; you will like it there if you go. The meals are better than the ones you get in the cop shop, and you get clean clothes and a shower. I was in for eighteen months and loved it."

He was next to be called, and the room was empty, except us and an officer.

"When will we be called? This is taking far too long."

"The court has stopped for a break for ten minutes, then you will get called when the judge comes back in."

We sat looking at the floor for what seemed an hour, then my heart sank as they called both our names. Everyone else had gone on their own.

"Come on then look lively, follow me up the stairs and stand beside me when we get to the top, for fuck's sake don't sit down, and remember what I told you earlier."

We appeared from the stairs into the small opening into the court like a Wurlitzer Organ at a cinema. We looked around at the crowds in the public gallery, but there was nobody we knew.

"All rise."

We were already standing but everyone else stood up and only sat after they were asked to. I remembered what they had told me and stood still with my head bowed.

"Right then what have we here then? A pair of ruffians I think after reading this."

The judge was not a big as I had imagined him to be, and he was a lot older. He seemed to be taking a long time to speak again as he was reading over the papers in front of him. He sat with his head leaning forward with his gold-rimmed glasses balancing on the very tip of his nose and periodically stopped reading and looked towards us and shook his head from side to side. Then he spoke with a definite change in the tone of his voice, a more authoritarian pitch more that of a teacher would use in her class.

"David, what have you to say for yourself then? Just enlighten me as I have probably heard the story a hundred times before. I am afraid I have half listened to every excuse known to man, and it is getting boring now, so begin."

"He put his hand up my girlfriend's skirt your honour, I tried to shove him away, but he was too big and picked me up and threw me over a wall."

"What happened next, I mean after he threw you over the wall?"

"I landed on the ground your honour."

The whole court burst out laughing, even a solicitor had a snigger."

"Silence in court or I shall have you all removed from this court. This is a court of law, not a school playground."

"Now David, we shall start again, won't we, we shall get a sensible answer this time?"

David was not trying to be funny; he was being honest and sincere. He did land on the ground, but that was not what the Judge wanted. He started recalling everything he could remember, and he was stopped mid-sentence.

"David, I had to stop you there, I have definitely heard this story in a previous case, in fact, I keep hearing it, and being drunk is no excuse not to remember. I am sure you can remember more than that. The truth is, you don't want to remember because then you would have to be responsible for your actions. Now let's start over, shall we?"

The Judge was getting riled, and I wanted him to stay calm for when he came to me to start asking for the truth.

"I hit nobody. I only pushed him twice to try to get him onto the ground, and it ended when I landed on the tarmac."

"I will come back to you David, now it's your brother's turn to spin his tale of woe, and what happened and it better be good, although this may take some while."

"I saw my brother flying over the wall. That's what started it."

"No young sir, what started it as you call it was when you were seen by reliable witnesses repeatedly kicking the man and rendering him unconscious, and not just once either. You returned to the wedding reception and did the same crime again, then you willfully ripped a fire alarm control from the wall, causing the whole wedding to be interrupted as they had to leave the building, you assaulted several other people, all to their injury, vandalised a private single decker coach and used the part you tore from its mountings as a weapon, damaged the interior of a police car, locked the officers out and continued to damage it. Then you have the two serious police assaults, which is another matter entirely. You injured an Inspector in the course of his duty as you tried to rescue your brother, blacking the officer's eye, and knocking his hat off. And then we come to the assault on the driver who was transferring you to the custody cells in Forfar, not only did you injure him about the head, you placed another officer travelling with him, and yourself in grave danger. You have generated so much violence and destruction in one evening without provocation, that I do not think I can sentence you today."

I stood there totally dumbstruck, he must be sending me to Perth Prison on remand or something, and somebody told me he might do that. The police had kept my belongings at the station, they must have known.

"All rise."

The Judge adjourned the court for one hour, and they led us down the steps to the holding rooms down below. The officer with us was shaking his head from side to side. I don't think he had believed what he had just heard, either. I had heard several gasps of disbelief from the public gallery and had thought they were being a bit dramatic.

"I honestly think you are a goner sonny; I have never seen Sheriff Kermack adjourning for an hour before he sentences someone. He must be finding out what the maximum sentence is before he calls you back to court, God helps you, that's all I can say, you are getting a one-way ticket to Perth that's for certain."

"David, if I get the jail, please look after the house and pay the rent till I get out, I can't afford to have nowhere to live when I get out."

"Aye, I will, me and Mags can move in full time until you come back, but I don't think you will get jailed."

The officer went to the back door for a smoke, keeping us in full view, eying us up and down like he could not trust us. They handcuffed us so would not get very far if we ran, it would be hard to mingle with the crowds with them on our wrists.

"Officer, can I cadge a few draws of your fag before you put it out? I am absolutely dying here smelling that fag

"If you come here and promise not to run, I will give you a cigarette all to yourself. I smoke myself so I know you must be suffering now."

He gave David one, and the officer lit it for him. He took a long draw and did not seem to exhale, something I used to do when I smoked hash. The look on his face was priceless. He was beaming from ear to ear and was enjoying every minute.

"At least I have had a smoke before we go to Perth."

"You have nothing to worry about David. It will only be me who is going there."

The clerk of court was shouting downstairs for us to come back to court. I stood back in the same place I was before.

"All rise."

The Judge appeared through the door at the back of the court and called a solicitor over to talk to him. They were talking so quietly that I could not hear them. He sat down and the solicitor wrote things on a sheet of paper. Then there was the deadly silence which followed. We stood there for a good five minutes before he talked again. It was agonising waiting to find out what was to become of me, but I did not want him to rush it either.

"David, you resisted arrest and not much more, you have spent a whole weekend in confinement, so I will not add any sentence to that, you are free to go, but if you appear before me again, I will have no hesitation to fine you heavily. Do you understand me?"

"Yes, sir, I understand perfectly well. I will never be in this court again, and I can promise you that.

"Please just stand there until I speak to your brother."

He looked over to me and he appeared to be studying me. He looked at me then at his notes several times before he spoke to me.

"After careful consideration, I am getting you admitted to Sunnyside Royal Psychiatric Hospital for reports. I read over your case several times today, and have concluded that no one of sound mind would have been capable of the crimes you have just committed. You are without remorse or emotion regarding everything that this case rests on, therefore, having your mental state evaluated is the only option open to me at the moment. You will be taken there today where you will undergo intense psychiatric evaluation for a minimum period of two months. If you do not stay in the hospital, I will have no other alternative but to send you to prison. This is not an option for you, it is compulsory."

"Court will be held here again in just over two months' time on an exact date yet to be confirmed, when you will be sentenced for your crimes. You have to attend the hearing in person, and we will send a letter to the hospital explaining this to you. Officer, take him away."

We almost floated down the stairs we were so elated at the sentences. David had got off scot free, and I was going on a holiday to Montrose. We were expecting the worst, but it never happened. David said his goodbyes after he had first lit a fag and smoked it with both hands, putting it first in his right, then his left hand, just because he could. They had removed his cuffs, and I was waiting on mine coming off. He was heading to the police station first to collect his wallet and whatever else he had handed over when he was detained, I would get mine on the way. The officer was away to check to see who was taking me to Sunnyside, and if I was getting my cuffs left on to go to the hospital given my previous incidents in the police car. He did not trust me and I did not blame him. Another officer appeared from a room along the corridor carrying what looked like my wallet, belt and laces from my shoes in a clear plastic bag.

"This will save us having to stop at the station

on the way to Sunnyside. You can get your cuffs off now, but any nonsense and they will go back on with no hesitation from us, do you hear?"

"Yes, I'm listening, one weekend in your lovely bed and breakfast ensuite cell is enough for me, and I never want to stay there again, never."

CHAPTER 21

The police van was stuffy in the back where I was sitting and no windows could be opened. The trip seemed to take forever on the narrow winding roads. It had been a long time since I had been admitted to Sunnyside and I was dreading it, and this time I could not just walk out if I wanted to, it would be my home for the next eight weeks even if I hated it. The van slowed right down and we went through the big gated entrance and I saw the massive red sandstone building towering high above the van. It stopped at the main reception, a place I remember well because my father crushed my testicles the last time I waited here. There had been a few minor changes since I was here on my previous visit. The counter was further forward than it used to be, and they had added a door to gain access to a side room. They had repainted the shabby light blue paint, with magnolia with white woodwork.

A nurse finally appeared, and I was glad. Being flanked by two officers was not much of a laugh for me. The officers handed paperwork to the nurse, and she signed it and handed it back. They asked me to sign for my meagre belongings, and I grabbed them quickly because I needed my laces for my shoes.

The officers, left me standing there alone in the room. I sat down and looked around me, and memories of this place came flooding back, not all good memories either. I wondered if Maxwell was still here or if he had recovered enough to move on. I did not have a good feeling about this place, and I was so looking forward to it earlier.

A door opened to my right and I could smell cinnamon, I recognised it as my mother used it for making cinnamon swirls. I was summoned inside by a man who looked around forty years old. His brown hair was immaculately combed to the side and his skin did not have a blemish; it resembled plastic, more like a doll's skin. He looked like someone out a catalogue with his chiselled rugged features. His accent did not match his image as he spoke with a strong Glaswegian accent.

I sat across the large green leather-topped desk from him and he began talking to me about anything that came into his head. He was trying to trap me; he must be because he is skirting round the obvious reason I was here for. Surely, he knew the reason they had forced me to stay here, somebody must have told him, and here he was talking about fishing and random shite I was not interested in. I bet he is recording my every word which he will give to the Judge.

I looked around the room at the pictures on the walls. They were all hand painted scenes of countryside views with old fashioned gold frames. They looked out of place in the modern elegance of the room with the magnolia painted walls.

"Look young man I am trying to relax you so we can have a proper chat about how you are feeling, and how you think you are coping with life in general. This is not a test and there are no right or wrong answers. If you see me writing, I am just keeping notes so I can remember our chats and refer back to them later."

I looked at him with suspicion, he was gathering information to give the court, not to help me, he was only interested in what the court had requested, and I did not trust him. He would get no information from me the sly bastard. I never responded to his senseless remarks; he was being ridiculous, treating me like a child, patronising me with his snide quips. I was an adult; I neither wanted nor needed this stupid shit. Not a word passed my lips the whole hour I sat in his room, I just sat and listened to his nonsense and his ideas of how my life was. He knew fuck all about me; he was obviously born on the other side of the fence than I had been. I bet his father never kicked him around the house or tried to drown him in a bath of cold water. He could not know, because he was not there; I had a front row ringside seat when discipline was handed out, the bastard always ensured that I had a front row when it came to a beating. The man across the desk turned out to be a psychiatrist, and he would get fuck all information from me, fuck all.

"Well, maybe next time, then, if you don't feel ready yet. If you want a chat any time, just tell my receptionist and she will organise it for you."

The man was a prick, I had decided that in the first five minutes after I met him. I was not a little boy, but he was treating me like one. I wanted to get out of his office and settle in for the night, plus I needed the toilet. He sat grinning as he asked me to follow the ward sister through to where I would call home for the next two months.

There was nobody in the ward when we went in, beds were obviously occupied because there were personal effects on top of the bedside lockers. Get-well cards and flowers in different stages of wilting, and probably given through a guilty conscience and not because people cared, were dotted around on a few of the lockers. At least they received a card regardless of how I imagined someone gave it. At least someone who cared actually knew they were here. I had never had a card in my whole life so far. My bed was in the middle of the ward in full view of everyone, they would look at me from both ends of the ward, scrutinising me and watching my every move, and there would be nowhere to hide.

"Do you not have anything with you, like a change of clothes or toiletries?"

"No, I did not have time to pack anything, and

need clean clothes because I have had them on since Friday."

"I will see what I can do for you. We can't have you looking like someone has dragged you through a hedge backwards."

The nurse told me to just call her Ruth, and she was kind to me expecting nothing in return. Her hair reminded me of my gran, when she was younger, there was something about her that drew me to her, but maybe it was only the fact she cared. I sat on the chair beside my bed and had a look in my wallet, the first time I had looked inside it since Friday, and there was plenty of money in it. Gwen's party had been a free night out, so I had not spent a penny all night.

"I have plenty of cash with me so I could buy something to wear if somebody can take me to the town."

"We do have clothes you can wear over in another ward store. You cannot go out until you have been assessed by a psychologist or the psychiatrist you spoke to this morning. They will decide when you can go out, but that won't be for a wee while yet, and even if they let you go you will have to have a staff member with you."

Ruth wrote down the sizes I told her for replacement clothing for me and went away to rummage in the store for me. She seemed to take ages to come back, but she came back with an armful of clothes, socks, and underwear, and they were all new. Ruth explained that a few of the bigger stores in the town donated clothing and toiletries to the hospital every year.

"Have a shower, then put the clean ones on, and put all your dirty ones in this bag. It has your name on it, so when the laundry washes them, they will come back to this ward. Come with me and I will show you where to go."

"I know my way around here Ruth, I have stayed here twice before when I was fifteen, and I know where everything is."

Ruth told me she would be back later to take me to see someone from the admin office to sort money out for me because I was unemployed now.

"Don't go wandering around after you have had your shower, stay in the ward until I come back."

I chose what to wear from the two changes of clothing I had been given and headed for the showers. I turned on the water and got undressed. As I went under the stream of hot water a sense of calm came over me. The feeling was rejuvenating as the grime and sweat from my time in the cells was removed from my skin. The pine smell of the soap was so refreshing, so good for my soul, I felt euphoric, never had a shower felt this good. I eventually stepped out of my shower heaven and got dried. My skin felt new, revitalised, and I felt good. I placed my dirty clothing in the bag, remembering to take my wallet and money out of my jeans. My new jeans felt starchy as I pulled them up over my legs because they were new. The socks, they had given me were a light yellow colour, more like a custard yellow, but they felt so soft against my feet. I got finished dressing and gave my hair a final rub with the towel and headed back to my bed. Ruth was already in the ward when I returned, busy writing up paperwork.

"I thought you had fallen down the plug hole you were away so long. Right give me your bag and I will put it in the big laundry sack before it gets picked up."

"Ruth is there a comb or brush I can borrow."

"No, we can't let you share personal items like that, come on and I will take you to the hospital shop to get some things like a toothbrush and toothpaste, and a comb, you better get your long hair brushed before it dries."

It felt strange getting accompanied everywhere I went, shadowed everywhere except in the toilet.

Ruth told me that there were around 400 patients throughout all the different wards and departments in Sunnyside. I had still not seen any of them since I had arrived from Forfar, but that was about to change. I was led into a large room with three rows of tables stretching the whole length of the room with a high dark painted ceiling coming to a peak in the centre. There was a long serving counter right at the back with two women wearing white overalls and hats. I filled my nostrils with the smell of fried onions, and something else I could not quite put my finger on. There were people sitting at some tables farther up who had been scrutinising me since I entered with Ruth. One of them came running the full length of the room to introduce themselves, she was hyper, and she was waving her arms in front of me and was trying to touch my face. Her eyes seemed to be unable to stay still, flicking up and down and side to side in quick jerky movements. I did not feel at ease around her, but at the same time, she did not appear threatening.

"This is where you will come for all your meals. We try to encourage everyone to mix.

You will get escorted over and back again when it is time to come eat."

"Where is everybody from my ward, I have seen none of them?"

"They are either in the lounge watching television or the arts and crafts rooms, we let nobody hang about their beds all day, and it is not good to be isolated so we encourage group pastimes."

I was shown into the lounge, which had a large television higher up on the wall on a metal bracket. Armchairs covered in a fake leather like material, some a light blue and some a dusky pink colour lined the room round all four walls. The ceiling was high with several windows along the one wall that were adorned with gaudy green patterned curtains. A man got to his feet to pull two curtains across because the sunlight was shining on the television screen. He did not talk or look at anyone as he did it, and he never saw me standing at the door.

"Who are you then? Why are you hanging about the door, are you eying me up?"

A female around my age had seen me; now I felt obliged to go right into the room. I did not want to go in, I felt out of place in here, and wished that the ground would open up and swallow me whole."

I told her my name, and she laughed out loud.

"Your voice is stupid, you sound foreign, so where do you come from?"

"I was born in Orkney at the very top of Scotland, and everybody there talks like that. You sound stupid as well, where are you from?"

"I am Lorna from Stonehaven, and I don't talk as bad as some of them from there, some have a really strong accent, especially my grandparents."

Lorna was stockily built with a chubby face covered in freckles, and half hid with her red hair. She was wearing a pair of jeans which were bright blue, and a T-shirt which was skin tight, showing any folds of skin she had. She could talk for everyone in the room, and she never stopped, which made it easier for me. I sat down a seat away from her and looked around at everybody sitting around the room. Some were engrossed in the television and others were just staring at anything, not really engaging in what was going on around them.

"Do you fancy going outside Peedie?"

"We aren't allowed outside. Someone told me that when I came in here."

"They allow us in the garden at the side; it is just through that door."

We went out to the garden and sat on a wooden bench. Lorna got to her feet and walked over to a small gate disappearing out of sight for a minute, then appeared back hiding something under her T-shirt.

"Get your lips round this Peedie. This will sort you out, I have a couple every day."

She had two cans of lager and handed me one, she was smiling at me. Her expression was priceless; she looked like a child who had just been given a lolly or some other treat. I took one from her and took a small sip, just to savour it for a minute.

"For fuck's sake min, let nobody see you with it, keep it kind of hidden when you drink it."

"How do you manage to get to the shops to buy this? It's not as if the hospital shop sells it?"

"There is a taxi driver who brings it for me when he is either dropping a fare off or picking one up. I leave the money hidden for him, and he hides the lager in the same place every time. I give him oral sex now and again to make sure he keeps bringing it. I've told him I would tell his wife, I shagged him, if he does not bring me lager, and I don't even know his wife."

That was a good can of lager, it was the longest a can had ever lasted me, and I savoured every last drop like it would be my last.

"Do you fancy another one Peedie? We can come back later if you do."

"Lorna, am I breathing? Do I look like I would refuse a fucking lager, of course, I will come back for one, as long as I have a pulse that is?"

We both walked over to a bin farther along and dropped the empty cans out of sight under some newspaper and headed back inside. I suddenly felt better; I had never felt this good since I arrived. My next can could not come soon enough.

"Come on, then let's ready to go over for our lunch. I can see vinegar tits coming over to get us. Pretend that you can't hear her when she shouts for us to come over, it really pisses her off. She sucks her cheeks in like she has just sucked a lemon and stands with her hands on her hips looking at us. Then just before she shouts again, we get up to go over, she just about explodes with a temper, it's fucking brilliant and she falls for it every time the silly cow."

When we entered the dining hall, most of the tables were full, but Lorna led me to our table, which was only for our ward. She showed me where to get a tray and we lined up waiting for our turn to get served. A small, older woman asked me what I wanted, and she shoved a plate in front of me which she had already filled. It was like a production line. There were two choices: beef olives or burgers with onions. You either or take it or leave it, that's what Lorna had told me before we came in, if you liked nothing you went hungry. We sat at the table and ate, the beef olives were like shoe leather, and it was taking a long time to chew and swallow. The burger Lorna had looked like it had been partly mummified it was that dried up, and it had been partially hidden under a thinly spooned layer of onions, which did not enhance the taste any, but Lorna ate it, and I eventually finished mine. That was always going to one of the problems is to be some of the last to dine.

"Come on you two, time to back over the road to the lounge, and Lorna you have medication to get. Peedie you have to go to see the doctor when we get over. He is waiting for you."

"OK nurse keep your wig on, we are just sitting talking, I am ready now, but I will need something to get the taste of that burger away before I take my meds."

"Lorna can't you just come without all the carry on, every day is the same, one day I will die with shock if you come straight away."

"Alright, then I will come first shout tomorrow."

I laughed and so did Lorna, but the nurse never saw what was funny in Lorna's last reply to her. I could see why they called her vinegar tits; she was straighter than a ruler and did not have an ounce of fun in her. Vinegar, was slimly built, and about fifty years old with short black hair cut into a style more suited to a man. She had a face which could curdle milk just by looking at it, that's what I had decided, and I would not change my mind on that. Her uniform was immaculate, but then she never leaned on anything, nor sat down in all the times I have seen her.

The doctor was not the one I was expecting, not the patronising prick from before. He was different from the prick, dressed like a tramp and was wearing a pair of spectacles repaired using Elastoplast to hold the legs on. I felt that I could talk to him and answered any questions I felt comfortable answering. He had an aroma about him, which I thought was a tobacco pipe smoke. His hair was untidy, and he kept flicking his fringe to the side with his hand, even though his hair had not moved. I think it was more of a nervous thing than for vanity.

"Right then, young sir, I have been looking through your records from your last visits, and the ones forwarded by your own doctor. You have what we call severe depression, and I have prescribed you a course of anti-depressants which will not seem like they are helping straight away, they may take some weeks or months to make a difference. Take this along to the nurse and she will get the drugs from the dispensary for you."

Lorna was waiting outside the doctor's office when I came out.

"What a fucking time you have been in there, come on we have a can of lager with our name on it. They are chilled as fuck, straight from the toilet cistern."

I did not enjoy this lager as much as the last one, my mind was elsewhere. The sun was lower in the sky now, and the sweet smell of tiger lilies was wafting through the garden, mingling with the pungent but nice smell of honeysuckle. The air was still, and not even the leaves were moving. Birds were sitting high up in a copper beech tree. I was not sure what kind they were, but they were noisy. In a split second, the noise stopped, and they shot into the air like a rocket and vanished out of earshot, leaving an eerie silence behind them. A car door closing broke the silence, and Lorna sprung to her feet and ran towards the garden gate.

"Stay here, I will be back in about three minutes."

I sat watching a red squirrel running around the branches and jumping from limb to limb above me. I marveled at the agility it had even though it was so small.

"Right, that's me back, another six cans of lager delivered, and a mouthful of taxi driver's sperm down my throat. As soon as he puts his knob in my mouth, he comes, the filthy dirty bastard. Do I have any sperm on my chin?"

"No, you don't Lorna, oh my God woman you are something else, definitely different, that's all I will say on the matter. I can't believe I just checked your chin for sperm."

CHAPTER 22

My first night in the ward was hell. Every hour felt like a week as someone from somewhere in the room either screamed, snored, coughed or talked in their sleep. The morning was a relief from the torment of my mind. The anti-depressants were adding to my sleep problem, and so was my thoughts. My home was foremost in my mind wondering if David had actually gone to stay there or if he had gone straight to Kirriemuir. I wondered if my parents had found out about me being here and if my father was laughing fit to burst about me being stuck here for two months awaiting psychiatric reports. My father had always told me I was not right in the head anyway, I did not need this place to tell me about my mental state as I had had it been drummed into my head all my childhood.

If that rope had not broken, I would not be in this awful place now. I would just be a memory and not a family embarrassment. He would be too ashamed to mention to his pub cronies, I was in here, no son of his would be off their heads. This would now finally prove to him I was not his real son, and that none of his blood ran through my veins. He will make sure he tells me again when he next sees me, he never misses an opportunity to remind me of my parentage, and that he only had my mother's word I was his son. I wondered why my mother had put up with all the years of accusations that she had got pregnant by another man, and why my father has always denied me as his own flesh and blood. Why was a seed of doubt planted in his twisted mind to start with, something must have triggered it? I did not care whose son I was now as it mattered nothing to me, as it did not affect nor change what I had become. Things had accelerated to a point where I did not really want to live now, and I did not see the point in carrying on.

"Oh, you are awake, are you? I have been sitting reading my book for ages as I could not sleep. My name is Bill, we have not really met properly yet."

"I could not sleep either, I hate this place as it is so noisy."

"You get used to it after a while, this was your first night and it is the same for everyone who comes in."

Bill looked semi normal, not like some of the other people, I had seen yesterday in the dining room and the corridors. He was a small man about my age, stick thin with not an ounce of body fat on him. I noticed scars all up his arms which were darker than his skin. His eyes were sunk deep into his eye sockets and his cheeks were nonexistent. He did not look like he had eaten in months, he looked sad and pathetic, and

I wondered how he had managed to get as thin as he was now.

Bill was back reading his book deep in concentration. He did not lift his eyes from the book even when two people farther along the ward were arguing loudly, resulting in everybody waking up. Two nurses came into the ward to stop the bickering, which could have become violent if they had left it. I could not lie in bed another minute; I just had to get out of the ward before my head detonated. My brain could not accept what was happening around me; it was like a bad dream and I was not sleeping. I was wide awake in this lunatic asylum, trapped, helpless and powerless to do anything about it.

The seat in the garden was slightly damp as I sat down, but I did not care. This place was my salvation, my retreat from the insanity and the screams inside. Birds were chirping in the copper beech above me, oblivious to where my mind was. I wished that I was not here but there was no way out of the hell I was in, I was overcome with the might of my thoughts.

I went back inside to the hustle and bustle of the ward and sat on the chair beside my bed and noticed that Billy was not in his bed, which was a relief for me because I was not in the mood to talk to anyone. There seemed to be a commotion in the toilets and there were frantic shouts coming from somewhere farther along. I went to investigate as I was bursting to use the toilet myself. A nurse was banging on a cubical door shouting on Bill to come out, she seemed stressed to the point of almost panicking.

"I can't get Bill to answer me, could you please help me get this door open."

My shoulder hardly rammed the door and it burst open, revealing Bill sitting fully clothed on the toilet with blood dripping from his wrist onto the floor.

"Right you better go out for a minute until we can get Billy fixed up, it won't take long."

"I am just going into this cubicle for a minute, I am almost wetting myself, and then I will go out and close the door."

A male nurse almost knocked me over as he rushed past me and into Bill's cubical. This was not a pleasant start to the day for Bill nor me, and I did not need any more negativity in my life at the moment.

Breakfast time was announced and a few of us headed across to the dining hall. I was not even hungry, but went along just to get a change of scenery away from the bedlam which was now my home. I picked up a tray and took it along with me because everyone else had one. The queue was not very long and soon I was getting asked what I wanted.

"Come on sonny don't hold everyone up, there are more people to get fed behind you. It is either porridge or cereal, that's not a hard decision to make.

"I will just have the porridge then, and a mug of coffee please."

The woman serving was obviously unhappy in her job and was just serving up food in a robotic fashion which probably came normal after dishing up hundreds of thousands of meals. I went and sat down at an empty table and put the spoon in my porridge, but I could not stir it round like I wanted to as it was just a thick, gloopy mess in the bottom of my plate, It had a thin rubbery like skin covering it, and it was beyond saving. I drank my coffee and rejoined the queue to get some cereal and to return my congealed plateful of porridge.

"If you didn't want it you should not have taken it, I am sick of all the food wasted in here. We all work hard to feed you lot, you had porridge, you can't have cereal as well."

"Well, you can fucking keep your plate of dried up shit you call breakfast, here have it back."

I tipped the plate upside down on the counter and it stayed on the plate.

"There you go, just as I told you it is shite, it won't even come out of my plate, ram it up your big fat arse and ram the plate in as well there will be plenty room for it."

The whole place erupted into laughter and did not stop even after I walked out the door. She deserved it, she thought she was better than me, but she was not.

Billy was sitting in the lounge when I got back to the hospital. He was looking unhappier than I was feeling, and I felt bad.

"What's up Bill, you look pissed off?"

"Look, sorry about earlier in the toilets you were not meant to see that. I just cut myself to get try to relieve the pressure I am feeling. It is something I have done for years now. I just want to sit here on my own just now."

I left him sitting in the lounge and wandered out to the garden to see if Lorna was around as I had not set eyes on her today, not even at breakfast. I would have known if she had been there because she would have been at the front cheering me on when I insulted the staff member in the dining room. I walked along the long corridor to look for the craft rooms, hearing every one of my footsteps echoing off the walls at the far end. The floor was covered with blue tiles, which were shiny as a mirror, but they were not slippy. There was a smell of pine lingering in the air halfway down the corridor, but no smell at either end. I peered through the small glass window in the door and saw where everyone was. This was not for me, this would be like going back to school, and I was too old to be sitting painting pictures, so I turned around and headed back in the direction of the lounge before someone spotted me.

"There you are Peedie, you know that you are supposed to stay in or around the unit. Staff has been looking for you, where have you been?"

"Ruth, I just went over for breakfast, then came back here."

"Well, I was a bit worried after what I heard in the dining room; the lady is very upset. You know you shouldn't go over on your own. With all the carry on we had with Bill, we never noticed you leaving."

"I will remember at lunchtime to wait for everybody else. Have you seen Lorna today, Ruth? I have not seen her since last night."

"She won't be with us today. That's all I can tell you at the moment. She can tell you herself if she comes back."

"If she comes back, that sounds ominous, is she in some kind of trouble?"

"Look, I can't reveal where she is, that would be a breach of patient confidentiality. Let's just leave it at that and forget that I that I revealed as much as I did."

The day dragged, and time almost stood still and it was time I tried to get some sleep. Lorna was still on my mind; she had cans of lager hidden and was not around to drink them. She told me she always had two cans a day and today she had not been here. I lay looking at the ceiling for ages picking out imaginary faces in the shadows which trees were making with the street lights shining through them. Bill had been sleeping for ages because a nurse had given him sleeping tablets, and as I looked around the room, I could see or hear that most of the men in the ward were asleep. The snores, grunts, and farts seemed to get less noticeable the longer the night went on. The sounds were almost melodic as they were played from bed to bed up the ward, backwards and forwards the length of the room. Random melodies of gaseous farting coming from a bed farther up made me laugh to myself as it seemed to go on forever in long and then short bursts. I would have absolutely hated to have been sharing a bed with his arse, and would positively not feel safe striking a match near him.

There were many things going on around me when I eventually woke up in the morning. I had fallen into a much-needed deep sleep. A nurse was making up Bill's bed because he had left Sunnyside for good. Someone told me that he had signed himself out of his treatment program thinking that he would get on better at home.

"Come on, lazy bones. It is time you had your medication. Everybody else has had theirs already."

Ruth unlocked the drugs trolley and handed me my meds to me in a small beaker.

"Right down the hatch with a sip of water. Make sure that you swallow them because they won't be any use spat out after I am gone."

It was ten thirty already, and I had missed breakfast, but that was probably a bonus after yesterday's attempt. Most of the ward was empty now, with only two nurses changing bedding chatting away about their planned night out at the weekend. I had already decided my weekend; I was going nowhere. When Lorna finally appears, I might get a can of lager, but that would be my lot, there would be no music or merriment for me.

The shower was just what I needed to waken me up, I was still a bit tired, but that had probably more to do with my new medication than lack of sleep. The water surged from the shower, down to my face with a force I had not felt before. It was probably because I was the only one using them. My mind was still going over the night out in Edzell and that I could not say goodbye to Gwen properly, and if I would ever see her again. The Judge had said some horrifying things in court about what I had supposedly done, but I could not picture myself doing them.

He was describing my father, not me, he was capable of a lot more than that, and had done depraved evil and sadistic things to me in the past, but it was me on trial, not my father. He was still walking about a free man, still drinking and living his life with no remorse or condemnation of his actions. But he did not have a conscience when it came to cruelty or violence and never thought what he had done to me all my life was wrong. It was acceptable and normal to him and accepted by everyone around him. Not one family member ever validated or aided me when I needed them, and as long as the violence and bullying were not directed at them, it was ignored.

My skin was tinged red after being in the shower so long. I got dressed and headed back to the ward for my shoes and headed out to the garden for fresh air. It was busy outside today because the sun was hot and people were out walking the grounds. The biggest proportion of them had dressing gowns and pyjamas on and was accompanied by staff. It was probably more the idea of the staff to come out in the sun than the poor souls they were escorting. This was a good place to sit, right against a wall sheltered from any breeze, and it faced south, so it got the sun most of the day. I could think here and relax away from everyone they forced me to share a room with, I could be transported away from here just by closing my eyes.

"Come on, Peedie we are all heading over for lunch."

I was brought back to reality and back where I did not want to be. The convoy of patients headed across for lunch and lined up like robots to await their food. I looked at the full plates passing me coming from the front of the queue and noticed that it was a stew of some sort with new potatoes, and the meal looked and actually smelled appetising. It was vinegar tits on duty today and not the ram the plate up the arse one so I was not going to get into an argument today. I did not even ask for stew, but that was what I got, the only choice was to take it or leave it. I made my way to the tables and sat down beside a man from my ward. He never talked to anyone and just sat looking around him. He looked a lot younger than me and had bleached blonde hair and black eyebrows. His eyes flicked round towards me, and he immediately picked up his meal and moved to the other end of the table, leaving a steaming gravy covered potato which had slid off his plate in the rush. I ate slowly taking in everything around me. There was such a vast assembly of people here with different needs and disabilities all trying to live together in harmony. It never worked, there was always a scuffle of some sort at mealtimes, and sometimes a random plate would be thrown across the room, causing fellow diners to take evasive action to avoid wearing the contents of it.

My belly was full, and I was content. I finished my first tasty meal and my plate and cutlery returned to the trolley for washing. I went outside to stand in the warm sunshine and wait for everyone joining me so we could return to the hospital. A familiar sight appeared from a door opposite. It was Lorna, and she was smiling fit to burst.

"I am back Peedie, have you missed my fabulous company?"

"Where have you been?"

"It's a fucking long story, but basically they called the police just because I battered a staff member and poured paint in her hair. She should have shut her mouth instead of pissing me off by telling me to calm down."

They had locked Lorna up until she had appeared in court and sent back here on bail pending a court date and trial. There was not one single fuck given by her about what happened before they arrested her; she just did not care. Lorna seemed more upset that the paint had washed out of her victim's hair than she had blacked her eye and was now off work because of her injuries. Lorna remembered everything in graphic detail, and she was proud of her actions like she had achieved something amazing. She was buzzing with excitement as she went over the assault in detail, blow for blow, right down to the colour of the paint she poured over her victim's hair.

I was different with my assaults, I recollected nothing much of the precise details of what happened, and just vaguely remembered minute parts of my night out. What they read out in court had to be true as witnesses had given statements to the police? So much had happened that night, which I thought I was incapable of carrying out. I had behaved like a wild animal attacking its prey, and I was so lucky that I had not killed anyone that night.

Much of my stay at Sunnyside was a boring routine which was depriving me of mental stimulation. I needed out of this place as it was making me feel ill. They sent Lorna to Perth prison for her attack on the staff member so she could not help me any longer, and I was lonely even although plenty people spoke to me.

I had an idea where Lorna had hidden the lager, so went to look for it. I went through the small gate, she used to use, but could see nowhere she could have hidden it. She said she kept it cold in a toilet cistern, but there were no toilets nearby. Lorna had only ever taken a few minutes to bring the lager back after she went through the gate. I went to sit on the bench we always sat on, got up and walked through the gate and timed myself and stopped. My eyes scanned the area like a radar, taking in every rock and plant as I swept the nearby area looking for my prize, then I spotted it, a large water butt with a lid standing proudly in the corner of the garden. I slowly opened the lid and there they were, hanging from a piece of string, deep in the cold water below.

A fanfare of trumpets played in my head, playing a melody fit for a King at a coronation. I pulled the string gently, running it through my fingers, and brought the cans slowly to the top, making tiny ripples across the surface of the water like on a large pond. My reflection on the surface of the water was broken, breaking my concentration and back to what I was actually doing. I pulled the string and fished the cans out, opened one, and dropped the rest back into the cold clear water they had come from. The seat was a better place with a cold lager in my hand, and I drank the golden nectar until the can was empty. I returned several times over the next few weeks until they were all gone except one, and I left that so that someone else may find it, or if Lorna ever returned.

I met with the psychiatrist several more times in my time at Sunnyside. He told me things which I already knew about myself and some which I would not even admit to myself. He only knew what I let him know, and what they had written during my last two stays in this God forsaken place. There was only so far, I would let anybody get into my mind. It was a fragile place and could explode at any time with the slightest trigger. I have always been a loner, and I have tried to blend in with the world and be sociable, but the more people I meet, the more disappointed I become. I have learned to close my mind to the word and shut most people out, only letting a tiny fragment of happiness through the barrier, which is my mind. My childhood has taught me to keep guard at all times, ready to react to any emotion thrown at me, and to deny any wrongdoing so I would not get beaten up. It was now an inbuilt natural reaction to deny and defend an accusation against me, regardless of how trivial it was.

CHAPTER 23

My last morning in Sunnyside had finally arrived, and I was happy, but also terrified as this was the day my fate would be decided in court. Ruth was fussing around me trying to get me to listen to her about the medication she had put in a bag for me, but my thoughts were elsewhere. There was no way of contacting David to let him know that I would be going to Forfar Sheriff Court today, and I at least wanted to wave to him as they took me away to prison. He was the only person I could trust now; he was my brother and only reliable friend.

"Peedie, remember to keep taking your tablets and to make an appointment with your GP to get more. A letter has been sent to your GP explaining everything, and we have sent another letter Procurator Fiscal at the court."

"That's a bit of a waste of time because I won't be going home, I will be going to prison, my solicitor has told me that there is a good chance I will end up there, and be ready for it if it happens."

"If it happens; you are giving in without a fight, you tell that Judge you are sorry, appeal to his better side."

The Judge was Sheriff Kermack and he only

had one side, and that was a reputation for being uncaring and harsh in his sentencing, even for first offenders. I had listened to too many stories about him to think otherwise, he would certainly not be believing me if I said that I was sorry.

The police car arrived earlier than it was supposed to, but I was ready. I said my goodbyes to the staff and headed outside with the officers.

"Right sonny, you have a choice of the way this will get done. You can promise to behave in the car, in which case you won't get cuffed, or we can go down the official road."

"No, I would not be as stupid as to start anything today, I am in enough trouble already."

"Right you go in the back seats and behave yourself."

The officers got in and we headed off towards Forfar and my uncertain future. The inside of the car had a smell of lavender in it, not the smell I would have expected. It was strange being away from the confines of Sunnyside and the security it provided. The car trundled along the winding narrow road to Forfar, throwing up chips from the newly tarred road and pinging them loudly on the floor beneath my feet. We stopped at the traffic lights to let someone cross the road. The buildings around us looked miniature compared to the hospital I had just come from. The car turned right up North Street and nearer to the court but stopped near the end of the road.

"Do you fancy a Forfar Bridie lad, you might as well, as we are having one before we go into court. My treat."

"Yes, please, I have not had breakfast yet, could you make mine an onion one?"

He appeared back with three bags with a bridie in each, and handed me one.

"Yours is the onion one, it has two holes in it, and the plain bridie has one, so this is ours."

The bridie melted in my mouth, I had forgotten what they tasted like. Flavours blasted around my taste buds like fireworks going off at a display. It was the best thing I had eaten in weeks, and I hoped it would not be my last.

"Thank you for that, I really enjoyed it."

"Not all police are the same you know, there are some decent ones with a bit of compassion. But I am afraid it is time to head to court."

The police car moved off and travelled the last part of the journey, and round to the back door where it parked up.

"Right son, you better come with us now. We have to be in early before the court starts. I am so sorry, but I will have to put handcuffs on you before you upstairs to the court, but I am just doing my job."

"Don't worry about me, you lads have been brilliant with me so far."

"Well, don't you be telling everybody; I can't keep everybody in bridies? Anyway, I don't know why I bother eating them, I always end up with bloody heartburn."

We sat in the holding room waiting on the Clerk shouting out my name for my time on the stand. There was nobody else with us in the room, and it was eerily silent. I sat trying to hear what was going on upstairs. The heavy door which was keeping me in, muffled the sound.

Then it happened, and my heart almost stopped. My name boomed down the stairs and reverberated in my head. The time of reckoning had come at last and it worried me.

"Don't worry, son. You can't change what will happen up there in the court. The Judge will probably have decided already what he is going to do with you, so no amount of worrying is going to change the outcome. Right, now for the bad bit, let's get these bloody cuffs on."

The stairs were steep, I felt like I was going to the gallows to get hanged, any minute someone would pull the trapdoor handle and I would die, but that would have been too quick and easy. The stand was my pedestal, where I was displayed to everyone in the public gallery. I was flanked by an officer, and his wrist, and mine, were attached by manacles of shiny steel. This was my show: my circus, and I was the star of the ring. People had come for miles to see me get my just desserts, they were baying for my blood, and for revenge and justice. Every eye in the court was boring into my head when I turned around to see if my father had come to gloat at me, to jeer as they led me away. I spotted David right at the back of the gallery, and I was glad.

"All rise."

The clerk boomed out my name and I stood up. I did not look behind me, I was trying to focus on what was about to happen. Then he appeared, the magnificent Judge, the star of the show, like a magician out of nowhere and sat down on his golden chair. They told me to keep standing, but everyone else sat down. He slowly looked me up and down, but I did not look directly back at him and drifted my gaze to the floor.

"What have you got to say for yourself then, you know and admit that you understand what charges have been brought against you? Do you plead guilty or not guilty?"

"Guilty your honour."

The Judge went over everything that had happened that night in Edzell in detail and asked if I had anything to add.

"Yes, your honour, I do."

"Well, let's begin, shall we? Let me get my handkerchief out before you tell me your sob story. Believe me, I have heard them all before, unless you spin me a different one, but I sincerely doubt it, but go on anyway try to amuse me."

"He put his hand up my brother's girlfriend's skirt, your honour."

"Surely that was none of your business."

"It was when he threw my brother over the wall and he landed in front of me your honour."

"You attacked him and rendered him unconscious, not once but twice, you wrenched a fire alarm from the wall setting it off so that the whole wedding party had to evacuate the hotel, you tried to rescue your brother from custody, attacked and injured an officer in the course of his duty, willfully and deliberately damaged a police car, and resisted arrest, and attacked and injured an officer driving you to custody and endangered not only their lives but also your own. What do you have to say for yourself?"

"I am sorry your honour. It was totally out of character. I have enquired about the poor gentleman I injured, but nobody would tell me how he was."

"That gentleman is in court today, and luckily for you that you plead guilty, or he would have had to give evidence today. You have spared him the indignity of that at least."

The Judge and the solicitor seemed to talk for what seemed an eternity. The whole of the court sat waiting on my sentence getting read out. He read page after page of reports, occasionally peering at me over his glasses, and straightening his ridiculous wig which looked far too small for his head. Every now and again the silence was broken by someone coughing, then somebody started humming a song. Half the court laughed.

"Silence in court or I will have you all thrown

out. This is a court of law, not a circus."

That's all I needed right now, some musical cunt getting the Judge in a bad mood as if things were not bad enough without some idiot humming a tune.

"All rise."

I got to my feet and looked quickly behind me. David made a thumbs up sign to me, and I saw the man who I assaulted staring at me with a smirk on his face. He was sure that I was getting sent to jail, and that made two of us.

"After careful consideration, and after reading your psychiatric reports, I have decided to imprison you for a period of twelve months, which you will have to serve in full."

My heart actually stopped beating for a few seconds. Time stood still and suddenly shit just got real, I was going to jail.

"Hold on a minute, I think I shall suspend that sentence for a period of twelve months. If you so much as drop a piece of litter you shall be summoned back to this court and serve your year in prison, plus time on top of that for whatever crime you commit. You shall return to this court after your twelve months of good behaviour, where I will decide what I shall do with you. Do you understand?"

"Yes, your Honour, thank you."

"You are free to go."

I sat down again, too shocked to move. I could hardly breathe, and my heart was nearly coming through my rib cage.

"You are free to go, now leave this court before I change my mind."

The judge disappeared through a door behind him, and the public gallery erupted into a noisy rabble. Everybody seemed to be in shock at my sentence, but not as shocked as me. I rose to my feet and headed towards the exit. I was free at last, even if there were conditions to my release, I was out. David was waiting outside as I entered the fresh air.

"I fucking told you that you would get out, I just fucking knew it. I almost smoked this fag to the cork with one draw I was so stressed when I got outside."

"You should have been sitting where I was sitting, you don't know what stress is, you cunt. I almost shit myself when that bastard told me that I was getting jailed for a year."

"Come on then, let's head for the bus and get back home where you belong, we have twenty minutes before it leaves, so we have plenty of time."

"Fucking poofter, come and hit me now you gay bastard, you should have been locked up for what you did to me."

"Just ignore him Peedie, he is trying to rile you up so that you will hit him and get lifted again."

I turned around and puckered my lips together and blew him a kiss. That stopped him in his tracks, he did not know what to do. I had not realised how big he was either, a large six-foot-tall streak of piss with some muscles thrown in for good measure. David burst out laughing at my antics. Normally he would have been kicked senseless, lying in a pool of his own blood or vomit for calling me names, but as hard as it was, I had to walk away. He would have been floored if there were no witnesses, but I could wait, that was something I was good at. I had waited all my life for recognition in my family group, but it had still not materialised, so another wait was not going to be hard. We kept walking and eventually he turned back and headed out of sight.

"You are going to have to ignore a lot more for the next year if you want to stay out of jail. Cunts like him will deliberately wind you up once word gets out about your sentence. This story will be in all the local papers."

"What's dad saying about it all?"

"He told me not to bother going to court because it would be a waste of my time. He said you would be going to jail to get your arse stretched, but he reckoned you would be used to that. He actually said that. I am not fucking exaggerating."

"So, he still loves me the same then. That fucking man actually hates me with an unnatural passion, but then he always has."

"Keep walking and don't look round. We have a party of arseholes behind us."

I felt a soft thud on my jacket as I walked

along, but I did not respond, then I felt it again. I kept on walking, but David stopped and confronted them with rage like I had not seen before from him.

"The next cunt who fucking throws something at my brother will get the shit kicked out of them, then whatever they throw will be rammed up their arse. I am not on probation so I have fuck all stopping me, now fuck off the lot of you."

David caught up with me looking pleased with himself, and the posse behind us headed back in the direction of the court.

"Fucking tosspots the lot of them, come on, let's get to the bus stop, fuck waiting an hour on the next one."

The Brechin bus was sitting at the bus stance when we arrived. The driver was sitting on the low wall at the bank having a smoke, so we asked him what time we would reach Edzell.

"This bus does not go as far as Edzell laddie, but I can take you as far as the bus stance, and you will have to hitch a lift from there."

We paid the driver and went to sit at the back of the bus. I always felt safer in the back seats as I could keep an eye on everybody, plus there was an emergency escape door which had already come in handy once before. An elderly couple came on board at the last stop out of Forfar, and he instantly recognised me, but I had never seen him before.

"Aye laddie, you were bloody lucky today. I always sit at the back of the court to fill in a bit of time now that I am retired. Learn to turn the other cheek, you have a long life ahead of you, so do not spend most of it in prison. I was like you once, and I was not proud of myself. You will meet some nice girl one day who will change your life forever. I did, and here she is."

His wife smiled at us but said nothing, but she did not have to as her face said it all. They got off at the same stop as us in Brechin and said their goodbyes. I never met him again, but I always remembered what he told me.

"Peedie there are no buses to Edzell for ages, and I can't afford a taxi. What do you want to do?

"I don't care what we do as long as I get home. I have been cooped up for so long that a walk would do me good."

We started to walk the five and a half miles from Brechin to Edzell, but were stopped after only a mile further along by someone in a lorry.

"Can any of you tell me where Inchbare is please, I have a load of steel to drop off? Some arsehole sent me on a wild goose chase up the wrong fucking road."

"We can do better than that if you give us a lift, we can take you to where it is going."

"Right hop in and watch and not sit on my lunch."

He looked like he needed no lunch, today or any other day. I sat looking across the lorry cab wondering how he had managed to squeeze his bulk of a body through the door. He talked with a wheeze in his voice, stopping and starting a conversation in between breaths. He had enough chins for all of us and a belly so large that it scraped on the leather covered steering wheel. Every time he turned the wheel, we could hear the leather scraping loudly on his shirt.

"It's just round the next corner, there it is, Edzell Engineering."

"Thanks, mate, you have saved me and David a power of walking."

The lorry reversed into the side road and came to stop. David opened the door and we both jumped down to the verge and waited for a minute before we headed along the last of the road towards Edzell.

"What are you waiting for David, let's get to fuck out of here?"

"I want to see how the fat cunt gets out of the lorry; he is a lard arse who has definitely got shares in a pie shop. He is bound to squeeze himself out the door like toothpaste out of a tube the fat fucker."

I could not help it and started to laugh and just could not stop. That had made my day, I had forgotten how sick in the head, David was, and how spontaneous he was with his sick comments. The driver hopped down to the ground with remarkable ease despite his bulk and thanked us for showing him the way.

The road seemed a lot shorter now we had managed to get a lift we had not even instigated. David was acting stupid as usual, and he turned around grinning at me.

"Do you want a ham and tomato roll Peedie? I have stolen more than half the rolls out of the fat cunts lunch box. There were seven rolls in it as well as fuck knows how many chocolate biscuits. We will be doing him a favour, honestly, we will."

We were both hungry, so we peeled off the tin foil, and devoured two squashed rolls each, and enjoyed every bite. That was followed by a half-melted chocolate penguin biscuit.

"Peedie he never had enough salt on the tomato the selfish bastard, I hate when a roll is like that. I bet you would love to be there when he opens that box, his whole life will be in ruins. Next, he will be flagging somebody down looking for a baker shop to empty."

We continued to walk in silence for ages, and my mind was focusing on what the Judge had told me. My name will be plastered in all the local newspapers for everyone to examine and dissect and to make up their minds as to who I am. My father would be cutting the article out and smirking at it, thumbing over the words until his fingers were black with newsprint. He would be praying that I reacted to someone badly and got sent to prison, and then he would be rid of me for a long time. Then he would have been right all along, he would tell all his drinking friends and they would buy him drink, he would be the man of the moment, the star of his own show. He will be so upset that I am out and free, he will drink until he gets violent tonight and gets some gratification out on an unsuspecting victim.

"Stop for a minute Peedie I am needing a piss."

"Well, go into the trees in case you get seen, that's all we need. There is a woman in the garden over there."

David disappeared into the trees and took ages to come out. He was smiling with that sick smug look on his face, that look he had when he was up to something.

"Wait until they drive off in their car. I have just tied their long dog chain to the back bumper of the car, and round one of the trees."

"Fucking brilliant, I wish I could stay here and watch it happen. It would be like something out of a film."

We laughed until we could laugh no more, my sides were aching and I could hardly speak. That was proof to me that I was sick in the head in thinking that tying a car to a tree was funny. But it was hilarious all right and it was a perfect pick me up, after my stay in Sunnyside. We kept walking, and soon the Edzell Arch was in sight at the end of the long stretch of road ahead of us. Large tubs of flowers adorned both sides of the road, planted by volunteers who probably nothing better to do with their lives. The arch was the gateway to the village and it was a pleasure walking under it.

A woman came out of the bank and disappeared quickly back inside, then she reappeared with another three people. I could read their minds, they could not believe what they were seeing, and I was walking up the main street a free man. Before we got much farther people started coming to their doors. There must have been a lot of rushed phone calls between houses for that to happen. They were stuck up snobby arseholes, who were so far up each other's arses that all you could see was the soles of their shoes dangling out. I did not mix with the likes of them, the born with a silver spoon in their mouth brigade. They wore clothes that you could not buy in shops, or anywhere else.

We waved at everyone who appeared to stare at my return to the village. I was famous and had not noticed before. The amount of excitement my sudden appearance had caused was amusing me. Because when you witness as I was first-hand, a street containing a cackling, finger-pointing, staring group, of over a dozen supposedly mature, well-educated adults, performing this act of passive aggressive intimidation of a man of my age, then it's jaw-dropping. Unbelievable and not what you'd expect at all from such people.

We made our way up the street without further incident. The pavement was lined with people from one end to the other right up as far as Smokey Joes. Our last part or our road home was the only part I was happy about. Jenny was standing waiting at her gate, and she was smiling fit to burst. Jenny never smiled, she just looked at everybody with a look of disgust, but I saw a different side to her.

"I have caught two thieving bastards trying to get into your house when David was away.

They soon left when they were looking down the barrel of my four ten shotgun. Word will have got around by now, so you won't be getting broken into any time soon. I have read about what happened in the newspaper, so you watch your back, there will always be some cunt or other trying to piss you off. If you have to kick the shit out of somebody, do it at the back end of Edzell Muir and make sure that there are no witnesses."

We thanked Jenny for her gun slinging security and headed home unhindered the rest of the way.

CHAPTER 24

There was something different about the house since I was here the last time, but I could not put my finger on it so I had to ask David.

"It's the new sofa and two chairs in the living room."

"David, I hope you don't think I am paying for them, where the fuck did, they come from?"

"Look, it's ok, they are from Liz, Malcolm's mums clubby. I ordered them from my Kirriemuir house and had them delivered just before I moved here, but I kind of forgot to mention to Liz that I have moved."

"Liz will be at mum's door giving her grief for clubby money, and mum will tell dad and he will go to Liz's door to tell her to ram her clubby money up her arse sideways, that will be the last it gets mentioned. Liz will write to the clubby and tell them you died or something, better that than dad kicking her husband to near death because that is what would happen."

Something as large as a three-piece suite, should have been an obvious thing to see. It had sort of blended into my brain as it if had been part of the existing furniture. I had overlooked the new smell in the living room as I had been away for so long.

"You should have ordered a hoover while you were at it."

"That's another story Peedie, wait there a minute."

David went to the hallway cupboard and brought back a box. He opened the lid to reveal a shiny new Goblin vacuum cleaner, complete with all the attachments.

"Look Peedie it's not actually stolen as such."

"It's either stolen, or it's not stolen. I can't have the fucking police here while I am on bail for a year."

"Well, I was passing a house when I saw a delivery man banging frantically on the door. I simply walked in the gate and said that I lived next door, he asked me to sign for it, and hey presto, and here it is. He posted a note through the door telling them that a neighbour took it in for them. That is bound to cause a dispute between them; they will be arguing like fuck. I have not used it yet, I was keeping it new in case someone spotted me carrying it up the road, but that was two weeks ago so I think we will be good to go now."

I made myself a cup of coffee, real tasting coffee, not that dodgy fake stuff we got forced on us at Sunnyside. They honestly thought just because we were all mentally infirm that we had no taste buds. I sat back on the new sofa and sank into a relaxed stupor, oblivious to what was going on around me. It had been so long since I had felt relaxed enough to close my eyes when I was awake, but I was safe here, safe from harm.

Sunnyside had been a dangerous place where I had to always have one eye open in case, I got attacked by someone. I was used to keeping an ear open when I was young, so was used to it. Dad's breathing outside the bedroom door always woke me up, or that single sniff he did when he was concentrating, listening for the slightest noise from the bedroom so he could dive in and batter me senseless for either me or my siblings talking or sniggering under the blankets. This house was safe from him; he would never be enlightened where it was, and he did not need to know.

The door was getting banged hard by someone outside. David peered out the window and saw Mags standing there with another female.

"Why the fuck did you not just come in Mags, you have a key?"

"David, I tried the bloody key, but it would not turn, you must have double locked it by accident."

It was me who had double locked it. I could not chance to fall asleep with the door unlocked. My mind was still in self-preservation mode, nothing from now on would be left to chance. Someone could have robbed Mags of her key and let themselves into the house. Mags could have been bribed to give it to someone, she could have had it copied a dozen times and sold all over Brechin. First thing in the morning the lock would get changed, and only David and I would have a key, I trusted no one.

"Who are you then, a friend of Mags?"

"Yes, this is my cousin Karen, she is up on holiday from Glasgow for two weeks and is staying at my mum's with me."

She was a good-looking woman of around twenty years old with jet black short hair. She had a strong smell of cannabis smoke coming from her clothing. I recognised that smell as soon as it hit my nostrils.

"Come on then Karen skin up if you have some."

"What are you fucking like Peedie, you are not backwards in coming forwards, are you?"

"David you should know me by now, I never turn a joint down."

"Peedie, Mags told me that you are into smoke, I have been dying for a stone since I left Brechin, but I have been too nervous to ask"

"Just skin up woman for fuck's sake, I have not had a joint for ages, and it is just what has been missing from my life."

Karen sat rolling a joint, her face was contorted by all the concentration. The tip of her tongue was just sticking out through her lips, and occasionally darting in again for a second before appearing again. Her eyes never lifted from the record sleeve, the intense scrutiny and meticulous rolling made the possibility of a stone seem very unlikely any time soon. Her head finally looked up and turned round to look at me.

"That's the joint to beat all joints Peedie, get a bit of that in your lungs min, that will blow any cobwebs out of your brain, here you can light it."

I took it from her and put it slowly to my lips. I did not want to rush this; my body was needing to be totally relaxed for maximum effect. My mind was about to be blown right open, and I had to be in the right place. My sanctuary was my mind, nobody could control what I was thinking, and people only got from me what I let them have. My father tried to control my every move and thought, but he could not tell that I had contemplated killing him as he slept, he couldn't have or I would be dead myself now. I lit the twisted end and took a long draw and nearly choked on the potency of it.

"What have you put in that joint, my eyes feel like they are spinning round like the dials on a slot machine, Jesus fuck woman, you almost killed me?"

"Peedie you wanted a stone, just you wait, this stuff is lethal with a delayed effect which will mess with your mind. It seems to shoot up from the soles of your feet, then up to your head last, so don't try to walk for fuck's sake."

The menthol minty effect started shooting out through tiny holes in the soles of my feet. The force made me remove my shoes and socks, rocket force, minty air thrust from my feet, across the room, hitting the opposite wall making the curtains move. My legs seemed to have a type of paralysis, and only able to move, when I did not try to move them. I sat as still as I could, as the settee was spinning slowly with me on it. It got faster and faster and I was hanging on with both hands. Karen grabbed me by the arm with a startled look on her face.

"Hang on to me, you bastard, Peedie, this fucking couch is about to go through the ceiling, don't you dare let me go for fuck's sake?"

"You hang on to me or we will both be flung off, try shoving your feet hard on the floor, it might slow us down."

"My fucking legs are stuck. My muscles have gone floppy, I could not move my legs even if I wanted to, you anus."

We were well and truly wasted, we had smoked only one joint and I was out of my sanctuary and into a place I had not been for ages. This was the most unusual stone I had ever had in my life, and I had smoked an assortment of joints before. The curtains were moving by themselves now, slowly parting to let some light in, and then closing just as you noticed. They seemed to have a mind of their own, making random patterns on the ceiling as the light sporadically darted through the gap between them.

David put a record on the stereo to play, but

did not switch the plug on, we did not need music, because our heads had a crescendo of music increasing in intensity, sending it through every nerve cell in our bodies, and shooting melodic sounds to join the menthol vapours coming from our feet below us. We were well and truly stoned. I looked around the room for David and Mags but they were not there, but I had not seen them leave. I tried to get to my feet, but my legs were getting held down by an invisible force too powerful for me.

"Karen help me up, for fuck's sake. I cannot move, my legs are stuck to the settee."

"That's because my legs are across yours, you silly cunt. I managed to lift mine off the floor eventually, so I put them across yours so they did not stick to the floor."

"Fuck, I'm wasted Karen, what a fabulous state to be in. I want a quarter of whatever you put in that joint. I have never been stoned on one joint in my life."

"I don't know what stuff it was, I scored it from an American from the base in a bar in Brechin. I have never seen him again to get some more."

"Karen, where are David and Mags?"

"Fuck only knows Peedie, they were here when you lit the joint. I seem to remember vaguely them not wanting a smoke and heading to the village or something. Do you want another smoke?"

"This will be the first time I have ever said no to a joint. You had better believe it, Karen, that has never happened before."

"Mags reckoned that I could stay here tonight. She said you were cool that way."

"Of course, you can stay, you have hash. No, I'm only joking Karen you can stay, but there are only two beds, and I will not give mine up, I have been looking forward to sleeping in it for over two months."

"That's not a problem with me. I can share if you can, and you can kick me out in the morning if you want to."

My immediate thoughts were that she was up to something. She had to have planned this in advance; she would stay here and never leave. I would have to get Jenny to threaten her with her gun like the last one who would not go. I had been in a psychiatric hospital for two months, and she knew that, why would she want to stay here on her own with me? Then when we woke up in the morning, she would make some excuse or some lies she had nowhere else to go. The hardest thing to do every day is to wake up. Every time I commit myself to be awake, everything is there again. A million thoughts flying around in my head, always feeling sick and just wanting it all to end. Trying to find something to push on for, is hard, without having emotional baggage hanging around my neck.

Despite the hash, I was in a low mood now

and I was in a state of utter confusion. This was all happening so fast around me that I felt out of control and unable to cope. I did not know Karen, and she was offering to share my bed. I could be a mass murderer, or a psychopath who cuts people up and eats them. She knew nothing about me apart from my stay in that lunatic asylum, yet she trusted me with her life, and yet I trusted nobody. I had learned that at a very young age. A smiling person was not always what they appeared to be. My father could keep a smile on his face when he was hurting me. He was good at that and had plenty of experience.

"Come on, then don't keep me in suspense any longer. Am I sharing a bed with you? Or am I sleeping on this hard couch?"

"Karen, of course, you can sleep in my bed, but no farting."

We both laughed at my comical remark. The romance was dead in the water already, but I was not looking for any either, and neither was Karen.

"Do you want a coffee before we go to bed, Karen? I always have one every night without fail. It keeps me going until morning."

"Only if you are making it."

We sat in silence drinking our coffee, and I was deep in thought. My mind was churning out thoughts that only I could think of. What if Karen was a murderer and had a knife in her bag? What if she stayed awake and gouged my eyes out when I fell asleep? I did not know her either, but I had committed myself now so there was no way out without appearing paranoid.

We eventually went to the bedroom; I could not delay it any longer. Karen sat on the edge of the bed and waited until I got undressed before she did the same. She seemed to take ages taking her clothes off and climbing in beside me. We lay in the bed, with an invisible force field up the centre of the bed. I wanted to stretch out, but the invisible line would not let me.

"I'm cold Peedie, can I cuddle in?"

"Yes, cuddle in and get to sleep, woman, I need all the beauty sleep I can get."

The sex after that was spontaneous and uninhibited, I was suddenly free of the guilt of letting a man pleasure me.

CHAPTER 25

I could not get to sleep after my night of passion, but Karen was fast asleep. I had a feeling that I had taken advantage of her, but at the same time, I knew that she had encouraged me. She rolled round to face me and then she put her arm around me and pulled me close. I lay there thinking about my life, or lack of it. There was nothing to live for now as I had to keep out of trouble for a whole year. Life was boring enough without having to watch what I was doing all the time, and now I felt obliged to Karen to let her stay if she wanted to. My fabulous stone had well and truly worn off and I needed more, but I also needed sleep, I was drifting into a dreamlike sensation, and only half aware of what was around me.

I woke with a voice shouting my name. It sounded like the voice was in the distance, but it was in the same room.

"Come on, you lazy cunt, I have been down to the village for some rolls and bacon. After all our hard work last night, I thought you might be hungry."

"Sorry, Karen. I could not get to sleep last night. I had too much on my mind."

"Probably about how you have nothing to live

for now. You were talking in your sleep, and Jesus you can talk. It's a good job you have no secrets."

Now she would definitely want nothing to do with me. How much had I said about my mental state, how much had I spoken about my past, there was no way of knowing, and Karen was not saying? She differed from most girls I had met; she was mature for her age and talked her mind. I liked her, and we had only spent a night together. I could smell the bacon getting fried in the kitchen so I got out of bed and went through. Karen was busy building a joint and keeping an eye on our breakfast. I did my bit by slicing open the rolls.

"You are not getting any smoke until you have eaten your two bacon rolls, then we can share a joint for pudding."

We sat on the sofa eating with a cup of coffee in one hand and a bacon roll in the other. I did not think I was hungry, but I ate both my rolls and one which Karen did not want. Then the joint got lit. Karen took the first draw, sending thick yellow tinged smoke into the air above us. She handed it to me and I inhaled a giant lungful of the pleasure giving cannabis. I held my breath for so long that no smoke came out when I exhaled. I filtered every morsel of pleasure through my body and oozed through my pores, hitting my T-shirt with a hollow thud. This was good.

"What are you planning to do today, then,

Peedie?"

"I am just not long out of bed woman, and my brain is still only half awake. I don't have a clue what to do."

"Well, we are not sitting here all day when the sun is shining. I fancy going to see Edzell Castle, I have never been there before, and it is not even half a mile from here. I have walked past it, but never been close."

Breakfast finished and dressed we set off for the castle and were there in only a few minutes. It was an impressive place built in the sixteenth century, but now mostly in ruins. The red sandstone walls towered above us as we stood in awe below the walkway above us. This place was spectacular, and I had never really looked at it with this depth of feeling before. We headed up to the viewing gallery and looked over the immaculate ornate walled garden below. I filled my nostrils with the rich aroma of roses coming from below. Box hedging neatly trimmed and laid out in intricate geometric patterns filled each section and was mirrored at each corner of the plot. I had looked at this garden, before, but had not actually seen it. Karen pointed out grey carved stones in the walls I had just walked past. They looked like some sort of a family crest. There were tall chimneys we could look up to see the sky above, ingle nook fireplaces with ornate seats built in, this place was fabulous. I would hate a family crest made for me. It would comprise a small naked boy hanging on a hook getting battered by a man standing on one side, and a woman standing watching it happen on the other. That crest would not look good above any front door, and you would probably get arrested.

We stayed for ages and sucked in all the information from all the information boards. I had never as much as glanced at them before. This was the best day I had lived for a long time, and it was not even lunchtime yet.

"Come on, Peedie let's get back home and top up our stone."

"Karen, my stone stopped when I came to the castle, and I will continue it when I leave. I have had only a couple of joints that I could do that with, both of them made with Nepalese Temple Balls. That was when I could turn off a stone to answer the door, then turn it back on when I sat down again."

A car horn sounded as we neared the main road, but I never recognised the car. It was a green Triumph Vitesse. It reversed into the road end and waited on us coming. The driver opened the window and smiled. It was David and Mags.

"Where the fuck did you get the car? I thought you were skint?"

"Mags's dad got a year's ban for drunk driving, so he has lent it to me to keep it running. The engine has six cylinders, and it still has tax and MOT for eleven months. Do you fancy going on a camping holiday? We still have the big frame tent."

"Do you fancy it, Karen? I don't fancy playing gooseberry with David and Mags. Nor do I want to lie on my own listening to the pair of them at it like fucking rabbits, through the canvas dividing wall."

"Fucking right, I do, when do we leave?" I will have to go home first to get some clothes before I go, but we could do that on the way."

We got into the back seats and David drove us the short distance home. It only took us ten minutes to load the car up for our trip, then we headed off. We never planned to go anywhere in particular and just sort of ended up in Fife somewhere called Leslie. The campsite was small and not too busy, it was right next to a car workshop which seemed to be part of the same business, so we paid for one night to see how we got on.

"I hope you young ones will not cause any bother. There are older people here for a quiet holiday. Don't come back from the pubs shouting and singing or you will get asked to leave when I get here in the morning."

"No, sir, we would never do that, would we David? We are here for a quiet change of scenery, that's all."

After what seemed a long time and so many campsite rules and regulations to remember, we built our massive tent right in the corner by the entrance. The owner Billy thought we would not have to pass other campers and disturb them on our way back from the pub if we camped there. He must have been reading our minds. It was the proximity of the surrounding bars that made us decide that this was the campsite for us, not his lush green grass he was so proud of, or the newly painted toilets which stank of paint fumes.

"Park your car in front of your tent like everyone else has with their tents or caravans, then the place looks tidy and you all get the same space. Shipshape and orderly, that's the happy camper's way."

David parked the car under the scrutiny of Billy, who was guiding David to the exact acceptable parking spot, parallel with the tent, and exactly four feet away from the narrow road which went all the way to the back of the campsite. Billy seemed obsessed with how square everything was, every pitch had a white painted peg in the ground, which lined up with the next one farther along. When you looked at them, they lined up perfectly, regardless of where they were in the campsite.

"He is a bit weird Peedie. I bet he watches women shower through a hole in the toilet wall."

"No Mags that will be David, after he shoves me out of the way first."

David laughed at the thought of us peering through a hole which just would not happen.

Both of us had great respect for women, we had been brought up in a household where the woman was the lowest in class, the one who cooked and cleaned and stayed home. Dad always maintained that the reason women's feet were shorter than men's feet, was so they could get closer to the sink.

"Bar lunch or filled roll from the Co-op, I just can't decide, what do you think Mags?"

"David, have I got a pulse? As long as I do, it will always be a pub before a supermarket."

"Come on, then Peedie lets head to the local lager dispensing establishment."

The four of us headed along the street and stopped at the first pub we saw. I was the first to poke my head round the Burns Tavern door, and the first to get scrutinised by the locals. The place was not too, so we went in and sat at the bar and were immediately questioned by the barman.

"I hope you lot don't cause any bother in here. This is a friendly pub, so we don't want any fighting in here."

I don't know what was wrong with the way we looked, but this was the second person to warn us not to cause trouble. We assured him we were here on holiday at the campsite and we did not want any bother either.

"Oh well, if Billy let you camp at his site, you must be alright. He is proud of his little sideline at the back of the garage. That's what he plans to keep him going when he finally retires, and he is sixty-eight years old as it is. His wife died a few years back, and the campsite was her hobby while Billy ran the garage."

Niceties out of the way, we ordered a pint of lager each and something to eat. The air was filled with smoke, which occasionally blew into the room from the log fire. It was warm and sunny outside, so there was really no need for a fire to be burning. Our meals arrived, and the barman set them down on a small table behind us near the fire. I sat in the seat facing the door so I could keep an eye on who was coming and going. I never sat with my back to the door. Our food looked and tasted good, so we ate it all. I sat there in silence, staring at the flickering flames in the log fire, only looking away when someone came into the bar. Karen gathered up our empty plates and set them on the bar counter. A wolf whistle emitted from the other side of the bar as she walked back to the table. Karen stopped in her tracks and stared in the direction of where the whistle came from.

"There's not a man among you lot who could handle me with your needle dicks. Come on, then flash your knob to see if I think it would be big enough."

The room went quiet, and then the barman laughed. Everybody else joined in the hilarity, except the one who whistled. He hung his head in shame after it humiliated him.

"Karen, he deserved that, he will not whistle at you again."

"Peedie if there is one thing, I hate it is getting whistled at like some sort of dog. I have always tried to shame men when they do it to me, fucking perverts. They would not be happy if someone did it to their daughters, and they would not wolf whistle you in the Co-op in front of their wives either."

It cleared the air in the pub after that, we felt that we were part of the locals now. Four pints appeared at our table from an anonymous donor. We accepted them even though we had not finished our first ones. The door opened and a man and woman I recognised from the campsite came in and ordered a drink. They were carrying a guitar and a banjo, and my immediate reaction was one of horror. I hoped that they would not be playing in here or I would have to move. I liked Pink Floyd style music and this would be nothing like it. I hated country music; I had endured years of Jim Reeves at home when I was young. They sat down across from us and set their instruments down, so it relieved me for now. A voice bellowed from across the room.

"Will you play us your tune again, please? That was amazing yesterday."

The couple did not reply and calmly picked up their guitar and banjo. They smiled at each other and I cringed for a moment as I waited for the music to start. The woman with the guitar started first, then the banjo, they did this slowly at first, time about until they picked up speed. I suddenly recognised the music they were playing. It was the music played in the film Deliverance by the hillbilly with a banjo and a man with a guitar. This was fabulous and soon everybody, including me, was clapping in time with the music. I wished it would last all night. We never moved from that pub until closing time. I could not remember a night as enjoyable as we had just had. We half fell out the door at closing time and promised that we would come back.

"I feel sick Mags let go of my arm."

Mags stepped away from David, who was immediately sick on somebody's door mat. It looked and smelt disgusting.

"There you go, I have left somebody a nice pavement pizza for them to stand on when they come out of their house in the morning."

The drink and fresh air were getting to us all as we staggered back to our tent. I struggled to find the end of the door zipper so we could get into our tent to collapse into a drunken coma. Karen was staggering about, then all hell broke loose. She tripped on a guy rope and fell full length on the two-man tent next to us, sending the hysterical occupants into a screaming frenzy. I stood there laughing until tears came running down my face. I could do nothing to help her as she writhed about on the tent trying to get up. She was lying at the door end of the two-man tent trapping the still screaming couple inside. Lights came on all over the campsite as startled campers came out to see what was happening. Someone caught David pissing on the side of somebody's tent when the occupants came out, which started another fracas. Children were crying, and dogs were barking after all the noise and excitement. Then we finally got into our tent. Mags got up and went outside and shouted across the campsite.

"Could you please keep your children from making a noise? We are trying to sleep over here, you inconsiderate cunts, the lot of you want to have some respect."

That was it for me and David, we could not stop laughing, that remark from Mags was hilarious. The hilarity in our tent continued until we felt the tent getting shaken by an angry shouting man.

"If you don't stop your noise, I will actually come into your tent and thrash you. You have a five-minute warning, then I will get really angry, and you would not like to see that."

That remark and empty threat started us off again.

"David, do you want a thrashing?"

"No, you bounder, do you?"

The tears were rolling down Karen's face. I could see them even in the dim light from the bollard outside our tent. Mags had fallen victim of the alcohol and had fallen asleep hearing nothing of what was going on, and soon we all settled down for the night. The campsite was all quiet at last and tranquility was recovered everywhere.

"Peedie I am going for a piss."

"Well, remember to go to the toilets this time and not on somebody's fucking tent."

David pulled the zipper door open, and slipped out quietly and headed for the toilets. He looked comical wearing boxer shorts and a pair of brown boots. He appeared back after about ten minutes and was smirking about something. I knew that look well; he had been up to something, but would not enlighten me.

The morning seemed to arrive too soon, and I was not quite ready for it yet. Karen was draped over me like a blanket, trapping me from sitting up, so I gently unfurled her arm and legs off me and slid myself to the side and slowly stood up. Memories of last night came flooding back to me, we would definitely get kicked off the site when Billy got to hear about our antics. I found the bottle of coke at the bottom of the pile of clothing and took a long drink, and God did I need it. David was already up, and sitting outside in the sun.

"Just wait for it. This will be fucking brilliant."

"What will be brilliant? Don't just say things and leave me wondering, you know I hate that"

"Just keep an eye on big boy thrasher's tent,

that's the hard man who threatened to come into our tent and thrash us last night. Look at the size of the little prick. He could not punch his way out of a wet paper bag. He has not looked in our direction since he appeared out of his tent."

I sat on the ground beside David, enjoying the warmth from the sun. Thrasher went back into his tent and appeared a minute later and went into his car. He started the engine and pissed around for a few minutes sorting his hair in the rear-view mirror. Then he looked at us and smirked as he drove off. Then I saw it, the car was tied to thrashers tent which lifted up into the air and came crashing down in a heap behind the car and got dragged along and out the campsite gate before he noticed. His wife was lying in her sleeping bag in the open air for all to see. She did not have her false teeth in, when she sat up; the poor woman had no clue as to what had just happened. She sat looking confused and bewildered until thrasher appeared, shouting abuse at us. He was actually blaming us for tying his tent to his tow bar. He was jumping up and down shouting at us with his ridiculous sounding posh accent and threatening us with the police if we did not pay for his twisted and broken tent. Other campers came to his aid and helped move the tent off the road and peace for a few minutes fell over the campsite.

"David, that is one cheeky bastard, blaming us for his fucking tent. He only blamed us because we made noise last night."

David did not have to admit to it; the answer was written all over his grinning face. I knew he had been up to something when he went to the toilets last night. This had to beat any other stunt he had pulled before. I could still picture that women sitting up looking confused, with the sun shining on her toothless face, which was priceless, and the frame tent dragging along the road like a sledge. Luckily for her, it did not have a sewn in ground sheet.

Billy appeared to open his garage, and we knew what was coming next. A crowd of campers leapt on him the minute he got out of his car, gesticulating towards innocent us. As far as we were concerned, we were well behaved last night; they had obviously not seen David and me on a noisy night out before.

"Look lads, I have had a lot of complaints about you. What have you all got to say for yourself?"

Karen appeared from inside the tent with no top or bra on, and she spoke to Billy who did not know where to look. She was deliberately doing it to embarrass Billy; he was stuttering and going red.

"Well, there had better be no noise tonight, then, this is your last chance."

"You mean we are getting to stay then."

"Yes, after that skinny snooty prick has told me that he is leaving, it is well worth the hassle.

He has been a moaning bastard since he arrived here over a week ago. A fucking bird twitcher or something he told me, what the fucks that all about?"

Billy winked at me as he left, he was an intelligent man and knew who was to blame for all the noise last night, and who could have tied the tent to the car. But he was also a kind human being who was young once himself and had not yet forgotten it.

CHAPTER 26

Thrasher packed up his mangled tent and drove away in the huff, and thank fuck for that. He had threatened us with the police so often that Karen offered him the money to go to the phone box. There was no proof anyway, Billy had said that some local had done it for a laugh, but thrasher did not think it was funny in the least.

"Peedie I am not having so much to drink tonight, are you?"

"No, David I'm not, and anyway you will be driving home if we decide to go tomorrow."

"Well, it's not like I will lose my driving licence, is it? Because I don't have one."

We went to a café for something to eat because David was starving after leaving his pavement pizza on a stranger's doorstep last night. Nobody talked as we sat and ate our fry up. They were all probably thinking the same as me. I was needing to get back home for some home comforts and a proper bed. A groundsheet on grass was alright to sleep on when you are full of alcohol and almost unconscious, but we would not be drinking tonight, that had been decided. There was no point in prolonging this trip just for an extra night away. We could go home and have a drink in Edzell if we wanted and then stagger home without having to worry about driving.

Breakfast finished, we headed back to the tent and sat down. It was unanimously decided that we were packing up and heading back to civilisation, back home where we could relax and have a bath. The showers were not the best here; they kept running out of hot water, plus there was always a queue regardless when you went.

It took almost half an hour to pack the tent up and cram everything in the boot, but finally, we were ready to go. We waved to Billy on our way past his garage and headed back towards Edzell. Karen suggested that we head for St Andrews to the beach for a look, but the tide was in when we arrived there. It was too cold to go in the water anyway, so we just had a walk around the shops. There did not seem to be any proper shops there, just tourist orientated one's selling nearly all imported stuff. I picked up a small sailing boat to look at it and turned it upside down to reveal the word made in China, the handmade soap made in Cardiff, and ornaments from all over the place, nothing souvenir of the town was actually made in St. Andrews. None of us bought anything because it was too expensive, well, except Mags, who stole two bars of Lavender soap, and a keyring, but that does not count. David bundled her out of the shop before someone saw her, none of us had noticed what she was up to except David, and he did not want her spending a night in the cells in the town. Fife was a beautiful place and we could have trailed about there for ages. We backtracked our journey and headed for Anstruther to get fish and chips and sat at the harbour eating them.

"Look Peedie there is a seagull dancing, I kid you not, look at the cunt over there."

"Karen, they all do that on the grass to bring worms up to the surface, you silly tart."

"Oh fuck, another one has joined in, do you think it is a male? And with no music either, aren't they clever?"

"It does not matter if it is male or female, they have to eat."

"It does so, two males dancing would make the seagulls gay, wouldn't it?"

I never answered her despite her staring at me inquisitively waiting for a reply, there was no reply I could give her she would have been happy with, nor would she believe that seagulls did the same dance in Edzell, or wherever they lived. We went from the harbour to a pub for a pint, and only one pint. The Ship Tavern doorway was low, tall enough for me to walk under, but anybody taller would definitely have to duck. It was full of local people and the odd tourist, you could tell who was who by the dress code, and their accents and the shorts and sandals with socks on being a dead giveaway.

The pub was old-fashioned with old ship lanterns for lights, and paintings of fishing boats adorning the white painted wooden cladding which covered the ceiling and the walls. When we first went inside the place seemed dark, but we soon got used to the light. The small original windows did not help either, as they were full of nautically themed ornaments, including a full-size copper diving helmet, and cuttings of fishing nets and floats made of green glass. The pub was amazing, and we were made welcome by the barman as soon as we went through the door.

"What can I get you lads, something to eat, or is it just a drink you want?"

"Four pints of lager please and get yourself one."

That was the drink ordered, and I paid for it and we all sat at a table near the window. I could not help noticing that most of the elderly men had at least one gammy eye. I did not stare, but counted eleven eyes afflicted by a droopy bottom eyelid, which hung down quite a bit compared to normal eyes. I imagined that this was due to years of being at the mercy of the sea aboard fishing boats.

"What are you lot staring at? Have you not seen people before? My name is Jessie Swankie and I can tell you a few things about us fishing families, and number one is no staring."

"What's number two, then Jessie?"

David was immediately slapped over the head with her handbag for his impudence, and everybody in the pub burst out laughing.

"I hope it's not me you are laughing at, I don't think to be cheeky is funny in the slightest, in my day we would not have gotten away with it, but then we were born with manners, not like you heathens."

Jessie joined some other women at a table at the other end of the room, allowing David to get his laugh over with, he did not want to laugh when she was still beside him for fear of another bash with her bag. We sat for ages drinking our pint. I had never had a pint last so long. We went to the toilet before we left, but David was not so sure.

"Look that Jessie woman is sitting there, and I will have to pass her to get to the toilets. Give me a loan of your shirt Peedie so she does not recognise me."

"Oh, for fuck's sake David, don't be such a girl just go past her like a man, she is an old woman, not a bloody psychopath."

David decided that his need for the toilet was greater than his imagined fear of Jessie, so he headed slowly past her, and just as he was right beside Jessie, she jokingly flicked her bag towards him, sending David cowering for cover into the toilets. That was funny and deliberate. Jessie was wanting a laugh, and she got one and so did everyone in the pub.

The rest of the trip home seemed to take forever. The twisted roads from Fife to Dundee were full of caravan owners either going on holiday or coming back. None of them realised that they could go over thirty-five miles an hour, and they did not have to slow down even further to look at something wonderful on the way past. We were not on a timetable to get home in time for an event or for anything special, which was just as well for us. There were no places to pass the creeping morons who were towing their temporary homes behind them, and if one materialised there was another moron heading towards us. I suddenly remembered why I hated travelling, and hated caravans getting towed behind underpowered cars laden with everything from their house they could not possibly need.

We had survived on a change of clothes and a bloody tent and sleeping bags which fitted into a medium sized boot. Lights getting flashed at them and horn blasting had no effect whatsoever in trying to attract their attention. They ambled along getting older by the minute with no clue nor care that a near suicidal driver was driving behind them. They were the only driver who mattered because they were going on holiday and dam the peasants who only had cars behind them.

Our car was overheating because we had been driving so slowly, so we drove into a layby to let the car and our tempers cool down a bit. Karen and Mags were needing the toilet anyway, so they walked across a field to a row of trees where they could get some privacy from all the passing cars. They appeared back after about ten minutes carrying a small plastic basket each full with strawberries, which they had borrowed from a field next to the hedge. We shared them out between us always hoping that our last strawberry would not be a sour one. Finally, the car had cooled enough to carry on and we pulled out of the layby with no traffic in front or behind us. The morons had vanished out of sight, leaving a fast drive to Dundee possible at last. Karen moaned that she had sat on a strawberry and that her pants were damp and stained red with berry juice, but nobody was taking any heed of her. We only had thoughts of getting back home to Edzell in as short a time as possible. Dundee was bad to drive in as well and seemed to be a never-ending town which we had no option to drive through, then on to Forfar and finally Edzell.

The farmer was peering through my living-room window when we drew up at the house. His face was pressed up hard against the glass so he never noticed who was in the car. I had to shoot past him to get to the toilet before I flooded my boxer shorts, then I went back to speak to him.

"Look Peedie somebody in the village told me you were in the prison for murdering somebody, but Jenny said that she had spoken to you recently."

"That's typical of the village. If you farted at

one end, you would have shit yourself by the time you walked the main street. Yes, I was in a spot of bother, but it is all sorted now."

"Well, with me being a church elder, it would not look good letting a murderer stay in my cottage. God would not approve if that happened. My lovely wife heard other stories at Vishal's hairdressers when she was in getting her hair coloured and set. And you know that he is a pillar of the church, so would not lie to her."

"Oh, I know his wife well and his two children, but I know his boyfriend better. I have seen the two of them out together a lot holding hands going up the street. God moves in mysterious ways, alright. His wife is ok with it though, Vishal has a large house, several hairdresser shops, and plenty of money, plus it means the empty flat upstairs from the salon gets used now."

The farmer could not answer after I told him about his pillar of the church. I bet he looked at Vishal differently now. The church should treat anyone different, but I bet they will now. Vishal told me that the only reason he went to church was to drum up a bit of local business for himself. God did not fit into his long-term plans, only money, and potential clients. Vishal told me that they named him after an Indian relative on his mother's side of the family, but he had no Indian blood. A very strange name for a man who was born in the North of England to white parents, but the name looked good above the shop, much better than Dougie or Shug I thought to myself.

"Well, I will go and give you peace Peedie, have a nice night all of you."

"Aye, and you too."

He headed back around the corner to the farm house. I bet he was dying to tell his wife, my little ditty, which would shatter her illusion of her upright hairdresser. She looked the type who would judge Vishal, whereas I took everyone for who they were. Vishal had cut and permed my hair several times, and we got on great. He never hid his sexuality from anyone, not even his wife. She looked good going to functions on his arm. The circle Vishal mixed in would not have accepted him coming in with Gary the boyfriend draped all over him. His wife, however, did, swathed in her expensive clothing and jewellery, impeccable hair, and driving a car which I had only ever seen in a magazine before. I had done a couple of decorating jobs in his shops, working through the night, so he did not have to close the salon, and he paid me handsomely.

"Fucking murder, who does he take me for, the fucking ripper?"

"Peedie there is no point getting annoyed at what he said to you. Many a time it has been sheer luck that some of your victims did not die, you never ever waited around to find out either. You always kicked them until they stopped moving and talking, so you are fucking lucky."

"That has changed now, though, I can't get into bother now or I will get jailed. I am reborn, a born-again human being."

"You are also full of shit; I can't see you turning the other cheek if some cunt clobbers you. I just can't hear you saying, oh dash, you have punched me, punch the other side now. That will be spiffing, old chap, tallyho."

"No, but I could bash the shit out of them if nobody was looking."

"I told you nothing has changed; you just can't help yourself."

Karen and I had a bath together, to save time, she said, but it actually took twice as long, as she kept molesting me, and lathering up parts of me which really only needed a wipe. I took ages to wash her, but she never complained either, except when we noticed that the bath water had gone cold. David was banging on the door telling us to hurry up, so we got out of the bath and got our clothes on.

"It's about fucking time you cunts came out of the bathroom, me and Mags need a bath as well, I hope that there is plenty hot water for us."

"Well the immersion is still on, so there had better be. We never topped the water up. Watch and not slip on any thick, creamy stuff lying in the bottom of the bath."

"You filthy bastard Peedie, there had better not be any of your bodily fluids in the bath. I hope you rinsed it out."

"Oh, look Peedie is only winding you up. There can't be anything in the bath because I fucking swallowed it, the whole lot."

"Karen, you are making me gag, shut up will you."

Karen was a cracker; she had no shame and did not care who heard her either. She dried her hair and finished getting her makeup on, and we started the mile walk to the Panny. I hoped that Gavin had not banned me, but I was near certain he would not have done something as drastic as that. I kept the peace in the pub because nobody ever started trouble when I was there, so he got an easy life and I got the odd free pint.

When I walked in, Gavin was grinning from ear to ear, something he always did, but he was happy to see me.

"A pint of lager on the house, it will be then, God I have missed you here Peedie. A lot of the younger ones have been taking the piss out of me since you have been away. I can't wait to see their faces when they walk in and see you sitting here."

"Aye Gavin, the usual, and one for my darling Karen."

"Less of the darling, Peedie, you only call me that when you are wanting something, or have done something wrong, come on, let's go and sit at a table, oh, and get me some crisps, anything except plain."

We sat down and listened to the music coming from the jukebox, fucking Frank Sinatra of all people. Gavin always puts that one on so we have to put money in the slot to put something decent on, and it always works, irrespective of who is in the pub at the time.

"There's your crisps, salt, and vinegar."

"I hate salt and vinegar crisps, what made you get them?"

"You said any kind, except plain, you vagina. if you said you did not like salt and vinegar, I would have got something else. Do you want me to go and change them?"

"No salt and vinegar are ok, but I would have preferred cheese and onion ones."

"And you wonder why men rule the earth Karen, that shit about the crisps said it all."

"As long as women have vaginas, they will rule men, so you have it all wrong. I could get you on your knees begging for sex just by touching you with one finger."

"Just eat the crisps, and I hope you choke on them woman."

We were always winding each other up; people listening were bound to wonder if we were serious sometimes. The lager was nice and chilled, and Gavin had given us both a pint for free. The pub got busy, so other people had put money in the jukebox. Gavin lifted his head and looked at the ceiling which was his signal that he needed help.

I calmly got to my feet and walked over and asked Gavin for a couple more lagers.

"Do you want some peanuts Peedie, this cunt thinks I do, he keeps spitting them at the back of my head when I turn my back on him."

"Aye Gavin give me two packets of the salted ones please."

I put the peanuts into my pocket and picked up my pints and went back to sit beside Karen. I sat waiting until the peanut spitter went to the toilet. Then I asked Gavin to keep people out as I had business to carry out. I went as silently as I could. He was standing to piss in the urinal so I pushed him against the wall making him wet his trousers.

"So, you like peanuts, then you bastard, well guess what, Gavin can't eat through the back of his head. So here is some just for you, open your mouth."

"Fuck off, I'm not eating them, and you can't make me."

That was the wrong thing to say to me. I rammed the whole packet of nuts into his mouth and held it shut. He was coughing and gagging, but they went down his throat without him chewing them, then I emptied the second packet in, but let him spit them out on to the floor.

"Now you can pick every one of them up. Gavin has enough to do without cleaning up after careless eaters."

"The floor is stinking and covered in piss."

"You either pick them up with your hands or your mouth, you decide, then you can go out and apologise to Gavin."

He picked up every peanut, even the ones which had landed in the urinals, and soon had the place tidy and to my liking. I left him in the toilets to get his shit together, then he appeared out and approached Gavin at the bar.

"Look Gavin, I am sorry about spitting peanuts at you. I hope you can forgive me."

"Aye, I will after you pay for the two packets you ate in the toilets. Peedie said that you stole them off him and crammed them in your mouth. That is not very nice, is it?"

He paid for the peanuts and sat back on his stool at the bar. I was back to where I knew best, and I knew that Gavin would deny that I had ever been in the toilets if spitter ever grassed me up. Deep down I knew that he would say nothing, he had seen me in action before many times. It felt good being in charge again, but I would have to be careful.

"You took a long time at the toilets Peedie."

"Oh, you know what it's like Karen, there was a queue."

Karen laughed at me because she knew that I had been up to something and that I would tell her later. Spitter was dabbing his bleeding gums with a tissue. They had been cut by him greedily ramming the peanuts into his mouth with a little help from me, and the abrasive salt in the nuts would also help clean his cuts up. Job done.

"Do you want another pint Peedie, this kind man has offered to buy you one?"

"No thank you, kind sir, my partner and I are going home, so I will decline your kind offer."

Gavin was laughing at my remark, but he accepted a pint without hesitating a minute. It would be the payback for spitting peanuts at him. Gavin did not drink a lot when he was on duty, but occasionally had a pint sitting out of sight under the bar. Then when someone offered him a drink, he just put the money for it in a pint glass behind the bar and took it home with him at the end of his shift.

Karen and I headed out the door and went to Smokey Joes for a haggis supper, there were two choices, white pudding or haggis, and nothing else. Davie was working by himself tonight because Mary had her sister up visiting, so things were a bit quicker than normal. He still cooked the chips in a tiny chip basket in the huge fryer and held the basket in place until they were almost cooked. He flicked the basket up to mix the chips up and then plunged back under to finish them off. Both Davie and Mary had similar rituals which only differed when Davie spat in the fat to see if it was hot enough. His haggis suppers were always good to eat, whether you were drunk or sober. He was proud of his cooking, but it always took ages to get ready. Even if there were ten people queuing at the counter, he still only cooked a small basket of chips; he would not change for anybody. He lost a lot of potential customers who were not prepared to wait forty minutes on haggis and chips, but neither Mary nor Davie cared.

The suppers were finally double wrapped to keep them hot until we got home, then tucked inside my jacket for more protection against the cold air.

We arrived home to meet David in the hall-way.

"How many people are queuing up at Smokey's?"

"There are only two."

"Well, they close in an hour's time, and that won't be enough time to cook three suppers, so fuck it, I will make something myself, it will be much quicker. That smell is fucking killing me. I love Smokey's food."

"We will share ours Peedie, give them here and I will split them up between us, there is plenty for all of us."

"Where is Mags, is she still here?"

"No, she has gone home to Brechin to stay at her mum's house for a couple of days, but she will be back."

We sat down on the sofa with our chips and ate them in silence, just staring into the flames of the fire. This was the life, we were happy for now at least, life was on the up.

CHAPTER 27

Karen and I went our separate ways after a while, but it was never meant to be a relationship in the first place. We had met by accident and had got on well together, but Karen had found a college course in Dundee. She would be sharing a flat with some other girls that her mum knew, so that was it, the temporary romance was over. Now I could plan my life to suit myself, not that I minded sharing it with Karen. She had kept me sane when I was feeling down, and now I would have to deal with the dark days myself. I had no doubt in my mind that I would slip back to the turmoil of my broken mind. David would stay with Mags for a while to keep her company, plus he reckoned that he would be well fed when he was there. I would be sharing the house with my demons inside me and there was nothing I could do to change it. Karen's mutually agreed parting was hitting me harder than I cared to admit, harder than I could ever have envisioned. I was suddenly home alone, and I felt vulnerable.

I made myself an appointment at my doctor's and luckily got a cancellation for the same day. It was not my usual doctor, but I needed to talk to someone, anyone. She spoke with a soft voice which immediately put me at ease.

"Have you been taking your tablets? According to when you last got a prescription, you have had none for around three weeks."

"I have been feeling fine, so I stopped taking them ages ago, anyway they made me tired."

"No wonder you are feeling the way you do. You can't just stop taking the tablets when you are feeling fine. You have a psychotic illness that needs constant maintenance with the correct combination of drugs. You have to keep taking the drugs, even if you feel like you don't need them. I will prescribe you more medication to get you healed again, and I am making you an appointment with a psychiatrist at Stracathro Hospital. You have to attend that appointment to get the proper help you need because drugs alone will not be enough. I don't think."

I sat talking to her for ages, pouring my heart out with tears running down my face. My life was over and there seemed like there was no way back from this. I told her about everything I was feeling and how black my mind was.

"Could you not move back in with your parents for a while just till you feel a bit more able to cope? That's one way you would feel less alone and vulnerable if you had familiar people around you."

I never responded to that remark. It would have taken the whole day to fill in the blanks in my medical notes if I went into detail. That would be the end for me if I went home, then I would definitely kill myself. The thought of sitting in the same room as my father with him knowing what was wrong with me now would be too much. He would milk it for months and make things worse. I would get called every derogatory name he could think of; I would be the shit on his shoe. He never had time for me when I was a child so he would never help me now; he absolutely despised me.

"Look doctor, they would not want me to move back home."

"How do you know? Have you asked them?"

She was just not listening to me. My parents did not have to tell me I was not wanted. It was as good as tattooed into my brain and had been since I was young. I would be as welcome as a paedophile at a playgroup, as I would be in that house.

"I can see that I am wasting my breath asking you to go home to your parent's house as you are not answering me. Just keep taking your medication and wait on your appointment with the psychiatrist coming in the post."

This has to be the lowest point in my life and I am just having to watch my whole world fall apart, and all I can do is stare blankly. As a survivor of severe emotional, physical and sexual abuse as a child, I thought that one day I would be completely healed from the abuse because doctors and psychiatrists had told me that. I lived every moment of my childhood years in my own personal hell at the hands of my father. I have spent most of my adult life so far validating, processing and trying to heal from the negative emotions and mental damage my father did to me as a child. I always believed that one day the abuse would be truly behind me. I have come to realise that I will probably never be completely healed from that abuse. There will always be some triggers that bring back the memories of the dark days and bring them flooding back. I will probably never be truly free until I die. This hell is mine and mine alone, and there is no one alive who can live it for me, and I hate myself for what I have let myself become. I have turned from a relatively carefree person into a morbid recluse since Karen and I parted company, and I have to get back to the real world to look for a way out of this abyss I am trapped in.

After a few weeks, my medication was slowly changing my mood even if it was brief. Some days were manageable for an hour or two, but not for much longer. I got off the bus from Stracathro after seeing my psychiatrist and headed for the Panny for a lager, and to speak to Gavin. He was a good friend and full of good advice even if I did not always agree with him.

"Where the hell have you been Peedie, I have not seen you for weeks?" Fucking look at you. Where has your body gone? You have lost a lot of weight?"

"Gavin, are you saying I was a fat cunt before I lost weight?"

"You know fine, what I am saying, you know me better than that, aye you were a fat cunt."

We laughed, a thing I had not done in ages. Life was not funny; it was pointless and depressing. I gave Gavin a brief explanation of what had been happening in my life or lack of it. He listened intently to me and did not interrupt until I was finished talking.

"Right then, that's the formalities over, what do you want to drink, or have you forgotten how to?"

"Right Gavin, I will have a pint of Stella on the house, please. You must have missed me, so this will let us catch up."

"One pint of Stella coming up, you skinny bastard, this will fatten you up to what you should be."

We sat talking about anything we could think of, putting the world to rights in our minds anyway. We were interrupted by a man in his thirties barging in through the door, who was followed by another three men. They were all drunk and very loud.

"Get me four pints of Tenants, you old bastard, and hurry up or else I will come behind the bar and pour it myself."

Gavin winked at me and carried on pouring the pints at his own pace, half indicating with his eyes to his right. Then I noticed what he was looking at, a squad of builders were sitting through in the kitchen getting a free meal from the owner to save them leaving the premises.

"I thought I told you to hurry up, grandad, well, I have waited fucking long enough, get out of my way."

He shoved Gavin to the side and grabbed the beer tap, and all hell broke loose. Two of the builders grabbed the man and physically picked him up and threw him over the top of the bar, and he landed on the floor shouting profanities at Gavin. His friends came through from the kitchen and headed for the three shouting idiots. One of them picked up a stool and threw it towards the bar, narrowly missing me and my pint of Stella. I saw red and picked up my bar stool and swung it at the one nearest me and hit him over the back with it. He crumpled in a heap in front of me. He was picked up and thrown outside onto the pavement; this was like something you would see in a Western movie. Within ten minutes there was a police car outside with blue lights flashing.

"Come on Peedie, get through the back into the kitchen, and for fuck's sake, don't come out, whatever you do."

"Thanks, Gavin, trouble is the last thing I need tonight."

The four of them were arrested and cuffed, awaiting a van to come and pick them up. I could hear one of them describing me, and how I had hit him so hard that he now had a cracked rib, he was lying through his teeth because I hit him across the back with the stool. Gavin stood listening to the injured man saying nothing at first, then he explained what had really happened to the officers.

"This man tried to rob my till. He jumped over the bar and unluckily slipped on the floor. The two kind workers helped him over to the other side of the bar and checked to see if he was ok. This other man he is describing is a figment of his imagination, too much drink if you ask me."

The officers knew Gavin and believed him over the drunken arseholes who barged in causing trouble. Two of them were taken away and two were waiting for a doctor to get their injuries checked over before they followed their drunken friends to the cells. Gavin gave me the all clear, and I headed back to the bar.

"Peedie, you will have to get your shit together, or you will end in the jail laddie. You should not have reacted to the trouble. If you were in here when the police came, you would have been pointed out and arrested. It would not matter whether you did anything, you would have ended in court."

I sat there listening to Gavin. He was right. I was violent towards anyone who was in the slightest bit aggressive near me. They did not even have to be directing it towards me and I retaliated. Things would have to change, and soon.

I had spent all my life witnessing violence, and most of that had been directed at me by my father. I had learned to defend myself even before I was attacked, either by attacking first or by rejecting any accusation against me as lies. Pain which I had hidden for years has suddenly become unbearable. Anger once successfully repressed has surfaced, causing me to become abusive myself, mostly to others and sometimes to myself. My psychiatrist had tendered that explanation to me, as one reason I was violent, but I was just not believing that. I admit nothing for fear of incriminating myself, even I have just been witnessed doing it, the fear of retaliation overtakes the reality of what is happening. To admit anything as a child was a guaranteed beating and hours of interrogation. It became instinctive to deny first, then to take it from there, and occasionally it saved certain pain and humiliation if I was lucky.

I headed back home, realising how lucky I had just been. I could so easily be heading to prison for a minimum of a year. Prison would definitely finish me off if they sent there me, and if I did not try to change, that was where I was heading. I knew that, but felt unable to control my anger when it started in me. I just boiled over with rage and could not control what was happening. It was as if I was an onlooker when rage erupted inside me and it never felt like it was me who was doing it. It detached me from reality and true life. I lit the fire and sat down with a coffee, contemplating my next move, but came up with no solutions. I could not hide away for much longer as it was having an effect on my health, I was not eating as I should, and it had become noticeable.

Morning arrived abruptly. David was banging on the door trying to get in.

"Peedie answer the door, it's me, David."

"What are you doing here at this time of fucking morning?"

"It's not morning, it's almost twelve o'clock, I never expected you to be in bed at this time. Gavin told me you were at the Panny last night when shit was going on. I checked to see if you were in there first before I came here."

"Oh, it was just some drunken arseholes who came in to start shite with Gavin."

"Mags have I got a flat from the council in Kirriemuir, only two doors down from mums. I am here for the rest of my stuff. Remember, if you get sick of here you can come and stay, there are two bedrooms. You don't have to ask, just turn up any time you want."

"David, I have to learn to be happy living by myself before I live anywhere. My head is fucked up just now. There is a lot of stuff I need to sort out for myself."

David and I finished loading the car with his stuff and some things Mags had left. He drove off and left me standing there stunned. I was definitely on my own now. The house looked and felt even emptier than it had before. Pictures belonging to David had been removed from the walls, and even his blankets from the bed were gone. I could almost hear the emptiness in my head as my footsteps seemed to echo as I went from room to room checking to see if he had forgotten anything, but he hadn't, even his favourite mug was away with him.

The pub was looking like a good option for some gossip with Gavin. He had a calming influence on me, and he was good company. I headed down past Jenny's house, trying not to get noticed by her as I was not in the mood for her pep talks; however, well meant they were. A familiar face was staring in my direction as I approached Smokey Joes. It was Bob, and he was not happy with himself.

"That cunt of a boss of mine has fucking paid me off, the bastard knew I needed the money. Just because I let the works van tyres down at night so I could get a longer lie next morning is no excuse, that can't be legal."

"Bob, you haven't changed a bit, have you?"

"Aye, he moaned like fuck because he had to wait for three hours for the tyre company appearing with the proper tyres. I don't know why he was moaning because he got to spend all that time looking after his prize-winning garden. The fat cunt has entered it into the Edzell in bloom contest again, he was second last year, and he is so sure he will win outright this time."

I sat on the wall and listened to Bob, then I had an idea which I knew would work as I had done it before. I asked Bob what he thought of my revenge tactic, and he was all up for it. We both walked up to the cottage and grabbed a few hessian sacks from the farm and headed up the hill towards the forest near the top. There was a fence at one corner of the forest which went into a very long, narrow v shape at the corner. I instructed Bob where to walk slowly along, and I told him where I would be. We walked slowly and quietly down the hill driving the rabbits into the long v at the end of the trees, then when we got to the end there were at least forty rabbits of all sizes, young and old. We blocked their escape and captured them easily and popped them into the hessian sacks, tied the tops and headed towards my house. The rabbits did not know it, but they were going on a holiday they would never forget; this was no Butlins; this would be a luxury for them all.

It was dark when we got down the hill and we were needing a drink and a rest. I never knew that rabbits could be so heavy, but there was exactly forty-three split between four bags, and they wriggled all the way. The kettle boiled, and we had a cup of coffee and planned our next move. We would have to go the back road through the village, cross the main road and take the darker paths farthest away from the street lights, then we could do our magic trick.

The rabbits wriggled the second we lifted the sacks, letting out noisy squeaks as we walked along. Eventually, they settled down and just before the village. If they had carried on, the mission would have to have been postponed. Someone was coming in the distance so we gently set the bags behind a wall until they passed us, then we carried on. The night was still, and every noise seemed to travel for miles and I imagined it sounded like a sonic boom, and finally, we reached the Garden of Eden, the prized garden, the eighth wonder of the world, the fat bastard's haven.

"Have a good look Bob, look at the lovely prize vegetables and look at the straight lines of fresh goodness, the root vegetables of paradise, and the green cabbages of tomorrow. Worth every minute the fat bulbous cunt has spent on them, he will definitely win a top prize now, aye for keeping fat rabbits."

We made sure that they could not escape and emptied the rabbits gently into the garden, one bag at a time until all four bags were empty. They ran about trying to get away from us, even though it was almost pitch black. We hid quietly out of sight until they settled. Nobody else would have any reason to come down to the allotments tonight, so our rabbits would have the banquet of a lifetime, a thickly set out feast of health-giving sustenance fit for a Queen, and they had all night to indulge.

Bob and I sneaked up the path to the village and went for a pint at the Glennie because the fat man gardener would be there. He had ten bellies and four chins, enough to feed a pack of wolves at a zoo for a month if he was lifted into their enclosure by a forklift. He was swilling on a pint of lager and eating a pie, but he always seemed to be eating. We ordered a pint and sat at the tables farthest away from him so we could watch him and have a laugh.

"Look at his fucking hamster cheeks Bob, you could fit a double bed in that mouth."

He sat there constantly munching on crisps, his deep piggy like eyes boring down to the bottom of the packet, searching for every last crumb, then he sat licking the residue from his fat fingers. We ordered another pint and continued watching the show, then we made plans to come back in the morning to see how the rabbits had fared through the night.

I had deliberately set my alarm and so had Bob. He was waiting for me at the Post office when I got there. The sight at the garden which was laid out in front of us was amazing. I never knew that forty-three rabbits could be so ravenous. They had felled cabbage like lumber jacks and devoured their prize, moving from lettuce to carrot like crazed hungry lunatics. The place looked like a war zone, they left nothing whole, and rows of chomped carrots which looked like landing strips at an airport gave the barren garden a bit of colour, a focal point where there had been none before. Fatso would be livid, jumping up and down hyperventilating with his lard arse bouncing up and down like a trampoline full of excited children. He should not have sacked Bob, then he would have a garden and not a private rabbit sanctuary, he would have rosettes instead of bunnies, and we would not be laughing like we were now.

He turned up at his usual time to tend his prized plot before he went to work, but he did not jump up and down, he fell to his knees and let out a wail.

"Bob, you little tosser. I know it was something to do with you. You are going to fucking pay for this."

"Try getting fingerprints off a rabbit, just don't even try to blame me, I was with Peedie at his house all night, so fuck off and get your facts straight, you cunt."

Bob stayed at my house, and I had Jenny as a witness. She had come to ask me a favour when Bob was there. But that was after our horticultural adventure, our hill walking extravaganza with our hessian bags full of night shift bunnies.

I nearly felt sorry for him and his garden, but only for a few minutes. He got to his feet and threw turnips at us, and one landed smack bang on Bob's back. Bob was laughing fit to burst despite any pain he was feeling.

"Right, you fat cunt, throw us a carrot and a leek, and Peedie and I will have enough vegetables to make soup."

We ran towards the village laughing at what had just happened, and left him frantically chasing rabbits around trying to get them out through the gate in his garden. That would definitely help him lose a few pounds. He was a bully of a man who made his younger workers lives a misery, so in my mind, he got what he deserved.

Tandem

CHAPTER 28

I was getting tired of having to look over my shoulders and having to stay out of trouble. It was nerve-wracking and humiliating always having to turn the other cheek any time something nasty was said to me. Eleven months had passed of my suspended sentence, leaving me a month to stay out of trouble. Gavin's advice had struck a chord with me, and I had for once in my life listened. He was different, more like a father than my own. There were never any patronising lectures, just kind advice, and friendship.

"Well, I think you should take your brother's advice and get out of this dead-end village if that's what you need to do to survive. I know a lot of the idiots around here have goaded you and tried to get you to batter them, but all credit to you, you never retaliated."

"I always feel a failure if I can't kick the shit out of them Gavin. It's weak if you don't stand up for yourself like a man."

"It is the bigger man who walks away from a fight, you are not weak by any means, plus you have no option but to do it if you don't want prison."

For a change, I had two pints instead of my usual one. I was enjoying speaking to Gavin too much to leave. I would not have a third one, because that would lead to more, and maybe trouble. If someone came to me, causing bother there was no way I could walk away from them if I had too much drink, they would certainly walk away from me wearing bruises.

"Right Gavin, I will probably see you around. I have decided that I am going to stay in Kirriemuir at my brother's house. It can't be any worse than here, and Bob has kept my house on for himself and he is getting all my furniture for nothing, well, except, the new living room stuff, it is coming with me."

"Well, do nothing to get yourself lifted; I don't want to be reading about you in the Dundee Courier getting banged up for something stupid. Come back and see me, sometime will you? Come here and give me a hug."

Gavin put his skinny arms around me and hugged me tightly; it was something I had never experienced before. Nobody in my family ever hugged each other and here was me getting my first ever hug at the tender age of twenty-four. I walked away towards the door with tears welling up in my eyes and a lump in my throat. I daren't turn to look at Gavin or I would have broken down in front of him and some pub regulars, which was something I could not let happen. I was brought up by my father who had instilled in me from a very young age that men don't cry, only women or gay boys cry.

My face must have been a picture coming through the door because somebody asked me what was wrong with me, but I could not talk to them. I crossed the road and walked home, and I could not control it anymore, the tears burst out and ran down my face, and I did not care if anyone saw me. I had phoned David from the pub and he was getting a loan of a transit van to pick up the sofa and armchairs, and all my stuff I was taking with me.

The van reversed right up to the gate, and David jumped out and opened the doors at the rear of the van. He had brought his old suite from his house for Bob to use. The van never took long to load, and soon we were on our way. I had only arrived at the cottage with a tent and sleeping bag and had spent many a happy time in the place. But there had been more sad times than happy ones. Bob reckoned that he would be happy there once I informed everyone that I had departed, then he would not live in fear of a violent gang at his door wanting blood. He asked if I could leave him the shotgun barrel to use if he was feeling threatened. I cleaned the barrel from top to bottom of any fingerprints, just in case the two halves of the gun were ever united and used in a crime. That would just be my luck, I would just have one week of my sentence left and someone would rob a bank with my prints on the gun, then shoot a policeman.

"Come on Peedie waken up, we are in Kirrie

now, and you have been sleeping since before we left Brechin."

"I am tired and getting hungry. We should get this stuff out of the van now while we can get parked here. Fuck humphing that heavy setee any further than we have to."

Mags was at home when we went in with the first armchair, and she immediately claimed it as hers.

"David, I have had nothing but a cushion to sit on since you took the old suite away, my arse needs be rubbed to get the circulation back."

"At least wait until we get all the stuff out of the van, or better still, come and give us a hand, then you will get all the rubbing you want."

The new furniture looked fabulous in this living room. It was a bigger and brighter room than the cottage with large a large window which looked on to a long row of two-storey houses. The block of flats I was to be living in now, had four storeys, but luckily our house was on the ground floor. I could see all the curtain switchers spying on us to see what was going on so they got a big wave from me, which always made the curtains shut with a bang. I placed everything where it was meant to be except my clothes which I would do later. David had to take the van back, he had borrowed, then we would get a fish cake supper on the way home. Bridget from the chip shop made her own fishcakes, and there was not another taste like it; nothing came close. We sat on a bench in the town square watching all the people walking past going about their lives.

"Look at that drunken arsehole Jimmy. He has just grabbed the arse of that posh woman who was in the chip shop."

"David she should think herself lucky anybody is touching her; I would not touch her with a bargepole."

"Peedie I have seen you with worse, what about her with the bleached blonde hair, the one in the Ogilvy Arms? She was definitely a double bagger if ever I saw one, you would have to put two bags on her head in case one burst."

"No, you're wrong David, she was a triple bagger, she was like a stalker before I managed to get rid of her. She used to be waiting for me whenever I got home from work and jumped on me trying to ram her hand down the front of my jeans."

A face I had not seen for ages, was suddenly looking at me with interest, and he looked like he had seen a ghost. It was Brian who sometimes stayed with me at my flat in Forfar.

"Peedie I was told that you were dead, that you had died in a car accident last year."

"Oh my God, what lying bastard told you that shite?"

"You're not going to believe me when I tell you it was your father who told me. I asked him where you were as I had not seen you for ages, he even told me what graveyard they buried you in.

We were all told in the pub not to mention you again as you were dead and gone."

"David, did you know about this fucking dead thing?"

"Yes, I did, but I never told you because you would have been upset."

"Upset, I think it is funny as fuck. I have always been dead to him; he has never been a father to me so that kind of talk is nothing to what he has said to me before to my face."

"Come on Peedie let's get home before you terrify all the kids with you being dead, and still eating a bag of chips."

"You should pop in to see dad on our way home. That would give me a laugh and would guarantee to ruin his happy home life up. He does not know that you are moving here yet, I wanted to leave that to you."

"No that won't be happening any time soon, I would rather stick hot pins in my eyes and poke a hole through my nose with a pencil"

David laughed most of the way home about the look on Brian's face when he saw me sitting there on the bench, and what dad would be like when he found out I was living just a few doors away from him. He would be furious that I had dared to move beside him and had challenged his authority. I would have needed his permission to move here for him to accept it, but that would never happen in my lifetime.

Mags was in bed when we got home, sitting listening to the radio.

"David your mum was round when you were away to the chip shop, she says you have to come round the minute you get home. She looks like she is in a cunt of a mood. You know the way she walks like her legs are moving but her body is still, that kind of mood."

"She can fuck off with her mood, some bastard has obviously told her that you are back in Kirrie, now her life with dad will be hell, especially if he ever finds out you are here. Let's forget about everybody else and have a housewarming party at the weekend, there are plenty of people who would come, well except dad that is."

The flat has been the pick-up I needed. My bedroom was large with a double wardrobe built in, not like the old-fashioned wooden one I left for Bob, and this house had a big kitchen with built in units. I put my clothes on hangers and tidied up the boxes I had brought them in. David had told me about the double divan bed, and he had not been exaggerating when he said that it was comfortable. I put my bedding on the bed and lay down and almost sank into a trance until Mags shouted at me.

"Come on Peedie, I have made us all a cup of coffee, and that is a rarity, so you had better come and drink it."

We all sat half watching the television, drinking our coffee, talking about dad finding out about my homecoming and what he would do to ruin it. I had already decided that my life did not include him, and it never had. Mum would get major shit if dad finds out that she has known before him and said nothing. She would be accused of everything dad could think of, and nag her until her ears bled. We all agreed that a party would be the best way to cheer me up, and that was it decided.

People arrived two hours before they were meant to, but they had brought a big carry out so it did not matter. Some people I knew, and some I had seen before going about the town. They all appeared happy and carefree and were in the party mood. Andy, a man I used to work with was there and he was not even invited, but he had heard the music and knocked on the door. He was an idiot when he had a drink in, and really funny.

The music got so loud that neighbours from the top floor came to complain, so we invited them to the party. One of them I recognised straight away as Tandem, she was around forty-five years old, and she was called Tandem because she was the local bike, and everybody rode her. She also liked two men at a time, hence the name. She was larger than life and weighed around fifteen stone, and she arrived in her pyjamas.

"There is no point in getting dressed as I can just climb the stairs later and go straight to bed. Right, who's got the vodka, I can smell it?"

The drink was flowing down everybody's throats like a waterfall and soon we all forgot our troubles for a while. Tandem was gyrating her hips like she was using an invisible hula hoop and dancing to the music like it would run out. She was the party.

More people arrived, but I did not have a clue who they were, and nor did David. They were laden with alcohol and that was the magic word at our door. Lights from some houses across the road came on, but we did not care. Our party was the only thing on our mind and if people were not happy, they could wear earplugs, and anyway, three am is not that late.

I was bursting for the toilet and had to squeeze past people standing outside my bedroom door. When I emerged from the toilet, I just had to ask what was happening.

"Peedie, Tandem is in your bed shagging somebody, I don't know who he is but she is loving it."

"In my bed, the cheeky bastards, well they will change the sheets when they are finished, fuck sleeping on sticky sheets."

"She won't be finished for ages, this is the queue to hump her, and if you want to empty yours, you better join the line behind us before it gets longer."

The room door was wide open and you could see and hear everything that was going on. The man just rolled off Tandem, and he shouted to who was next in line, put on his boxers and trousers and walked past us grinning.

"Right will the next man hurry up and come to shag me."

The next in line went in and climbed on top of her and she was getting annoyed with him.

"What do you fucking mean, you've come; we have not even started. I will have to call you trigger from now on, fuck off and let somebody else have a turn."

He came out of the room past us with a look of shame and humiliation at his lack of staying power. He would be remembered as trigger by everyone at the party. The line was not getting any shorter, not because the sex with her was taking too long, but that more people were joining the queue. I had already decided that I was going to sleep with her, all this time watching her at it had turned me on. Now I was next in line to go in, and Andy was busy humping her, but he was taking too long and Tandem was started to look bored.

"For fuck's sake, Andy, are you nearly coming?"

"No Tandem, I can't think of anybody."

"What do you mean, you can't think of anybody?"

She shoved him off the top of her and slapped him senseless, she was livid with him and all Andy could do was laugh.

"Well, you are so slack it is like throwing a

sausage up a close. I would have had to throw a pound of mince up your fanny to take up the slack."

"Aye more like you have a needle dick. I never even noticed you inside me."

"Nor did I, it was like humping fresh air."

Andy came past me laughing, and Tandem got out of bed, the shag fest was over, but I had lost my libido, anyway. There was no coming back from that last romantic encounter with Andy. Everybody went back through to the party, disgusted with Andy for ruining their chance of sex, especially young Tony who was a virgin.

If Tandem got pregnant, she would need a crystal ball to see who the father was as there were so many blasts of semen inside her, but luckily, I would not be on the possible list, and nor would David.

I stripped my bed while I was still sober enough to do it and put clean bedding on. I shut the bedroom door and warned everybody to stay out. If anybody was having any romance in that bed it would be me, but definitely not with Tandem. I shoved the offensive sheets straight in the washing machine and left them there to be dealt with in the morning. Tandem disappeared suddenly and she could only have gone home because she was not dressed. People were going home except for anyone who had fallen into a drunken stupor and could not move unaided. David and Mags had vacated the living room and had gone to bed. I was the only one who was still reasonably sober, everybody else was either snoring or trying to stagger out the door to go home. The place was an utter tip with empty cans and bottles littering nearly every surface, but I was happy. I had gone a whole night drinking and had not punched anybody in the face, that was the best evening ever.

"What time is it?"

"It's nearly four o'clock."

"Morning or afternoon."

The voice had come from the sofa, and she had just woken up.

"I can hardly remember being here. Did I do anything to embarrass myself?"

"Not yet, but you should have seen Tandem at it all night like a rabbit, she will definitely be walking funny when she gets up tomorrow, she is bound to be sore. Andy totally insulted her feminine feelings, which made her stop sleeping with more men, or else or she would be even sorer."

"That was my mum, she is a total embarrassment, and she has legs like a twenty-four-hour service station because she is always open for business. I hope she wasn't charging anybody tonight, not at your party. She usually goes to Dundee to a flat she shares with her pal. This is the first weekend she has not been because she was at the doctor yesterday getting medication for painful thrush, and to get checked for genital warts."

Her name was Milly, and she looked about eighteen years old. I was shocked at first at what she was saying, but it got me off the hook for slagging off her mum. We had a cup of coffee and talked for ages about her mum and the effect it had on her since she was a little girl, and about the constant new dads and uncles who appeared out of the bedroom every morning. The dodgy sleazy looking men who were only paying for sex. Milly always bolted her bedroom door at night to stop the perverse men from taking a wrong turn and ending up in her room by mistake. Her mum had asked her if she would have sex with men, but luckily, she had refused.

"Right Peedie I am away home now, good luck with your court case on Thursday."

"I will need all the luck in the world for my case, but thanks. You remember to look after yourself."

Milly was too nice to get mixed up in her mother's shenanigans. Tandem would probably end up riddled with some incurable venereal disease and spread it to half the population of Angus and beyond. Milly was away upstairs to her house to lock her herself into her own bedroom and try to get back to sleep, and I was going to mine. It was strange having people living all around me, and so much better having street lights. The cottage in Edzell was dark all around it when the outside lights were turned off.

I lay in bed, but could not settle. The lights were reflecting shadows as people passed the window on their way home. Voices seemed closer than they were as they rebounded off the steep banking behind the block of flats, we lived in. I was used to no noise and no light. My mind was going over my court case and what the outcome might be because of my good behaviour. It had seemed a long year, avoiding trouble at any cost, and having to dodge and hide from my enemies to avoid an altercation, but now my judgement day was only three days away and I was terrified.

CHAPTER 29

I was first up out of bed and I had hardly had any sleep. My thoughts were on my court case in Forfar at ten o'clock. The day of reckoning had finally arrived, and I was not mentally ready for it. If things go wrong for me and I get jailed, I will not cope with prison life. Life living here is bad enough staying almost next door to my father and my family. I had been told that he was hoping that I would be jailed so that he could get his life back. He hated the thought of me being the slightest bit happy. An arrangement set up by him to try to get me to fight with someone had gone wrong. The person he had paid to do it was Shug, and Shug was having none of it but still took the money. Now it would be Shug who was a marked man, but he did not care. We had been good friends for several years, but my father never knew it. He took no interest in any part of my life, nor what I was doing from day to day. He was devoid of any feelings towards me.

"What an absolute cunt your father is Peedie, when he offered me ten quid to start a fight with you knowing fine well you would hurt me and get arrested just before your fucking court case.

He hasn't changed since our schooldays has, he, what a fucking arsehole."

"You watch yourself Shug, he will break your arm for a fiver, never mind ten pounds. You have betrayed him now and no amount of pleading will change things for you. He will pick on you in front of the whole pub and crush your hand until he hears a bone break."

"Fuck him, I don't care about what he does, I have enough of my own shit to deal with just now. I will just avoid him until he forgets."

"I have the court at ten o'clock. Do you fancy coming for a laugh at me in the dock?"

"Peedie you won't be fucking laughing, you will be shitting your pants in case you get sent down, my brother has been to prison, and he hated it because he got put in the same cell as a murderer. He slept on the top bunk, listening to him going to sleep before he slept himself. The place is full of cunts like that, and the screws are all idiots out to impress the governor."

The bus was on time when it drew up at the stance and already had passengers on board from Dundee who was getting off. We waited on them all exiting the bus and went on board and I asked for a single ticket to Forfar

"You would be cheaper if you paid for a return ticket sonny."

"It is ok driver I already know that, but I only want a single because I may not be coming back for over a year."

We sat at the back of the bus because it was empty there. The bus took off and wound its way round Kirriemuir and then headed for Forfar, the place where I was dreading to go. Shug and I reminisced about our school days and my German jackboots and had a laugh about them. We had known each other for a long time and had kept each other's secrets about our family lives. Shug knew why I did not like my father because he had seen the bruises and the mental strain I was under, and my time spent at Sunnyside Royal Hospital.

The bus stopped just below the court, and we got off, followed by another man. I looked up at the massive building and my heart sank. The judge had better be in a good mood today for my sake, because I was shitting myself with the thought of heading to Perth on a one-way ticket to stay with murders and violent criminals. I never considered myself violent despite my aggressive past. I had left a lot of people lying in their own blood not knowing if they were alive or dead, but that was different, that was me.

The steps seemed steeper than they normally did because I did not want to get to the top. People were standing outside the front door smoking and laughing, but I was not in any state of mind to find anything remotely funny. Shug tried to lighten the moment by lifting his leg and letting out a loud watery sounding fart, but it did not work. Panic was setting in now, this was real and not a thing which would happen in a year's time, it was looming in the next half an hour or so, and it was happening to me.

"Come on Peedie we had better go in because most other people are away inside already."

I never answered Shug and just followed him up a flight of stairs, to court one, and stood outside the door for a minute before I went inside. It made a change going in without handcuffs on like the last visit, shackled to a police officer. But I had no choice this time either, I had to go in under my own steam and pay for what I had done in Edzell.

I sat at the end of the second row of seats so that it would be easier to get to the dock when my name was called. The graffiti on the back of the pine wooden seats in front of me had dozens of names on it, probably carved by people like me waiting to get called.

"Court rise."

The clerk of court had shouted, the Judge was on his way, my case could be heard any minute. The Judge appeared through the door behind the dock, and he did not look happy. He sat down first, then we were asked to be seated. He sat scanning the court looking for the person who was chatting away somewhere behind me.

"Silence in court or you shall be removed from this court immediately. I will not stand for disrespectful behaviour, discontinue the talking or else."

Trust somebody to get on the wrong side of him, and today, when I was up in front of him of all days.

"Call Mike Smith."

A small man walked up to the dock and was asked to confirm who he was. His crimes were read out to him, and he pleads guilty straight away. What he had committed was not even half of what I was charged with, and his prospects looked good as far as I was concerned.

"Stand up, Mr. Smith. You have pleaded guilty to the charges read out to you in court today, and although the offences are not of the most serious nature, I am sentencing you to six months in prison. Officer take him away."

That will be me fucked then I thought. There would be no hope for me now; he was in the foulest of moods already. I sat staring up at the high ornate dark pine ceiling, wondering how they ever managed to paint up there, then it happened without warning. The bottom fell out of my world, my name had been called. I walked in a daze up to the dock and was asked to sit down.

The charges started to get rattled out, and they seemed to take ages to read. The Judge looked bored stiff waiting on the fiscal finishing, then it happened.

"Stand, please."

I got to my feet even though my legs felt like jelly and my heart was nearly coming through my chest. My mind had semi locked down ready for my sentence getting read out to try to lessen the blow.

"You have previously pleaded guilty to all the charges read out in court. I asked you to come back here today with a clean report for good behaviour, and you were admitted to Sunnyside psychiatric hospital for reports which you carried out in full. I am not sure that a long term in prison would do your mental health any good, nor does your consultant psychiatrist. After careful consideration regarding your years prison sentence and your good behaviour, I will admonish you on all charges. If you appear in front of me again, I will not be so lenient next time. You are free to go."

"Thank you for believing in me Your Honour, I will not let you, nor myself down. I promise."

Shug was smiling at me when I turned around to leave the dock. Nobody else moved a muscle as I headed out the door, followed closely by Shug. I was still in shock at my sentencing and it had still not really sunk in yet. The year's suspended sentence had been the longest I had ever been out of major trouble since I left home, apart from breaking someone's rib in the Panny, but that did not count, as I was never caught. I was a free man, at last, free from the imminent threat of a spell behind bars, but still not free from my state of mind.

The year waiting on the court date, had added to the burden of what was already occurring in my head. The repercussions of what had happened today would be something I would never forget, and I now had to get out of the spiral of mental self-destruction which had been a part of me since I was young. Everybody who had ever managed to get close to me eventually drifted away. Nobody could cope with my mood swings and depressive tendencies, and my learned defensive habits I had carried on with since my childhood. An invisible barrier was round me all the time repelling any chance of happiness which came my way, and I could not get out of the rut I was in.

"Come on Peedie, this calls for a pint, the pubs are due to open in the next ten minutes."

"You can if you like Shug, but I am heading home on the next bus, my body could not cope with the effects of a drink just now."

"Well, I am going for one or maybe six pints. It will depend on who is in the pub. You can have my return bus ticket because I will go to my brother's house after I come out of the pub. Now go home and try to chill out for a while, and stay away from your dad, because he has already got into your head and you don't realise just how bad yet. I'm no psychiatrist, but I have known you long enough to see the big change in you since we went to school together."

"Don't you worry about me Shug, there is no chance that cunt will piss on my parade today. Part of me wishes he had been in court just to see his expression when I was admonished, and to see you sitting in the court after he had paid you to start trouble with me, that would have been priceless."

The bus arrived on time and I showed the driver Shug's return ticket and went to sit at the back. The bus was almost half full as it had just come from Dundee. Everyone was chatting away to each other, and I sat and listened to how happy some of them were. Children sitting beside mothers all well dressed and clean were arguing between the seats and were ignored by their mother. I would have been slapped half the length of the bus if I did that. The world I lived in now was so far removed from the one I grew up in, apart for one thing; my father. He still drank heavily and despised me breathing the same air as he did. Twenty-four years of my life have almost passed, and he has still never had a proper conversation with me, and if it ever happened, I would not know how to react. It would be such a shock if he actually talked to me instead of at me. I would probably stand looking at him in shock.

We finally arrived in the square in Kirriemuir and I was glad, it had taken ages. I wanted to get home to sit down and chill before I thought out where my life was going. I needed a plan of action; my doctor had told me that. Instead of drifting from idea to plan and never fulfilling what I really needed in life.

There was a police car parked outside the flats when I got there, and they were not here to see me and that was a change. I was on first-name terms now with most of the local police force from Forfar and Kirriemuir, but not quite on their Christmas card list. I squeezed past the crowd of onlookers expecting to see a body lying on the pathway, but it was only what looked like David's vacuum cleaner and a lot of broken glass scattered everywhere. Someone broke our living room window, and it looked as if they had done it from the inside.

"I'm sorry Peedie you can't go in there because there is a domestic ongoing inside the property. We cannot get the occupant to respond to us."

"Well, I actually live here, Constable Henderson and I have a key, so I will go in and sort it out for you. He's not getting arrested, is he?"

"No, it's only a domestic, and the broken window is between him and the council. You can go into the property at your own risk."

"As long as you lot don't barge past me when I open the lock, I don't want you going all heroic on me."

"Just open the bloody door and go in. If I don't hear from you in five minutes, we will come in."

I turned the key and went inside, screaming and shouting were coming from David's room. I opened the door slightly and was almost hit by an ashtray. Experience had taught me never to open a door fully if he was inside in a foul mood.

"That was close, you bad tempered cunt, it's me."

"Oh, your back, how did you get on at court?"

"Fine, they admonished me, but what is going on here that's more an issue now. The cops are coming in if you don't come to the door. Plus, they will want to speak to Mag's because they heard her screaming."

"Fucking screaming, I'll give the cunts screaming. Your brother has just been caught red handed, buried testicle deep shagging another woman in my bed, and he is lucky that screaming is all he got. I came back from my mums in Brechin and there she was, howling like a wolf, so loud that she never heard me coming in."

"Mags, just come to the door and speak to the cops before they come in, they think he was strangling you; people heard a woman shouting and she sounded like she was getting strangled."

"She fucking was, but it was his slut who was getting the life choked out of her, not me. Then David tried to get me to stop hurting her, and got in such a bad mood he threw the hoover out through the bloody window."

Mags opened the door to speak to the police and ensured them that she was in no way harmed, and David followed her through. They asked him if he wanted them to call the council to get the window boarded up temporarily to weatherproof it until it could get repaired.

"Well, David, you had better ensure that every fragment of glass is picked up before too long before a child or animal gets hurt. Now we don't want to have to come back here tonight again. So sort your differences out."

The police car drove away back up the hill to the town, no doubt talking about what had just happened.

"David, I will phone my uncle to come and get me. You can gladly have your slut to stay. Before that, I am going round to your mums to tell her before you fill her head with lies."

"Mags it was only the once. Don't try to make it seem worse than it was."

"I am not listening to your crap David, Dave the rave, you just can't tell the truth, can you? All your family is the same; they skirt round the truth and embellish bits to make it sound plausible. You cannot lie to me this time. I caught you with your dick inside her, that's if she even noticed the slack arsed prostitute. It's lucky for her you threw the hoover out the window and distracted me enough so she escaped, I would have kicked her vagina so hard it would have ended up on her forehead."

I could not help laughing at what Mag's had just said, but I was the only one who thought it was funny. David went to the kitchen for a can of lager and came back and handed me one before he opened his.

"It's her fault for coming home early, she said she was not coming back until tomorrow. She has never found out before, and what does she expect if she is going away for a few days?"

We could hear mags crashing about in the bedroom shoving things into black bags, clattering things down hard for effect. Things went quiet for a few minutes and then she went stamping past the living room door and out the front door without slowing down."

"There she goes round to mum's, she will be adding arms and legs to her story, and mum will suck it all in. Dad won't give a shite about her leaving Kirrie, he does not give a fuck about anybody."

"David just talk to her; she might change her mind if you tell her the truth."

"No, I would rather she went. I have had enough of her hiding in the bedroom all the time. Visitors to this house think I am single because they only ever see me. I cook, clean, wash and iron, and do everything except doing the toilet for her, and I have had my fill of it, she can fuck off."

Mags appeared back and slammed the door hard behind her. She stomped up the hall and carted black bags to the front door ready to get picked up.

The door opened and a small man appeared. He did not look old enough to be an uncle, never mind old enough to drive a car.

"Are you nearly ready Margaret? I have to be at work in two hours' time, and I cannot be late. I'm on my final warning for timekeeping."

Mags came through from the toilet after she

had finished plastering another coat of makeup on. She never left the house without touching it up it even if she was going next door to mums. She was dressed as she was always dressed, tarted up, like she was going on a night out with high heels she could barely walk in, carrying a bag in each hand and taking it out to the waiting car. The car was loaded quickly and Mags left and never even said goodbye. The door closed behind her and that was the last I saw her.

"Well, she can go and stay in Brechin for all I care, there are plenty more fish in the sea. What about us having a celebration party because your court case went well, and because Mags has fucked off back to her mums, it can be a double celebration, a fresh start for both of us"

"On one condition; we don't invite Tandem."

Thankfully, not many people turned up for our party because there was only enough vodka for us and some lager in the fridge. A bottle of vodka each did not last long if we were in full party mode. David had invited a few female friends he knew and a couple of his workmates, and only the women turned up, which meant our vodka took a hit. After only about an hour had passed, our door was getting hammered aggressively.

"Open the fucking door. I know she is in there."

"Peedie you go and answer it; I think I know who it is. It is Peg from the Southmuir."

"And let me get a bang in the mouth when I open it? If she starts, she will get a crack in the jaw as anyone else would get."

"She won't hit you, just go and answer it."

I stood up and went to see who it was. I opened the door only enough to speak to her, and the irate woman barged past me like a steam train with her nostrils opening and shutting like bellows in a blacksmith's furnace. Her face was contorted with rage, as I had only ever seen in my father.

"I was told she was at the house with the wooden windows, and this is the only one boarded up, so, where is she?"

"Peedie, tell her she isn't here, for fuck's sake, she is putting a damper on the party."

"I just know that she is here, I can sense it."

She barged past David and looked in the bed-rooms and even searched the wardrobes. She came back into the living room and stood with her hands on her chubby hips and looked David up and down with suspicion.

"A clatter of something falling came from the kitchen, even although we were all sitting down, and that was it, she shoved the kitchen door open and stood with a vacant look on her face. Nobody was there, but she must have had a parent's intuition because she walked over to a cupboard, and wrenched the door open with such force it was a wonder it never came off the hinges.

"There I told you she was here. Audrey get home you little slut you are only fifteen years old, and you should know better to let her come here, you pervert."

"You obviously don't know your daughter very well then, she lets men in through her bedroom window when you are asleep in the next room, and she humps behind the bike shelters at school, at lunchtimes, or down the den if it is raining. I am sorry Audrey, but I am not getting accused of being a pervert, not when we were only having a drink together."

"Look David, I know what she is like, that is why I came here looking for her. Yes, I admit that I thought she would be in bed with somebody, and this time I was wrong. Right, Audrey, we are going home."

Peg and Audrey left, and the party fell flat, the show was over and despite being full of vodka nobody was in the mood now.

"Wooden windows, that's a good description of our house. We have maybe started a new trend."

Two of the women went home, leaving just Moira, who was already draped round David's neck, and Hazel, who just sat looking at me for ages before she spoke.

"Come on, then Peedie get your clothes off, you have pulled. Which room is yours because that is where we are heading?"

It had come as a shock hearing that words

come out of her mouth. She was a beautiful woman with a chiseled unique look about her; she could easily have been a model. Her long black hair was immaculately kept and held in place by a red clasp on each side of her forehead, and she had absolutely no make-up on because she did not need it.

We headed off to my room and she was insatiable, no amount of sex was enough for her, so I was happy. She stayed until morning and left early because she had to go to work. I lay in bed not believing what had happened, she had literally thrown herself at me not even knowing anything about me, but I was not complaining.

David was first up from his bedroom and he looked rough and still half asleep. He sat on the sofa and picked up a half-drunk can of lager which must have been flat, and downed it in one.

"What a fucking racket coming from your room Peedie, no wonder I am tired, every time I drifted off, your bed would start squeaking again."

"Stop being jealous, you had somebody sharing your bed as well."

"Well, if you humped her only once you had more sex than me. She told me I was too pissed to manage, and it was her that fell asleep, not me."

"Hazel wants to see me again tonight, so I will try to fix my bed before she appears. The noise was driving me mad at one point through the night, so you must have been well pissed off."

I spent the day tidying the house and hoovering the minute specks of glass from the pile in the carpet and washing the bedding so it smelt fresh for tonight. Amazingly the hoover still worked after its airborne trip through the living room window and not so perfect crash landing on the pavement below. I cleaned the bathroom and so was the kitchen. David was not the most domesticated of people and did not really care if all the dishes were dirty, or there was no clean cutlery left, but I had a guest coming to stay and I did not want her to see it a tip two nights in a row.

I walked up to the co-op to get more milk and six cans of lager and met Shug who was smiling like he was actually happy for a change.

"What are you looking so self-righteous for Shug?"

"Oh, I met Audrey on my way home from the Ogilvy, she had given her mum the slip. Well, she ended up staying the night, and I broke her virginity. She told me that I was her first."

"Aye first shag last night she meant, you did not actually believe her, did you?"

"I kind of wondered when she was asking me to do things to her that a virgin should not know, but I did not care because I got them emptied, at last, they were starting to get heavy."

"Right Shug I'm heading home because I am on a promise later today and I still have to make up my bed, the most important bit of all, nobody wants to sleep on crusty sheets."

The washing was dry on the line so I took it in and made the bed. I pulled the sheets tight and made sure that there were no creases anywhere. David's friend was still in his room sleeping last night off, and David had decided to join her. His head was pounding, and he had a sore throat and he reckoned that sleep would sort him out. It was probably the undiluted vodka that burned his throat. He had acquired his bottle from some dodgy character in the pub who went out to his car boot to collect it for him. It would probably have removed paint from any surface it touched, and it smelt toxic. I had sniffed the top of his bottle and had to gasp for breath at the noxious smell. Yes, vodka had a smell, but not as that did, it would probably make you blind if you drank enough, and I certainly would not taste it.

Hazel arrived very early, and we both sat down on the sofa, just saying nothing for a minute or two. She looked nervous today, not like the rampant sex maniac, she was last night.

"Have I done something wrong, Hazel? I know that there is something wrong."

"No Peedie it's me. I started my period this morning. I feel a failure for ruining our second night together."

"Look, Hazel. It does not matter; you can still stay if you want. We can just actually cuddle in and go to sleep."

Hazel wanted to go to bed to watch television just in case David came through, so we went taking our cans of lager with us.

"Look, Hazel, you are on my side of the bed, that's where I sleep, come on move or I will drag you across."

"Aye, if you think you are man enough, go for it."

I pulled her by the ankles and dragged her across to the other side of the bed. She struggled and fought like she was not wanting to move, then she grabbed me and fought back, and one thing led to another and we were having sex again like it was going to be our last time ever. The oral sex was fantastic, and she moaned and groaned like she was really enjoying it, and so was I.

"Look, I am going to have to go home, I start early shift tomorrow and I don't want to sleep in, and if I stay here, I know I won't get any sleep."

Hazel got up and dressed quickly and just left me lying there. The front door closed behind her and she was gone, I would be sleeping alone tonight after all, but I was not caring in the slightest after the fabulous time I had just had. I got up to go to the toilet and had to wait for David coming out.

"About time, you cunt, I have been bursting for ages standing here."

"Well peedie you had better wear a gas mask to go in there, it is absolutely rancid, I have dropped a big one tonight which I have been baking in my back oven all day. Oh, my fucking God, what the fuck has happened to your face? You look like you have been in a bad car crash."

"Fuck off David, I am not that fucking ugly; you want to look in a mirror yourself sometime."

"No seriously it's you that should look in a mirror, not me. Are you telling me you can't taste what is all over your face?"

I looked in the mirror and recoiled back for a split second and stood there just looking without blinking. My entire face was covered in blood from Hazel, and I had not even noticed. I had tasted blood like when you prick your finger and lick it, but the taste was fantastic and I thought no more about it and carried on.

"Peedie there is no point in ignoring me, I know you have been at it on her period, you must be a vampire to handle all that blood, for fuck's sake go and wash it off you are making me feel queasy."

"Look David, you don't know what you are missing, take it from me, you don't even notice and it is a fabulous taste, a delicacy even."

I filled the sink and washed my face and the water turned red, so I had to fill it again to rinse it properly. David had been right. I had looked like I had been in an accident. Luckily, I had not walked Hazel home and met people outside the house.

CHAPTER 30

Despite meeting up several times Hazel and I never really became a couple, she was too busy a personality for me, and her work was always shift work so we drifted apart. I had started back bouncing in the Ogilvy bar, which was excellent wages and cash in hand, and it had its perks like a free drink after my shift.

Nothing had changed much in my life and I was finding it difficult existing almost next door to my parents' house. I met my mother as I was passing their house, and she asked me to come inside. Their house was a different house to the one I left when they lived on the other side of town, but it had the same unwelcoming feeling when I went inside. It was like the house was trying to repel me from its walls, but the feeling was in my head, and it was me who wanted to run out the door. Mum made me a cup of tea and I sat drinking it looking at all the pictures of my siblings dotted around the furniture and walls, but there was not one of me there. It was like I had not been born into the family. I remembered why I could not live with them now, not only because of my father, but because I was an outsider in my own family. They did not know who I was now and they never would, I was somebody who walked past their house on my way home. I saw mum ducking out of sight several times as I passed her house on my way home, but there was never a knock on the window nor a wave. There was nothing but a vacuum emitting from the house, sucking any happiness from me it possibly could

"Your dad was wondering when you are coming to visit us."

"I live almost next-door mum, and it is the same distance to both houses no matter which way you go, so you could come to us just as easily."

"I know that but we visit nobody in the family because they always come to us, and we don't want to interfere in your life. What about maybe coming round for your tea tonight then?"

"I don't know about that, he will just start his crap like he always does, then I will end up walking out the door, and he will shout abuse at me and humiliate me in front of everybody."

"No, I have told him not to. I am sick of all this bloody nonsense."

"If you have had to tell him not to start anything, then there is definitely no hope, and anyway when did he ever listen to you."

"Just come and see how you get on, that's all I am asking."

I headed straight home after my cup of tea, desperately trying to understand why I was getting lured back to the family home with the offer of a meal. Something must be looming in the distance they are needing me for. I have gone years without them in my life so why now, why the interest in my welfare. My mind was trying to make sense of what had just happened, and despite imagining it my head dozens of times, the reality of what mum had just asked me was surreal? It was not in my imagination this time, she really had asked me to come for my tea, and there had to be a hidden agenda because there was no love lost between us and the passing years had widened the gap even further.

I had told David about my invitation and he thought I was imagining it, or hallucinating and on drugs. Dad hated me and David knew it, so there was no way they would ask me to go there, ever. David often went round for his tea if he could not be arsed cooking, or if I had already eaten.

"Well, fuck it, I am coming to my tea and the fireworks after it, because there is bound to be friction between you and dad. He just won't be able to dampen his mouth filter for long, something hurtful will slip out of his vile mouth".

"If you come as a witness to the debacle then I will go with you, I want to see his face when I sit at the other end of the table out of his reach."

I had learned to sit at the table as far as possible away from dad as a young boy, always out of the reach of his huge fists. Even then it did not always guarantee an injury free meal, because he threw his cutlery at me intent on damaging my flesh. Perhaps now he had changed into a new man, a loving father, but I knew without a reasonable doubt he had not, and as long as I lived, he would only get worse. His unnatural loathing of me was rooted so far into the depths of his subconscious it would need a Divine intervention to remove it or death. I recalled all the times I had wished him dead, the times I was going to cut his brake pipes on his car but had bottled out at the last minute. I had always feared him because I knew firsthand how abnormally violent and sadistic, he could be. I had been his flogging boy all my life, his stress release, and his personal punch bag.

Dad was still not home when we went round to the house. Mum was busy mashing potatoes in a huge pan, I had forgotten how large her pans were when we all lived at home and she had to cook meals for nine people. Her spectacles were all steamed up when she turned around to see who had entered the kitchen, but she just carried on doing what she was doing and never acknowledged that we were there. I almost turned round and walked out the door again, but stayed because David had sat down at the large kitchen table. That table used to give me nightmares about incidents which happened to me in the past like the time when I was forced to eat my sister's vomit, and when my head was deliberately bashed against the table for eating a bit of white chicken meat. Memories of times at that table came flooding back as I sat looking around the kitchen, the fighting and bickering, the humiliating and derogatory name calling, and for a few minutes I was living that past. The table was not a place where we talked because talking was not allowed unless it was him. We ate in silence because nobody was interested in what you had been doing all day at school. Nobody was interested in me as a person either, I was just that pain in the arse who imagined everything, that pansy who was never ill, that family embarrassment who was not his flesh and blood.

"If you pair want a cuppy you can make it yourself, can't you see that I am busy?"

"I'll make it Peedie you won't know where anything is."

I sat looking at mum who still had not spoken directly to me since I had come in. It was like I was invisible, like it used to always be. Nothing had changed since I last saw her. It was like time had almost stood still but I had moved on and we had collided in the middle somewhere. Dad would be home soon and then the test would really begin when he saw me sitting in his house at his table. The stew was ready to serve up, and she mashed the potatoes, all mum needed now was for dad to appear through the door then it could get served up onto the plates.

The front door opened and dad walked in and sat down in his chair and switched on the television. He never came into the kitchen to see mum, nor did he talk to any of us. Mum took him a cup of tea and handed it to him.

"I think I will have my tea in my armchair for a change tonight. I'm too settled here now to go to the table."

"You usually sit at the table every night. What changed tonight?"

"Oh, nothing's changed. Can a man not come home from his work and sit where he wants without the grilling?"

There was a change alright, and that change was me. He just could not get over the fact I was in the house for my tea, and he could not bring himself to sit at the same table as me. That would be too much for him to take in at once, too much to have to bite his tongue when he had to sit looking at me sitting opposite him.

"Well, I hope you are keeping out of trouble Peedie, all that stuff in the paper about you shamed us, and your dad had to drink in the pub with everybody talking about you. He was black affronted having to sit there and listen to everybody, and he ended punching two of them in the mouth because of you. He was nearly lifted by the police and then you would have been in real bother with your dad. All he wanted was a peaceful night out without you getting involved."

There was no way of replying to that remark from mum, that's what dad had told her so it had to be true. Dad always said that I could cause trouble in an empty house, and here I was, causing trouble when I was not even near him, not even in the same street.

"Peedie are you wanting more stew?"

"No, David I have plenty because I have lost my appetite."

"You pair leave some for your father. He has been working hard all day, not loafing about like you."

He ended up with half a pan full of stew and a mound of mashed potatoes. David and I had both felt the lifeless and empty atmosphere since dad came in. There had been no conversation from dad, not even a forced look in my direction. Dad hated me, and no one is born to hate their children. He must have learned to hate me, and if he could learn to hate me, he should have been able to learn to love, for love comes more naturally to the human heart than hate does.

"Come on Peedie let's get out of here and get a can of lager. I have got a sour taste in my mouth with being in this house. The silence is almost deafening, and I feel awkward."

"David, I thought you would never ask. Let's get out of here."

"Peedie why did I even bother going there? We were totally ignored the whole time. If I am there by myself, dad talks to me about everything, and so does mum, it is you they don't talk to."

"Look at it this way, we had a cooked meal and no dishes to do, and it saved us a bit of electricity."

David lifted his leg up and farted. The living room filled with the disgusting odour, which had seeped through the material of his trousers releasing the offending stench all around the room.

"I better get to the toilet fast, because that was not a fart, it was a shart. It is nearly touching cloth and I can't nip it any longer, stand back, I have to run."

David half shuffled, half hopped his way to the toilet and just made it in time. He let out a groan of relief, which I heard from the living room.

"Peedie, that shit was almost nine inches long with not a crack in it. I had to poke it with the toilet brush to break it because it would not flush round the bend. Four times I had to flush it, before the last bit disappeared. The drains will get a clear out when that flows down the sewer, and if that beauty hits a rat it will definitely kill it."

"David, that was too much information for me, and too much smell. It has drifted through here like a fog, like a toxic mist floating at head height, and it is thrusting up my nostrils. You are fucking disgusting."

"I am going up to the Ogilvy for a pint. Are you coming?"

"No, I am staying home tonight. I am laying

low for a couple of weeks until Peg gets over her daughter coming to our party."

"Well, I am heading up the road and I won't be late for a change."

I walked up the hill to the town centre and passed the Gairie pub. There was music coming from inside, and I could hear a familiar voice above everybody else's. Dad was inside having his usual pint of heavy and a nip of whisky. He had his usual entourage around him, listening to the stories of his violent past, but never divulged his lifetime of abuse towards me, mainly because he never believed that he had done anything wrong towards me. I stood and watched him through the window just out of sight and was disgusted at his antics with a woman standing next to him. His hand groped at her chest, trying to get a peanut out of her cleavage which he had just thrown in. The smile on his face was something I had not seen for a very long time, he was laughing, and so was she. Mum never saw that jovial side of dad, nor did any of us. I could not look any longer. I had seen enough of his drunken hilarity and walked the rest of the way to the Ogilvy. The bar was busy when I went in, full of the usual drunks and dubious characters who I would never trust with anything. They were the type that would steal the sugar from your tea and then come back for the milk. One of them tried to sell me a zippo lighter, which had a name inscribed on it, and the owner of it was still sitting at the bar.

I had to get some peace from the constant boasting and banter between the arseholes at the bar. I got a handful of change from Davie at the bar and went through to the small lounge to play the one-armed bandits. A few people were sitting at the tables watching me.

"You are wasting your time playing that one-armed bandit. I have put nearly five pounds in it, and it just won't cough out any money. I think it is rigged."

"I will give it no more than a pound, then I will play another bandit."

I put twenty pence in the slot and pulled the handle and it disappeared into the abyss below never to be seen again. I added another two before I heard the noise, and so did everyone else, I had hit the jackpot. The coins came flooding out like a silver waterfall landing in the tray below with a metallic tinkling, like hailstones on a tin roof. The crowd gathered round to watch me scoop the money up with sheer delight. I was filling up my jersey with it because there was too much to carry.

I sat counting it up and stacking it in pound piles and counted forty-seven pounds. Davie at the bar changed it into notes for me and I had a willing woman hanging on to my arm offering to help me spend it. Marlene was different, her hair came out of a bottle and this time it was a yellow tinged blonde. Her hair looked so brittle and dry that it would probably snap if you touched it.

"Come on, buy me a pint, and I will shag you later."

"Marlene, come on now you could be a bit more subtle than that, everybody at the bar must have heard you."

"They will be fucking jealous because I just don't hump just anybody."

"No, only the ones who will buy you a drink, or the ones with a pulse."

Marlene laughed at what I had just said to her because she knew that I was only joking. She was not known for being an easy lay but had had some dodgy looking characters as partners over the years. Marlene was a single parent and because of her ex partners, she did not have much luck on the man front. Men were terrified of getting involved in case they got themselves into some sort of trouble.

"So, am I getting a pint or not Peedie, I am as dry as an Arabs sandal?"

"Marlene you can get a pint, two pints even but I don't want anything in return."

"So, my fanny's not good enough for you then. I thought you would hump anything. Come on man, my fanny is chewing at my knickers so you better help me out."

"I just want a pint in peace, I will catch up with you later."

I was not the type who liked the full-on approach even though I had succumbed to it before. Standing at a bar packed full of drinkers is just not Romeo and Juliet's type of seduction. Wherefore art thou Peedie, do you want a skelp at my pisher; just does not cut it for me. I am no prude but a little bit of mystery definitely helps.

My second pint did not seem as good as my first, but it probably had something to do with the female attachment on my arm. She was stuck to me like a limpet, and totally refused to let me go. She was wanting my body, and she was having it at any cost, plus I had emptied the bandit.

"Right Marlene I have to go to the toilet so you will have to let me go. I will be back to drink my pint in a minute."

Finally, her grip was released, and I disappeared through the toilet door in the bar, and emerged out the other door which led into the small lounge and escaped outside to freedom. I walked up the small, alleyway beside the Ogilvy, and vanished into the Airlie Arms unseen by my prey. Shug was there with his brother, and I told him about Marlene.

"She is all yours Peedie, you can have her with bells on. Once she gets her clutches into you, you will never be free of her, never."

"Shug, you will be doing me a favour if you go to the Ogilvy and sort her out, she is your type all right, and she is blonde now; you like blondes. It is guaranteed sex on a plate, with second helpings if you want."

"Peedie, I would not touch her with yours, never mind mine. She is your babe now if you bought her a pint, buying one is like an engagement ring to Marlene, and if you buy two, it's like a wedding invitation. It will be kids next you'll see; another pint will see to that."

We stood laughing about my brush with Marlene and played a game or two of darts and soon forgot about her. I needed someone in my life to share it with, but not her. My life was still on a downward slope and getting attached to someone like Marlene would do nothing to pick me up. If I took her round to meet my family, dad would probably think she was the business; she was definitely more the type he ogled in the bars. I finished my drink and said my farewells and headed back towards the Ogilvy. The small lounge only had two people sitting in it, and they both appeared to be almost eating each other's faces off, totally oblivious to me sitting at the next table.

"Oh, hiya darling, your back then. I thought you were not coming back."

"Marlene, I had to go to meet Shug. It was important. I am just getting one lager, and then I am going home."

"Get me one as well."

I came back and sat at the table, and so did Marlene, except she sat on my knee. Her cord trousers were now covered in small flecks of white fluff, in the time I had left to go to the Airlie Arms, but I did not ask where from. She started to slowly writhe about on my lap, pretending not to notice she was doing it.

"Come on Peedie, make my seat lumpy."

"Marlene for fuck's sake sit still, you are making me nearly spill my pint,"

Then it happened, a vision of beauty walked past where I was sitting, and headed towards the bar. Her hair was long and flowing behind her in red waves of lustrous opulence. I was transfixed and immediately in love, and I had never even spoken to her. Marlene was sitting on my knee so my chances were blown out of the water before they even had the chance of beginning.

"So, you're ignoring me then, I saw you eyeing that lassie up, you will have no chance with her, she comes from a good family, not one like yours or mine, and anyway you're sleeping with me tonight"

"Never mind her, come on Peedie, get your coat, you have pulled."

She had planted the seed, and I headed home with her on my arm. I had plenty lager in my system so she appeared better looking than she had before, or maybe it was a trick of the light, but we both ended up in my bed. The sex was so boring and dull; she had shouted that she wanted sex, but she really did not participate as promised. I would never have a repeat performance with her, which was a certainty. Plus,

I had another woman on my mind, that thing of beauty who floated past me earlier, I just could not get her out of my mind. The image of her slim perfect body was engraved in my mind. But there was more to her than her beauty; she had something other than that about her. There was a radiance of something special emitting from her, and I just hoped that I would get the chance to see her again.

Marlene stayed the night so I put my wallet inside my pillowcase for safety. I trusted nobody when it came to money. We fell asleep in minutes and woke up early. I wanted her gone from my house as soon as I woke, and before anybody saw her here. Having her in my bed would definitely not improve my morale if word got out, so she had to leave.

"Ok, one coffee, then you had better go, Marlene, I am getting picked up soon."

She left, and I went back to bed. I was disgusted with myself for taking her home with me, but she instigated it and drove me past the point of no return, and I had to see it through. This was the first time I had slept with someone and there was nothing there, her body was there but not her mind.

I woke late in the afternoon and my throat was dry. David was crashing about in the kitchen doing the dishes, which was a rare sight. The kettle was already boiled, so I made myself a coffee and went to sit in the living room to drink it.

"Who was that who went out the door this morning? I was waiting on her mooing, Jesus where the fuck did you find that cow. I have slept with some beasts in my time, but yours takes first prize."

"I thought you were still sleeping. You were imagining it all because Marlene was a beauty you jealous cunt."

"I never imagined that blonde brillo pad hair, so I will be able to pick her out when I see her."

We sat laughing about my night of detached sex and the fact that he had heard me calling out someone else's name in my bed instead of hers. It was definitely one of those can't think of anybody moments, one which I had to get out of my mind. I imagined that was what necrophilia must feel like; she definitely lay as still as a corpse with no emotion whatsoever.

I finished my coffee and stripped my bed and watched as a cluster of bleached blonde hair landed on the floor. It had snapped off her head like trampled on twigs on a forest floor. I hoovered the offending thatch off the carpet in case it made its way back into my bed, there could be no evidence left of her ever being here.

"Peedie are you going out tonight, not with her I mean, just out for a drink?"

"Yes definitely, I saw someone last night who I really want to meet. She went past me when Marlene was sitting on my knee."

"That will fuck up any chance if that howler

was seen sitting on your knee, no self-respecting woman will sleep with you after her being in your love nest."

"David, they will only find out if you tell them, my lips are sealed on this occasion. I won't be boasting about that night ever, only having nightmares."

CHAPTER 31

"Peedie let's go round to mums for lunch because these rolls are stale. Dad's away so we will be sorted."

"I will come with you just for something to eat because it will save me going up the town to Starkies."

Mum was sitting reading when we went in. Every book she read was Mills and Boon. She lifted her head to see us coming in and delved straight back into the depths of her story. David had already put the frying pan onto the cooker, and had dumped six pork sausages in oil to fry, before we even had time to sit down.

"Mum, we are starving. Where are your rolls?"

"Your dad took the last of them to work, but there is bread in the cupboard."

Mum came through to the kitchen to see us, minus her book. She was half staring at me, which made me feel uneasy for a minute.

"There is something different about you, but I can't quite put my finger on it. You look different today for some reason."

"Mum, I have not seen you for a long time. I have grown a lot in so many ways. The problem is that you never really knew me then either."

"I might have known you would start if I mentioned it. You just can't mix in with the rest of us, and you have always been different. Your father said you would start trouble in an empty house, and he's not far wrong."

"Peedie is right mum, you have never even bothered to try to see things from his side. You just take dad's side even if it is obvious that he is at fault."

"Look David I have to live with him, you don't know how much I have to put up with night after night with him coming home stinking of drink, and the moods he gets into if I say anything. It is easier for me if I just shut my mouth and just accept it."

"You never even went to see him in Sunnyside Hospital when he was in, not even once."

"There was dam all wrong with him. It was all in his head, so there would have been no point in visiting him. Plus, I hate that nuthouse, since Peedie was in there when he was fifteen, the place and the people gave me the creeps."

I sat listening to them both discussing my mental state like I was not even there. That had been one of my problems since I was four years old. I hardly existed in my parent's life, then, so now was no different, I was the scum of the earth, the lowest in the pack, even although I was the oldest sibling.

"Mum, you know that dad has never liked me. He has hated me since I was born for something I cannot change. Whatever happened between you and him before I was born has affected my whole life."

"Peedie nothing happened, he was stationed in London doing his National Service in the Royal Air Force, but I got pregnant just before he left Orkney. He found us a house to share with an old lady in London and I moved there to be with him, and not because he could not trust me either. His mother had sent him a letter telling him lies about me and an ex-boyfriend, but then I was never good enough for her precious son, her first born."

"So why has this had to be directed at me my whole life? I have been to hell and I am only half way back yet, I have suffered for years with mental health problems and I am still struggling to get out of the rut he put me in."

"Stop blaming your father for the mess your heads in. There is nothing wrong with you, and there never has been. All your brothers and sisters have got on with their lives, but not you. You always had to be the one who made your dad and me fight, night after night you caused us nothing but trouble with your lies. Always ill, always looking for bloody attention, well, I had another six of you to look after so I would not have had time even if I wanted to."

"I have always known that you thought like that, that's why I have never bothered talking about this stuff before. You will never believe me, over dad because you can only see his side of things, and you never saw half of what went on, and the other half you totally ignored because it was easier."

"If you were to stop wallowing in self-pity, you might get on better. It's your gran's fault that your dad says nasty things to you, she planted the seed in his head in the first place."

Mum stopped talking abruptly because dad appeared home from work.

"Right, Peedie, this shit stops now. I don't want you upsetting your father when he is just home from work. Stop living in the past for a change."

"What are you doing here, Peedie? I hope it's not for money?"

I nearly fainted on the spot; dad actually talked to me without using a derogatory remark. He never got a reply from me straight away, because he had caught me off guard. Maybe he was changing towards me, twenty-four years too late, but he had been civil.

"No dad, I am not after money because I have plenty of my own. I am working in forestry with David now for Gerald, and the pay is cash in hand as well."

The truth was that I was earning twice what dad was earning every week and that would be a proper kick in the teeth if he found out. Marion was always getting cash and clothes from me as she was my only sister with no money. She deserved to be dressed in nice modern clothes. I did not want her ridiculed any longer for wearing cast offs from older siblings. She could now go to discos and have at least some normal life. Shopping in Dundee for nice things was now a reality for her.

"Well, David, I am heading home to get a bath, because I am going out tonight for a few pints, are you coming?"

"No, I will be round in ten minutes, leave the immersion on for me."

That was the first time in years my dad had spoken to me directly even if it was only briefly. I filled the bath and sank into it and relaxed lying on my back. It was going to be my personal mission to find my red-haired vision which had passed me in the Ogilvy. I just could not get her out of my mind. For the first time in my life, I had actually fallen in love at first sight, and that was before I had even spoken to her.

"Peedie, hurry up in the bath. I want to get out of the house before the pubs shut."

"You just want to get out to look for Marlene to get my sloppy seconds."

"And I know who you are looking for as well, but you will have more chance flying to the moon than getting a date with her with the red hair, she is well out of your league. And I heard that her parents moved into our old house, and you know the state that was left in. The odds are stacked against you before you start, imagine if she took you home to meet the parents, and you walked in, they would call the fucking police to get you arrested."

"And how do you know so much about her?"

"I am getting so sick of hearing about her from you that I asked Margaret about her, she knows her, and so does Marion."

The Ogilvy was busy as usual and old Jimmy was leaping towards women shouting his usual Cow, Cow, Cow, and delving his hand into his jacket pocket pulling out pieces of gritty looking slices of luncheon meat. Gracie with her patent leather red shoes with her skirt so short, nothing was left to the imagination. The regulars were like part of the furniture in the Ogilvy because they only ever drank in there and nowhere else. I got myself a pint of lager and sat in the small lounge waiting on David coming. After only ten minutes in the place, my vision appeared before me and she was heading through to the bar.

"Hello, you have a beautiful young body just ready to explore."

I could not believe that I said that, what a chat up the line that was, that was my chances ruined now, and she would probably run for the door any minute. She smiled back at me and I was totally in love, and I was not dreaming; this was real. Marlene homed in on me the minute she spotted me when she came into the small lounge.

"Marlene, I am going out with someone else.

Last night was a one off."

"You are looking single to me Peedie, there is nobody with you and only one drink on the table, and that is yours."

She barged past two people standing in the doorway, and dumped her arse on my knee. I was horrified, my red-haired reality was due back from the bar at any minute, and Marlene was on my knee.

"Marlene get off, you are hurting me; my legs are sore."

"That's because you were giving me one last night. Surely you remember, no wonder you have sore legs. But I will go a bit easier on you tonight Peedie."

"Look Marlene, there won't be a tonight, or any other night. I slept with you last night because it just happened."

I had just spoken, half my sentence when my red-haired wonder walked past and she must have heard me. She looked at me and smiled, probably because I had the equivalent of the bride of Frankenstein sitting on my knee, compared to the vision before me. Marlene left the lounge in disgust at what I had said, but it had the desired effect. Then my vision spoke to me, and I could hardly answer.

"I know your brother James, and some of your sisters, but I don't know you. I have seen you around the town, but I did not know that you were related to James."

"I have been away from Kirrie for a few years. That's probably why you don't know me."

"Yes, James and I have been friends for ages. We went to school about the same time, and Margaret and Marion know me as well."

"You don't look very happy tonight. You were smiling when you came in, but I just know that there is something wrong."

"I have fallen out with my parents and have left home; I think I am staying at my friend Karen's house tonight."

"Look, if you're stuck, you can come to stay at my house tonight, no strings, just come to the door."

"Ok, I will, but only if Karen lets me down, oh and my name is Yvonne."

Yvonne was shy and so polite when I gave her my address. She left, and I thought no more about it. She had seen Marlene on my knee and she was not to know that we were not an item, my chances were blown. There was nothing for it but to accept that my life was not about to change any time soon. It would be the same routine of going for a pint, going to bed, and going to work. I needed someone to come home to, someone who would take me for who I am, not for what they had been told about me. The stories were most likely true, some probably exaggerated, but with truth in them. I actually regretted some things I had done in the past, but not all of them, because some people deserved everything they were given. Yvonne did not know me at all, but she talked so she could not have feared me as some women did. I showed no mercy when I was working as the bouncer on the door, male or female they got lashed out the door if they were causing trouble, even if they were sober. I was big built with huge arm muscles after working in forestry and I was heavily built with long hair and a beard, but she talked to me. My night was boring, I was just no longer in the mood to stay out; Marlene had ruined it sitting on my knee, at just the wrong time. I finished off my pint, and one somebody had bought me and headed round to Vissochis chip shop for a chicken supper to take home.

I was sitting eating my chips in the living room, when there was a knock on the door, so I got up and opened it. Yvonne and someone else were standing there.

"That offer you gave to Yvonne earlier, is it still on?"

"Of course, it is, I would not have offered otherwise, come in."

"I am Yvonne's friend Karen, and my plans have gone tits up, there are cousins coming to stay at mine tonight, so my mum says, but it is probably a pack of lies."

"Yvonne, why did you not just come yourself to ask?"

"I'm not like that, I may not look it, but I am shy."

"Do want some chips or a lager?"

"I don't drink alcohol, but I will have some chips from you."

"My brother David lives here as well as me, but he is ok to get on with, and he doesn't bite."

"Where are the rest of your brothers and sisters now?"

"Ann is married to a farmer. Charles is married as well. Both of them live in their own homes, and Margaret, James, and Marion still live at home."

"So, you don't mind me staying then?"

"No, I don't, but I am going to work tomorrow and so is David. But I will leave you a key so you can come and go as you please."

"I will have to try to get some of my clothes out of my mum's house so that I have the stuff to change into, but if she won't let me in, I don't know what to do."

"Don't you worry about clothes. It won't matter if you get them or not. There is plenty of money to buy more, I have more than enough cash so we will never be short."

We got on so well together and Yvonne moved in to stay for good. She came to work with me some days and sometimes stayed home. She got on with my parents better than I had ever done, and my mother taught her how to knit fancy patterns. I was in love with someone who was a genuine person and who felt the same as I did.

My first visit to her parents was trouble free

and the cold shoulder I expected did not happen. I was treated like royalty from day one even though they obviously knew about my violent past and my time spent in Sunnyside psychiatric hospital they never mentioned it. We visited them every week and had our tea there often. I was closer to them than my own family. For the first time ever, I saw how a real family lived their day-to-day life, and it was so far removed from the way mine lived theirs. Her father was a real man, not a violent thug. He had never hit Yvonne her whole life, which I found difficult to imagine. I had always thought every family, acted as mine did, and it took a long time talking about my upbringing to realise that not every father was like mine. I had become so used to the extreme abuse and bullying at his hands that it became normal. My brain accepted it for so long until it could not cope any longer, and it had shut itself down.

Having Yvonne in my life was the start of something special for me, and I suddenly found true happiness. Our first daughter was born, and she was treated to a special relationship with Yvonne's parents, who showed me how to bring a child up just by watching them. We ended up having two daughters and two sons, and have been together since I met her when I was twenty-four years old, and I am now sixty. We have had our ups and downs as most couples have, but we are closer now because of it.

My father died from cancer aged 78, the morning after I visited him in hospital, when he finally admitted that he had been wrong, and he apologised for his actions. He had been asking for me to visit him on his deathbed for a long time. I think he had clung on to life until I went to see him so that he could try to fix his wrong doings. It had been such a waste of his life and mine that he had never properly known me. If he had, he would have forgotten that there was a chance that I was not his son and saw me as a boy yearning for acceptance and love, and he would have enjoyed his time with me instead of a life of bitterness and hate.

My mother developed Alzheimer's three years after my father died

David sadly died aged only 53 years old from cancer and has left me a legacy of happy memories. When life is getting me down, I think of him and realise how lucky I am to still be alive and able to support my family.

Sadly, James committed suicide in 2018. He was only 52, and it happened a month before his 53rd birthday, and my mother died a year later, not aware James had died.

All my other siblings are alive and well and are successful in what they do for a living. I never had the confidence like they did to gamble and take a chance on a business venture, but then it has taken me until I reached sixty to be totally confident in myself. I achieved that mostly because of my time spent living with Yvonne, and writing my first book called, Stanley's Coat.

Writing my life story has helped me to finally come to terms with my abusive childhood, and hopefully, it will help someone else. Revealing my abuse saved my life. It took most of my life to accept the fact that I never had a loving family, as a child, or as a man. Everything in my life was built by me. I redeemed myself, and learned that I am truly a good person, in spite of my childhood.

When this healing journey started, I was totally oblivious to how it would turn out. Unfortunately, it is also here on the journey that I come to know my most devastating pain, my strengths and how to fight my way out of the darkness that mental and physical abuse left me in. As I sit here thinking of what I have shared or what I have written, I feel the little boy within me overwhelmed with so much joy because I have finally come full circle in my life. It has been such a long journey of highs and lows and I cannot explain to you how challenging this life has been, to a man, who has had to learn to be a normal human being. I did not know how to live, love, be a proper parent, nor handle normal, everyday situations. Being a father was also very scary because I did not know what was normal, or what wasn't, because I never had any good role models. I lived all my childhood and teenage years living with a violent and dysfunctional family. I had to learn to live the hard way, and I have made so many regretful mistakes, and I have hurt so many people, mentally and physically, before I came to the understanding of all the important things that I missed out in my developing years, and well into into my life.

People just don't understand that no matter what good or bad experiences happen during their childhood, they will influence and affect them in adulthood. When you accept, embrace, and learn from the change, you inevitably grow stronger without realising it. I have learned that my life is my life and I refuse to let the past control my happiness or the man I have become. I am no longer a victim; I am a survivor and proud of what I have achieved so far. Since meeting Yvonne when I was twenty-four, I have never been in trouble; she has been my savior and without her; I do not know what path I would have taken.

No matter what has happened or what is still to come, I will never lose my value as a person, husband, and proud father. I will always have to nurture and support my inner wounded child, to remind myself that I have travelled a long hard path, and have emerged happy.

Whether you are dirty or clean, no matter what religion you are, or what your sexuality is, you are still priceless to those who love you. The worth of our lives comes not in what we do or what we know, but by who we are, and how we act towards others around us.

I am so blessed to be loved by a beautiful woman, who supports and understands me, and has stood by me in this journey to get me where I am today, and without whose encouragement my story would never have been written.

Printed in Dunstable, United Kingdom